The
Quest for
Rananim

The Quest for Rananim

D. H. LAWRENCE'S LETTERS TO S. S. KOTELIANSKY 1914 TO 1930

EDITED WITH AN INTRODUCTION BY

George J. Zytaruk

McGILL–QUEEN'S UNIVERSITY PRESS

MONTREAL AND LONDON 1970

This work has been published with the help of a
grant from the Humanities Research Council of Canada
using funds provided by the Canada Council.

SBN 7735-0054-5
Library of Congress Catalog Card No. 79-96841
Printed in Great Britain by
William Clowes and Sons, Limited
London and Beccles
Designed by Robert R. Reid

Acknowledgements

I WISH TO MAKE the following acknowledgements: to Laurence Pollinger Limited for permission on behalf of the Estate of Frieda Lawrence Ravagli, owners of the copyrights to Lawrence's letters; to the British Museum for granting access to the *Koteliansky Papers* and for permission to make use of the illustrations; to Marshall Best of the Viking Press for allowing republication of the previously published letters to S. S. Koteliansky and thus enabling me to make this volume complete; to those well-established scholars, Harry T. Moore, the late Edward Nehls, Warren Roberts, and E. W. Tedlock, Jr., whose previous research has made my own work possible, and to the two anonymous readers of my manuscript for their valuable suggestions; to Mrs. Catherine Stoye for permission to copy previously unknown letters from D. H. Lawrence to S. S. Koteliansky; to Mrs. Sophie Jacobs, Mrs. Esther Salamon, Mrs. Beryl Samson, and Mrs. Rickard Donovan, friends of S. S. Koteliansky, for answering my many questions, and to Mrs. Pauline Smith for allowing me to read some of her letters from S. S. Koteliansky; to the Society of Authors for permission on behalf of the Estate of Katherine Mansfield to quote from the letters of Katherine Mansfield to S. S. Koteliansky, and to Messrs. Constable Ltd. for permission to quote from Beatrice Lady Glenavy's memoir; to the Board of Governors of Nipissing College for financial assistance which made this work possible; to the Research Committee of the University of Alberta for a travel grant which enabled me to spend some time in England completing my research; to William C. McConnell for his early interest in this book and his encouragement; to the Editors of *The Malahat Review*, the Editors of *The D. H. Lawrence Review*, and the Editor of the *Bulletin of Bibliography and Magazine Notes* for permission to reprint materials formerly included in these periodicals; to Professor Henry Kreisel and to Dr. M. Wyman of the University of Alberta for their willingness to support this project; to the Staff of the Rare Book Room of the Cameron Library, University of Alberta, for the opportunity of making use of its fine collection of D. H. Lawrence first editions; to Dorothy Gardner and the secretarial staff of Nipissing College for invaluable assistance in the preparation of the manuscript; to my wife, JoAnn Zytaruk, for initially transcribing the letters and for many hours of encouragement and of additional labour far beyond those which any husband has a right to expect.

Nipissing College
North Bay, Ontario

Contents

S. S. Koteliansky photographed in the garden of No. 5 Acacia Road,
St. John's Wood

Courtesy of Mrs. Beryl Samson

Beau Soleil
Bandol
Var

15 Jan. 1930

Dear Kot

Just a word to say
I have the Inquisitor & will try to do a nice
little introduction — though I shall never be
able to squash myself down to a thousand
words.

Pollinger arrived today,
but we haven't talked business at all yet.
He says he must leave Monday. Dr Morland
arrives with his wife on Friday. Shall let
you know what he says.

wr D.H.L.

By the way, how do we stand with regard to copies
of my novel? Did the Leon have them all? and did
he sell them all?

Facsimile of one of D. H. Lawrence's letters to S. S. Koteliansky
Courtesy of the British Museum

Courtesy of the British Museum

S. S. Koteliansky as a young man, c. 1910
Courtesy of Mrs. Catherine Stoye

Illustrations

Phoenix *Ex Libris* inscribed "To Kot from D. H. L."

S. S. Koteliansky as a young man, c. 1910.

S. S. Koteliansky photographed in the garden of No. 5 Acacia Road, St. John's Wood, London.

Facsimile of one of D. H. Lawrence's letters to S. S. Koteliansky.

Introduction

IT IS FORTUNATE for students interested in D. H. Lawrence that he lived prior to the commonplace availability of the telephone, that throughout the course of his life it was still essential for him to conduct his affairs, both business and personal, through the medium of letters. Had it been otherwise, much of the Lawrence we now know would have been lost. The novels, stories, poems, and essays have ensured the survival of Lawrence the artist; but it is the letters that have told us most about Lawrence the man. True, we have a large number of reminiscences by people who knew D. H. Lawrence, and these reminiscences as they are presented, for example, in the three volumes of Edward Nehls's *D. H. Lawrence: A Composite Biography* (1957–59)[1] help immeasurably to provide us with details concerning Lawrence's distinctive personal character. As everyone knows, however, reminiscences are not entirely trustworthy; and the student must try to obtain evidence from other places to verify personal accounts. A writer's letters are among the best sources of reliable evidence. It is amazing that so many of Lawrence's letters have been preserved—letters, after all, are made of perishable stuff. Were it not for what appears to be an instinctive recognition on the part of the recipients that a letter from D. H. Lawrence was indeed a precious memento, a great many of the letters we can read today might never have survived the onslaught of time.

I

Lawrence had been dead for only two years when his onetime friend and fellow writer Aldous Huxley published *The Letters*

---

1 *D. H. Lawrence: A Composite Biography*, gathered, arranged, and edited by Edward Nehls, 3 vols. (Madison: University of Wisconsin Press, 1957, 1958, 1959). In subsequent references this work will be cited as *C.B.*, with the appropriate volume and page number.

of D. H. Lawrence (1932),[2] that remarkable volume which helped to correct the one-sided memoirs which were spawned by Lawrence's friends and enemies. Because the Huxley volume was so large (889 pages), few people suspected that there were still many unpublished letters of Lawrence. Since 1932, however, sporadic publication of new Lawrence letters has continued for more than thirty years. Most of these letters appeared in the following memoirs of Lawrence: Mabel Dodge Luhan's *Lorenzo in Taos* (New York: Alfred A. Knopf, 1932); Knud Merrild's *A Poet and Two Painters* (New York: Viking Press, 1932);[3] Frieda Lawrence's *Not I, But the Wind...* (New York: Alfred A. Knopf, 1934); and Earl and Achsah Brewster's *D. H. Lawrence: Reminiscences and Correspondence* (London: Martin Secker, 1934). Somewhat later appeared *D. H. Lawrence's Letters to Bertrand Russell* (1948), collected and edited by Harry T. Moore.[4]

With the new interest in Lawrence, during the '50's, Harry T. Moore, who was spearheading Lawrence studies in the United States, turned up 200 new letters in the course of writing Lawrence's biography, *The Intelligent Heart: The Story of D. H. Lawrence* (1954). In the *Composite Biography*, Edward Nehls also included a great deal of material from hitherto unpublished letters. Nor was this all, for Lawrence was a prolific letter writer. In Liverpool in 1959 Kenneth and Miriam Allot discovered more of Lawrence's letters, letters which were written to Blanche Jennings, a postmistress,[5] who had known Lawrence while he was still struggling with *The White Peacock*, his first novel.

When ten new letters from D. H. Lawrence to S. S. Koteliansky were published in *Encounter* (1953),[6] it is surprising that few scholars seem to have had their curiosity aroused considering the editorial note which preceded the letters: "These letters are

2 *The Letters of D. H. Lawrence*, edited and with an Introduction by Aldous Huxley (London: William Heinemann, Ltd., 1932). The Introduction is reprinted in *The Collected Letters of D. H. Lawrence*, edited with an Introduction by Harry T. Moore, 2 vols. (New York: Viking Press, 1962). See Volume II, pp. 1247–68. In subsequent references *The Collected Letters of D. H. Lawrence* will be cited as *C.L.*, with the appropriate volume and page number.

3 This book has now been reissued as follows: Knud Merrild, *With D. H. Lawrence in New Mexico* (London: Routledge & Kegan Paul Ltd., 1964).

4 *D. H. Lawrence's Letters to Bertrand Russell*, edited by Harry T. Moore (New York: Gotham Book Mart, 1948).

5 All of these letters are now available in *C.L.*

6 *Encounter*, Vol. I, No. 3 (December 1953), p. 29.

selected from nearly four hundred written by D. H. Lawrence to S. S. Koteliansky, from 1914 to 1930, the year of Lawrence's death." Yet here was the key to a treasure trove of Lawrence's letters. Three years later K. W. Gransden reported in *The British Museum Quarterly*[7] that in his will Koteliansky had bequeathed to the British Museum ten volumes of letters, three of which were made up of Lawrence's letters to Koteliansky. Subsequently, Gransden estimated the Lawrence-Koteliansky correspondence at "over 300 letters."

In 1962 came the finest collection of Lawrence letters yet made available, *The Collected Letters of D. H. Lawrence* in two volumes, edited by Harry T. Moore. Although severely criticized in some circles and unjustly censured, Moore had done a magnificent editorial job, and there is no doubt that he succeeded in the task he set for himself, which was to print as many Lawrence letters in their entirety as could be included in two volumes designed to serve both a popular and a professional audience. Moore was, therefore, forced to keep footnotes down to a few essentials and did not give the source of each letter which he included in the collection. From the impressive list of persons and institutions given in Moore's acknowledgements,[8] we can only marvel at the enormous editorial task he performed. But when have literary critics been grateful?

The Collected Letters of D. H. Lawrence makes no claim to being the "Complete Letters" of Lawrence—that editorial feat has yet to be accomplished; for the bringing together, in several volumes, of all the existing Lawrence letters is needed for the advance of Lawrence scholarship, which must still tackle the relation of Lawrence's letters to his creative work. The size of Lawrence's correspondence presents a unique opportunity to explore this relationship. The dilemma, in the twentieth century, of the artist, his problems, and his work is revealed in Lawrence's correspondence perhaps better than anywhere else. His letters are a vital record of the artist's struggle as he attempts to translate into art the meaning of his experience. We may no longer regard Lawrence's personal problems as significant, but the importance of his artistic struggle will not diminish with the passage of time.

7 *The British Museum Quarterly*, XX (1956), 83.
8 See *C.L.*, I, xxiii–xxvii.

II

Nearly all the letters which make up this volume were bequeathed to the British Museum in 1955, the year of S. S. Koteliansky's death. Dilys Powell, who had been one of Koteliansky's intimate friends, and who wrote the article in the *London Times* (27 January 1955)[9] on his death, recalls that Koteliansky talked of his intention to make "a thank-offering for being a British subject." More specifically, Koteliansky had stipulated in his bequest: "The requests in this my Will in favour of the Trustees of the British Museum are made as an acknowledgment of my affection for England and of the friendship that I have enjoyed with many of her writers and citizens for nearly half a century." The bequest of ten volumes of letters, which are now in the British Museum, is the tangible result of Koteliansky's gratitude to England.[10] Before discussing the Lawrence-Koteliansky letters, however, let us review what we know about the recipient. Who, after all, was Koteliansky?

Perhaps something of the formidable nature of this man is conveyed by the name itself: Samuel Solomonovich Koteliansky, a name unpronounceable for most Englishmen, and which was therefore soon shortened by all his friends to "Kot." The Hon. Dorothy Brett, who was an artist, has left the following lively description of Koteliansky: "... so broad-shouldered that he [looked] short, his black hair brushed straight up 'en brosse,' his dark eyes set perhaps a trifle too close to his nose, the nose a delicate well-made arch, gold eye-glasses pinched onto it. He [had] an air of distinction, of power, and also a tremendous capacity for fun and enjoyment."[11] Leonard Woolf, who knew the man and worked with him, likens him to the Old Testament prophets Isaiah, Jeremiah, and Job. "If Jeremiah had been born in a ghetto village of the Ukraine in 1882," says Woolf, "he would have been Kot." "When he shook hands with you," Woolf recalls, "you felt that all the smaller bones in your hand must certainly have been permanently crushed to

9 My authority for this statement is Beatrice Lady Glenavy in '*Today We Will Only Gossip*' (London: Constable, 1964), pp. 191–92. Subsequent citations to this work will be given as *B.L.G.*

10 For details see "The S. S. Koteliansky Bequest" by K. W. Gransden in *The British Museum Quarterly*, XX (1956), 83–84.

11 Quoted from *C.B.*, I, 341.

fine powder. The handshake was merely an unconscious part of Kot's passionate intensity and integrity." [12]

If there is any way to account for Lawrence's extraordinary friendship with Koteliansky, it probably lies in the "passionate intensity and integrity" of Koteliansky, those qualities which Lawrence admired most in people. Leonard Woolf has, I think, focused accurately on the basis of the Lawrence-Koteliansky friendship: "Kot's passionate approval of what he thought good, particularly in people; his intense hatred of what he thought bad; the directness and vehemence of his speech; his inability to tell a lie—all this appealed strongly to Lawrence." [13]

Koteliansky was born in the little village of Ostropol in Volhinia Province in the Ukraine. The year is given by Gransden as 1880; Leonard Woolf gives it as 1882. However, the documents which I have examined, among them Koteliansky's Russian passport, give the year as 1880, and the date of birth is April 1. Kot's father was Arzum Shloima Koteliansky; his mother was Beila Geller. [14] Kot was very proud of his mother's side of the family, and he would sometimes cite his famous ancestors as indicative of the stock from which he had descended.

Koteliansky's parents were well off. Mrs. Pauline Smith, his niece, has told me that the family owned a flour mill and that the mother also ran a prosperous retail business. Besides Koteliansky, there were two brothers and one sister in the family. One of the brothers, Mrs. Smith's father, was killed by the Cossacks when she was only a girl of five. With help from Koteliansky, the second brother escaped to Canada and made his home in Montreal. What happened to the sister is not known, but it is likely that Kot's letters from his mother, who died in 1929, record much of the history of the family he left behind. These letters were willed to the Hebrew University in Jerusalem, but I have not examined them.

Despite his adoption of England as his second homeland, Koteliansky kept in close touch with the members of his family, both in the Ukraine and in Canada. I have read some of his

12 See Leonard Woolf's memoir "Kot" in *The New Statesman and Nation*, XLIX (5 February 1955), 170–72.

13 Leonard Woolf, "Kot," p. 172.

14 S. S. Koteliansky's "Certificate of Naturalization," however, records the parents' names as Solomon and Beila Koteliansky.

letters to his niece, and these reveal an almost fatherly concern for her children, particularly with regard to the children's education and their choice of careers. The letters also tell us of Kot's experience in the London of the Second World War, and they record his suffering from ill health and intense feelings of depression during his later years.

Much could be written about Kot's life in London and of his deep affection for England, and especially about his relations with such prominent literary figures as Leonard and Virginia Woolf, Katherine Mansfield (for whom Kot had the highest regard), J. M. Murry, T. S. Eliot, W. B. Yeats, H. G. Wells, E. M. Forster, G. B. Shaw, James Stephens, Ralph Hodgson, and Dorothy M. Richardson. Kot's letters from all these people are preserved among the *Koteliansky Papers* in the British Museum. In addition there are letters from J. W. N. Sullivan, Mark Gertler, Gilbert Cannan, and Philip Heseltine. Koteliansky continued to be associated with Lady Ottoline Morrell after Lawrence's death, and there are some interesting letters from her to Kot as well. Among his dearest friends were Beatrice Lady Glenavy (formerly Beatrice Campbell) and Marjorie Wells. Perhaps the most surprising of Kot's correspondents is Jessie Chambers. When in 1936 she published her memoir of Lawrence, Kot apparently wrote to her and told her how much he appreciated her book; later he tried to influence her to write a more definitive account of her relationship with Lawrence.

Although Kot's own story is well worth telling, let me now turn to his arrival in England and the beginning of his friendship with Lawrence. It is not clear why or under what circumstances Kot came to England. Gransden mentions "a three months' university grant," [15] but Mrs. Esther Salamon, who was Kot's intimate friend, denies that there was any such sponsorship. According to Mrs. Salamon, Kot was sent to England by his mother, and it was she who supported him during his first few months there.

Koteliansky's Russian passport was issued in Kiev on 17 May 1911, and he appears to have left Russia on 23 June 1911. He arrived in England on 7 July 1911, but where he stayed or what

15 K. W. Gransden, "*Rananim*: D. H. Lawrence's Letters to S. S. Koteliansky," *Twentieth Century*, CLIX (January 1956), 22.

he did at that time I have not been able to discover. The basis for Kot's decision to remain in England was political and was associated with the revolutionary movement going on in Russia. England was an asylum for Kot as it was for a great number of Russian émigrés. To attempt, however, to untangle his political affinities during that uncertain period would be a major undertaking. What is obvious is that it was safer for Koteliansky to remain in England than to go back to the Ukraine.

In 1914, when Lawrence first met Koteliansky, the latter was employed at the Russian Law Bureau at 212 High Holborn, London, E.C. The Law Bureau was only a rather pretentious name for a law office run by a Russian named R. S. Slatkowsky. In 1914 the Bureau included Koteliansky and another man named Horne. What sort of business was handled by the Law Bureau has not been recorded by anyone who was directly connected with it; however, Witter Bynner recalls:

> When I asked Frieda twenty-nine years later about Koteliansky, she beamed back at me: "He did not like me, but he loved Lawrence and he used to cheer Lawrence by roaring Russian songs at him. He was a mystery because he was supposed to be in a law office but he would take us there and bounce his boss out of the place and mix up sour herring and mashed potatoes for us on the spot with any old plates and then sing for us. Yes, he loved Lawrence. Ja!¹⁶

Mark Gertler, one of Kot's closest friends, is reported to have facetiously remarked that Kot's job at the Bureau was "to black his boss's beard." Slatkowsky was apparently a Russian lawyer, and Horne had some training as an English barrister; Koteliansky, who could read and write both Russian and English, must have worked as a kind of secretary and translator in the whole business. Beatrice Lady Glenavy has left this record of her visit to the Law Bureau: "I once went there with Katherine [Mansfield] and [John Middleton] Murry and was delighted with the hideousness of it all: the darkness, the horsehair-covered furniture, a picture of kittens playing in a basket of pansies, and an even more incongruous picture for such a place, a Christ surrounded by little children."¹⁷

16 Witter Bynner, *Journey with Genius* (London: Peter Nevill, 1953), p. 201.
17 *B.L.G.*, p. 75.

Katherine Mansfield has left a more vivid recollection of Koteliansky's days at the Law Bureau: writing to him on 19 February 1921, she reminisces:

What has happened to the inkstand with the elephants on it—mother-of-pearl, inlay—or was it ivory? Some of the inlay had begun to come off; I fancy one of the elephants had lost an eye.

And that dim little picture of a snowy landscape hanging on the wall in your room. Where is it now? And where are the kittens and the children and Christ, who looked awfully like a kitten, too, who used to hang in the dining room? And that leather furniture with the tufts of horsehair stuffing coming out?

Where are all the hats from the hatstand? And do you remember for how long the bell was broken.... Then there was the statue on the stairs, smiling, the fair caretaker, always washing up, the little children always falling through her door.

And your little room with the tiny mirror and the broken window and the piano sounding from outside.

Those were very nice teacups—thin—a nice shape—and the tea was awfully good—so hot.

"At the Vienna Cafe there is good bread."

And the cigarettes. The packet done up in writing paper you take from your pocket. It is folded so neatly at the ends like a parcel from the chemists.

And then Slatkovsky—his *beard*, his 'glad eye'—his sister, who sat in front of the fire and took off her boot. The two girls who came to see him the Classic Day his Father died. And the view from your window—you remember? The typist sits there and her hat and coat hang in the hall. Now an Indian in a turban walks up that street opposite to the British Museum *quartier*.

It begins to rain. The streets are very crowded. It is dusky. Now people are running downstairs. That heavy outer door slams. And now the umbrellas go up in the street and it is much darker, suddenly. Dear friend—do not think evil of me—forgive me.[18]

It is the Koteliansky of this recollection that Lawrence met in 1914, when the two men went on a walking tour in the Lake District. There were four men on that historic occasion: Horne, whom we have already mentioned; Lewis, a Vickers engineer, whom Lawrence had met in Italy in 1914 and whose parents lived in Westmorland; S. S. Koteliansky; and D. H. Lawrence. This was a memorable occasion for Lawrence, and for Koteliansky, for it marked the beginning of their relationship,

18 Quoted from *The Letters of Katherine Mansfield*, edited by J. Middleton Murry, 2 vols. (London: Constable, 1928), II, 94–95.

and it is the story of this relationship that is told in the letters printed here.

Owing to the research already carried out and published by such Lawrence scholars as Harry T. Moore, Edward Nehls, and E. W. Tedlock, Jr., it is possible to trace most of Lawrence's movements even though Lawrence was a ubiquitous traveller. We can, for example, give the exact dates of the walking tour; it began on 31 July 1914[19] and lasted until 5 August 1914. Writing to Koteliansky several months later, Lawrence recalls this time: "Do you remember coming down to Barrow-in-Furness & finding war declared?" (No. 34).[20] And more than ten years later, in a letter dated 18 December 1925, Lawrence still remembers the excursion with Koteliansky: "I remember very well the famous walk in the Lake district, how you suffered having to sleep in the same bed—& how we got water-lilies— and came down to Lewis' unattractive home, & it was war, & you departed in a cloud. It's part of one's life & we don't live twice" (No. 250).

Meeting thus on the eve of the First World War helped to fix the occasion permanently in Lawrence's mind; not an auspicious beginning for a lasting friendship, and Koteliansky was apparently upset about something on the tour and left the party. Lawrence did not take offence, as his first letter reveals. From Barrow-in-Furness, he wrote a brief note to Koteliansky, and the unique correspondence between the two men began.

How many letters were there? And what were they about? According to my count, 343 letters from Lawrence to Koteliansky are preserved in the British Museum in the collection called the *Koteliansky Papers* and designated Add. MSS. 48966 (Vol. I), 48967 (Vol. II), and 48968 (Vol. III).[21] In addition, I recently discovered three more letters from D. H. Lawrence to Kot when I examined some papers in the possession of Mrs. Catherine Stoye of Hollywell Ford, Oxford. These three letters, which in this volume are designated by the numbers 175, 176,

19 See Harry T. Moore, *The Intelligent Heart: The Story of D. H. Lawrence* (New York: Farrar, Straus and Young, 1954), pp. 167–68.

20 Numbers of letters cited here and elsewhere refer to the letters published in this volume.

21 These three volumes of MSS contain other material as well. There is, for example, a large number of letters from people who wished to subscribe to *The Signature*.

and 247, were not among those bequeathed to the British Museum, but they are included here to make the collection as complete as possible. Whether there are any additional letters is impossible to say; but the MS catalogued in the British Museum as Add. MSS. 48975 (Vol. X), which is reserved for fifty years, may very well contain more Lawrence letters to Kot. Koteliansky's respect for Lawrence was obviously such that he preserved every bit of correspondence that he received. He was also by nature an orderly man, one of those bachelors who are adept at housekeeping. Beatrice Lady Glenavy recalls the cleanliness of his residence at No. 5 Acacia Road, St. John's Wood:

> Kot used to say that a man's house is himself. His house was scrubbed and polished and dusted, with a special place for every cup, plate, book or piece of paper. He was an expert launderer and did all his own washing, even the blankets. He was also a good cook and enjoyed cooking little suppers for his friends. He once showed me how a Russian servant polished the floor; he had dusters tied round his feet, and slid about on his hall-floor swishing from side to side in a sort of wild dance.
>
> The polish on his hall-floor was really dangerous. There were a couple of small rugs and it was almost fatal to step on one of them, they just flew from under your feet and you sat down with a bang. When Kot opened his hall-door he had to warn the visitor to be careful; he clung on to you and you clung on to him till you could get a grip on the banisters and work your way into the sitting-room. The danger of breaking your bones was so great that I gave up going to the hall-door. On entering the little bit of front-garden you could see Kot sitting at his kitchen table through the half-basement window, then you made a sign that you were going round by the side-door which led into the scullery. There he would meet you and say, 'It is good that you have come,' and lead the way into the kitchen where so much Russian tea was drunk and where the conversation went on almost as if there had not been any break since the last time.[22]

That the letters have come down to us is to some degree a result of good housekeeping, unspectacular as that may be. The preservation of the letters is also attributable to Koteliansky's prudence; he left them to the British Museum, a public institution which has always served scholars well. Had the letters passed into the hands of uncooperative relatives or into the hands of

22 *B.L G.*, p. 161.

collectors, their availability for scholarship might have been greatly reduced.[23]

III

I have arranged the entire correspondence in chronological order and assigned a number to each letter in order to simplify references to any of the letters. Many of the letters, as the editorial brackets indicate, are undated, and in the "Notes" I explain some of the problems which had to be solved. In preparing the texts of these letters for publication, my aim has been to arrive at an accurate reproduction of the contents of each letter; however, I have not attempted to reproduce the form of each of the letters. The kind of paper used by Lawrence, whether the text appears on one or both sides of the paper, whether ink or pencil is used, and a host of other such considerations have not been my concern. The originals are available to those who may have an interest in these matters. Nor have I differentiated between letters proper and postcards, or letters and brief notes. My concern has been with what Lawrence wrote to Koteliansky and on what occasion the material was written.

By regularizing the originating address in each instance, I have hoped to make it easier for the reader to determine quickly from where Lawrence wrote each of the letters; however, editorial brackets are consistently used for the material which has been added to fill out the originating address. As for the dates, I have used those which are given by Lawrence and have supplied others on the basis of evidence gathered from a variety of sources. In the "Notes" I have given credit to the sources, where they are used. As for the form of the date, sometimes the order used by Lawrence has been changed, although his preference in this matter is generally the same as that which has been adopted. When the day of the week appears in the original, I have retained it; but where a date has had to be supplied, or where the day of the week does not appear in the original, I have dispensed with this element. In addition to regularizing the originating address, I have also tried to be consistent in reproducing the so-called complimentary close, by placing it in

23 The original Lawrence letters to Mabel Dodge Luhan are still not available to scholars. See *C.L.*, I, xviii.

each instance immediately above Lawrence's signature, even though the words or phrases are often included by Lawrence as part of the body of the letter.

Because Lawrence was in the habit of adding to the main body of his letter after he had written it, these additions have been printed consistently as postscripts because in several instances Lawrence employs this form and because the "added thought" is, I think, better communicated in this form. It would be a mistake to read a postscript as part of the body of the letter. This, to be sure, is a small point, but not insignificant, since it often provides an additional impression of Lawrence's mood or frame of mind at the time of writing.

As for the content of each letter, I have tried to be faithful to Lawrence's text, as regards both the language and the punctuation. His fondness for using the dash and the ampersand has been preserved because these help to convey the informal tone of the letters. In instances where Lawrence refers to specific time, however, I have used the conventional method as it is practised in the United States and Canada. Lawrence's spelling of words has not been altered, and unusual spellings are followed by [*sic*]. Italics are employed for the titles of books, names of periodicals, and foreign words, although Lawrence was not consistent in using this method; however, when italics appear elsewhere, it is to be assumed that these are Lawrence's and not the editor's italics.

With respect to the annotations, my aim has been to supply enough material to make the letters intelligible to both old and new readers of Lawrence's correspondence. Because Lawrence is a writer who has been well "researched" by others, I have thought it advisable to refer the reader to my sources of information regarding the many items which have had to be annotated. To the seasoned Lawrence scholar the notes may at times seem superfluous, but it is hoped that at least some of the notes shed new light on Lawrence's life and work. Although there are many opportunities here for extensive excursions into Lawrence's literary history, these have been avoided because most of the information regarding his literary work is available elsewhere and because such discussions would detract from the correspondence printed here. I have been unable to supply the answers to all the questions posed by the letters, but I hope that other readers of Lawrence will fill in the gaps in this work.

IV

The texts of the letters, as has already been indicated, are taken from the originals in the British Museum MSS and from the originals in the possession of Mrs. Catherine Stoye. Of the 346 letters that are printed in this volume, only 126 have thus far been published; the details of previous publication are given in Appendix III. The first letters from Kot's vast collection were published in *Encounter* (1953); there were ostensibly ten letters from Lawrence to Kot, but in fact there were only nine letters, since one of the letters included in *Encounter* (and now designated in the British Museum collection as a letter from Lawrence to Kot) is a letter from Lawrence to his wife Frieda.[24] Two of the letters (Nos. 43 and 294), which had already appeared in *Encounter*, were reprinted in *The Selected Letters of D. H. Lawrence*, edited with an Introduction by Diana Trilling (New York, 1958).

The largest selection of the Lawrence-Kot letters was published in *The Collected Letters of D. H. Lawrence* (1962). Here, for the first time, were included ninety-eight previously unpublished letters and six of the letters which had already appeared in *Encounter*, making a total of 104 letters from Lawrence to Kot in *The Collected Letters of D. H. Lawrence*. Three of the letters, Nos. 89, 216, and 328, were still available only in the *Encounter* issue. *The Malahat Review* (January 1967)[25] published twenty letters from Lawrence to Kot; but inadvertently I had included one letter (No. 104) which had already been published in *The Collected Letters*; thus there were only nineteen previously unpublished letters in the *Malahat* selection. The total number of letters from Lawrence to Kot published so far is, therefore, 126; published for the first time in this volume are 220 new letters, which brings the Lawrence-Koteliansky correspondence to 346 letters. By bringing together in one volume all of the available letters from Lawrence to Koteliansky we can, I think, see Lawrence in an unusual perspective. The letters are fairly evenly distributed throughout the years 1914–30, except for 1924 and 1925, during which there are only a few letters. In the "Notes"

24 The complete text of this letter is printed in *C.L.*, II, 762. Part of the text was omitted in the *Encounter* version.

25 See "D. H. Lawrence: Letters to Kotelianky," edited by George J. Zytaruk, *The Malahat Review*, I, No. 1 ([University of Victoria, B.C., Canada] January 1967), pp. 17–40.

I attempt to account for the paucity of correspondence in these years.

To readers familiar with Lawrence's letters, it will be apparent that the number of letters to Koteliansky exceeds easily that written by Lawrence to any other person. Apart from the impressive size of the correspondence, there are other reasons why the letters are significant, for the part played by Koteliansky in Lawrence's life has not yet been sufficiently appreciated by people who have studied Lawrence. This lack of scholarly attention to Koteliansky may be the man's own fault, or it may be just one of those historical accidents.

To begin with, Huxley's edition of *The Letters of D. H. Lawrence* (1932) did not include any letters to Koteliansky. Why? We now know that Koteliansky had all of Lawrence's letters in his possession at the time; it may even be that he had assembled them at that time for inclusion in Huxley's book. Koteliansky and Frieda Lawrence were seldom on good terms, and one suspects that some kind of disagreement took place, the result of which was Koteliansky's refusal to supply any of the letters in his possession for inclusion in Huxley's edition. My only basis for this conjecture is a remark which appears in a recently published letter from Mark Gertler to Koteliansky dated 26 March 1930, in which Gertler alludes to the possibility of Koteliansky acting as a joint editor with Huxley on the 1932 edition of Lawrence's letters:

> I saw the Huxleys on Monday and talked to them about your taking part in the editing of Lawrence's letters, etc. He seemed genuinely agreeable. In fact he seems anxious that there should be someone in London to collect letters. The only trouble is Frieda. Apparently she keeps changing her mind about everything, publishers, etc.—keeps promising first one publisher and then another. She is in Paris at present. I have written to her to phone me or write, but so far she has taken no notice. But I may see her yet. She is going to London, so you will be able to see her yourself.[26]

The disagreement with Frieda over the letters in Koteliansky's possession was still going on in 1953, when the first of the Lawrence-Koteliansky letters were to be published in *Encounter*.

26 *Mark Gertler: Selected Letters*, edited by Noel Carrington (London: Rupert Hart-Davis, 1965), p. 232.

In an undated letter to John Middleton Murry, Frieda Lawrence says:

> Spender (did I tell you this already?) has a new paper *Encounter* and Kot wanted him to print L's letters to Kot. Spender says only 6, but Frere and Pollinger resented that he did not send his letters to Aldous's book and when I was in London he had tea with me every Tuesday at 4 o'clock and I thought he was a friend, but he had written a nasty letter to Aldous about me a little while later. Kot has 500 pages of L's letters! Kot wants 75 per cent for himself—he has no right to anything, he might at least *ask!* He must be unbelievably sour![27]

Through some kind of misunderstanding, therefore, the first letters from Koteliansky's collection were not published until 1953, and as we have seen only nine of the letters were published at that time. When Harry T. Moore's *The Intelligent Heart* (1954) appeared, there were excerpts from over 200 letters not in the Huxley collection (eighty new letters were published in full), but there was still not a single new letter from Lawrence to Koteliansky, although the latter's name appears frequently in the biography. Later, from 1957 to 1959, came Edward Nehls's three volumes of *D. H. Lawrence: A Composite Biography* in which, once again, many new letters or parts of new letters were printed, but except for excerpts from the letters which had appeared in *Encounter*, there was still no sign of more of the Koteliansky letters.

So the matter stood until 1962, the year of *The Collected Letters of D. H. Lawrence*, when the first substantial representation of the Koteliansky-Lawrence letters was published. In selecting the letters for this edition Moore attempted to include what he considered to be the more important letters, stating that "the omissions, as far as the editor could control them, are chiefly of less important letters";[28] but Moore was no doubt aware that the criterion of "importance" was not an absolute one. He confessed that for "the minority of Lawrence scholars, who are hot after clues as to dates and places, some of those letters which have been left out might have been helpful."[29]

27 *Frieda Lawrence: The Memoirs and Correspondence*, edited by E. W. Tedlock, Jr. (First American Edition; New York: Alfred A. Knopf, 1964), p. 355.
28 *C.L.*, I, xvi.
29 *C.L.*, I, xvi.

The present edition makes no attempt to discriminate between the importance of one letter and another; *all* the letters are included in their entirety, and the question of which are important and which are not will be left for time to decide. The kind of scholarship which is being applied to Lawrence today makes it imperative to have every authentic document made available for examination. What new insights the publication of the letters in this edition may supply is difficult to predict, but let us now look at some of the ways in which the present edition is already relevant.

V

Because we have for the first time an opportunity to examine a substantial number of Lawrence's letters to one individual, written over a period of some sixteen years, we are in a better position to assess Lawrence's capacity for sustained human relationships. A reading of these letters does much to dispel those impressions of Lawrence created by memoirists who have presented him as predominantly irritable and temperamental. No one who reads Lawrence's letters to Koteliansky can fail to be impressed by Lawrence's sincerity, consideration, generosity, and understanding—all qualities for which Lawrence is not generally remembered.

It will be recalled that Lawrence came to know Koteliansky on the eve of the First World War, and everyone who is knowledgeable about Lawrence's career as a writer knows that it was the period of the war that was the most difficult for Lawrence. Not only were Lawrence's efforts as a writer frustrated, but he and Frieda suffered from poverty and political persecution as well. Throughout this period, Koteliansky was a constant friend on whom Lawrence could rely.

Koteliansky's friendship for Lawrence had some very practical results. Just shortly after they met, for example, Lawrence was already seeking assistance from Koteliansky in typing the "philosophy" with which Lawrence struggled as he attempted to formulate his basic beliefs (No. 6). But it was not merely the secretarial assistance that Lawrence sought: "You must tell me more particularly what you think of it" (No. 11), and "What do you think of my MS?—have you read it?" (No. 12). It is unfortunate that Lawrence did not save Kot's letters, for it would be invaluable to have the other side of the correspondence.

One aspect of Lawrence's activities which is directly attributable to the friendship with Koteliansky is Lawrence's role as a translator of Russian literature. Since I have investigated this role at length elsewhere,[30] I need say here only that Koteliansky was instrumental in placing before the English reading public no fewer than thirty-three works by Russian writers. Among these are two works by V. V. Rozanov, whose "phallic vision" Lawrence greatly admired and which had an important effect on some of his later work.[31] The bibliography of Koteliansky's translations is given in Appendix I, and a glance at the works listed there reveals how Koteliansky's translations of various Russian writers must have formed part of the reading experiences of such writers as Virginia Woolf, Katherine Mansfield, and J. M. Murry, all important figures in the history of twentieth-century English literature.

The role played by Lawrence in the translation of Shestov's *All Things Are Possible* (1920) and of Ivan Bunin's "The Gentleman from San Francisco" (1922) is revealed clearly in the hitherto published Lawrence letters, especially in those letters included for the first time in Harry T. Moore's *The Collected Letters of D. H. Lawrence*. This role is that of an "editor," rather than that of a translator proper. What the additional letters published here help to do is to fill out the picture by giving us added information. In the case of *All Things Are Possible*, for example, we can now read the story from the inception of the project to its conclusion, as well as beyond that, when years later Lawrence suggests a possible re-publication of Shestov's book. Lawrence's role as an "editor" would be much clearer, and probably more significant, if we had access to Koteliansky's original translation of Shestov's material; we could gather something of Lawrence's attitude if we could document the changes that he made in Koteliansky's text.

30 See Chapter II, "D. H. Lawrence's Role as a Translator of Russian Literature," of my unpublished Ph.D. dissertation entitled "D. H. Lawrence's Response to Russian Literature" (Seattle: University of Washington, 1965). For an abstract of this work see *Dissertation Abstracts*, XXVI (Ann Arbor, Mich., February 1966), 4678–79.

31 See my article "The Phallic Vision: D. H. Lawrence and V. V. Rozanov," *Comparative Literature Studies*, IV, No. 3 (1967), pp. 283–97.

But so far as I have been able to determine, this text is not available, although it may come to light some day. The same thing is true of Lawrence's revisions of Koteliansky's original version of Bunin's story "The Gentleman from San Francisco."

The letters published here also reveal that Lawrence was involved in several other "editorial" jobs for Koteliansky not hitherto suspected. The first of these is alluded to in Letter No. 288 and may involve the work of the Russian writer Kuprin, some of whose stories were translated by Koteliansky and J. M. Murry in 1916.[32] In Letter No. 288, Lawrence writes: "I'll try & work the stories up, when I have an inspired moment, & let you see what I can make of them." That the stories may be those of Kuprin is suggested in Letter No. 289: "—Then if you want to do Nonsuch Press stuff, you must leave out Kuprin & me."

There is, however, very strong evidence that the "stories" referred to in Letter No. 288 were not Kuprin's at all but two stories which Koteliansky's mother recorded for him in Yiddish. Koteliansky's English translation of the stories was published in *The London Mercury* (February 1937), pp. 362–70 under the general title "Two Jewish Stories." In the prefatory note, Koteliansky says:

> It must have been in 1926 or 1927, when I sent the two Jewish stories, in my translation, as given here, to D. H. Lawrence, saying, would he try either to render them into better English, or—which would be finer still—tell them in his own way. He replied at the time that he liked the stories very much; that he would try to remake them; and, having done so, he would send them to me to see how I liked his version. I heard no more from him about them. There seems to be no MS. left by him on *The Salvation of a Soul*. But *Maimonides and Aristotle* he did try to remake, although he left it unfinished. The fragment recently appeared under the title *The Undying Man* in the volume *Phoenix*, published by Messrs. Heinemann.

It is my contention that it is these "stories" that Lawrence refers to in Letter No. 288. Lawrence's re-writing of "Maimonides and Aristotle" reveals very clearly what Lawrence could do with raw materials furnished by another writer.

32 I. A. Kuprin, *The River of Life and Other Stories*, translated by S. S. Koteliansky and J. M. Murry (Boston: Luce, 1916).

The second case of Lawrence's involvement in "editing" Koteliansky's translations is not only easier to document but is also certain to arouse curiosity, since it has hitherto been assumed to be the work of another writer, and an important one at that. The evidence contained in Letters Nos. 229, 230, and 231 proves conclusively that it was Lawrence who put the finishing touches on another Koteliansky text. Since this is a new fact, perhaps I should explain it more fully.

In 1924 *The Adelphi* published in three instalments *Reminiscences of Leonid Andreyev*, by Maxim Gorky, authorized translation by Katherine Mansfield and S. S. Koteliansky. The *Reminiscences* appeared as follows: *The Adelphi*, Vol. I, No. 9 (February 1924), pp. 806–20; Vol. I, No. 10 (March 1924), pp. 892–905; Vol. I, No. 11 (April 1924), pp. 983–89. Two months later *The Dial* also published in serial form Maxim Gorky's *Reminiscences of Andreyev*; these reminiscences appeared in June 1924, pp. 481–92; July 1924, pp. 31–43; and August 1924, pp. 105–20. As published by both *The Adelphi* and *The Dial*, the work was ostensibly translated by S. S. Koteliansky and Katherine Mansfield. The latter had died in January 1923, but the *Reminiscences* had been translated by Koteliansky and edited by Katherine Mansfield during 1922.

If we examine Letters Nos. 231, 232, and 233, we learn that on 7 August 1923 Lawrence, who was in New York at that time, wrote to Koteliansky that he would obtain the MS of the *Reminiscences* from *The Dial*. On 13 August 1923, Lawrence received the MS, already accepted for publication, and was "going through it at once." And on 17 August 1923, Lawrence wrote to Koteliansky as follows: "I went through your Gorky MS. & returned it to [the] *Dial*. I made the English correct—& a little more flexible—but didn't change the style, since it was yours & Katharine's [*sic*]. But the first ten pages were a bit crude." Here, then, is conclusive evidence of Lawrence's part in revising the Koteliansky-Mansfield MS of Gorky's *Reminiscences of Andreyev*. Were it possible to recover the MS from which *The Dial* set up the type for these *Reminiscences*, we would be able to document the alterations which Lawrence made in the original version prepared by Koteliansky and Katherine Mansfield. Although *The Dial* ceased publication in 1929, there is still a chance that the MS may be found.

As a further note to this interesting discovery, I should point out that in 1931 there was published a deluxe limited edition of the *Maxim Gorki Reminiscences of Leonid Andreyev*, authorized translation from the Russian by Katherine Mansfield and S. S. Koteliansky (London: William Heinemann, Ltd). The edition was limited to 750 copies, and a note informed the reader of the following "facts": "This translation, which is authorized by Maxim Gorki, was made by Katherine Mansfield and S. S. Koteliansky during the last stay of the former in England, August-September, 1922." In addition, the title page featured a "facsimile of the handwriting of Katherine Mansfield, the words being re-arranged to avoid the necessity of reduction."

The motive behind all of Lawrence's activities as an editor of Koteliansky's translations is the same—he was out to help his friend, who was often just as badly off financially as Lawrence. The reason for Lawrence's desire to remain anonymous in the Shestov translation is given in Letter No. 166; he tried not to have his name appear in connection with Bunin's "The Gentleman from San Francisco," as we see in Letter No. 209; and he certainly gives no hint of wishing to have his part in the Gorky *Reminiscences* acknowledged. When Koteliansky offered him half the Shestov receipts, Lawrence insisted that one-third would be more than enough, for Lawrence was not one to appropriate what belonged to another. For his part in translating "The Gentleman from San Francisco," Lawrence received £12.1.0., half the proceeds,[33] but he felt that one-quarter was as much as he really deserved.

Lawrence's readiness to help with Koteliansky's translations shows that Lawrence did not forget the kind treatment he received in his times of adversity. During the First World War, for example, when Lawrence felt completely hopeless, it was Koteliansky who encouraged him. In Letter No. 138, Lawrence says: "You, my dear Kot, are a tower of strength—a real tower of strength to us both—and a solitary tower in the land, at that," and when Lawrence became gravely ill during the influenza epidemic in February 1919, it was Koteliansky who sent him food (grapefruit, tea, sweets, and brandy) and helped him through

33 See *The Frieda Lawrence Collection of D. H. Lawrence Manuscripts: A Descriptive Bibliography*, by E. W. Tedlock, Jr. (Albuquerque: University of New Mexico Press, 1948), p. 95.

a difficult time.[34] Perhaps one of the most touching instances of Koteliansky's concern for Lawrence's welfare is to be found in the letter quoted above in which Lawrence acknowledges the gift of a pair of "boots" that he has just received from Koteliansky.

The correspondence printed here is filled with instances of favours bestowed and favours received; in the correspondence there is ample evidence that Lawrence gave as much as he received. It is true that Lawrence is quite often asking Koteliansky for assistance: some typing, perhaps; the use of his rooms for a night in London; a book or two to be bought by Kot and sent to Lawrence's out-of-the-way cottage; a packet of paper; a typewriter ribbon; and so on. But there are always invitations to Koteliansky to come and pay a visit, to stay for a few days. Lawrence never omits thanking Kot for doing an errand; and when Lawrence begins finally to make some money old debts are paid off, and we read about gifts of Lawrence's own books and of money, tactfully sent to Koteliansky. The reader of these letters will have no reservations about Lawrence's generosity.

Although the personal element permeates the entire correspondence, there are, as we have already seen in the case of Koteliansky's translations, other activities of a literary nature in which Lawrence and Koteliansky were involved. The letters printed here enable us to see more clearly the extent of Lawrence's involvement in *The Signature*, the periodical founded by Lawrence and Murry in 1915. Although the paper ran to three numbers only, there was a great deal of work involved; and much of this work, as can now be seen, was done by Koteliansky, who served as business manager of *The Signature*.

Subsequent publishing schemes met the same fate as *The Signature*. Lawrence's scheme for "The Rainbow Books and Music"[35] came to nothing; and Koteliansky's venture into "expensive limited editions" (Nos. 289, 290, 291, 292) of an "intimate series" also failed to get off the ground. Yet if Lawrence and Koteliansky harboured an instinct to achieve success as publishers, the last venture in which they collaborated must have satisfied this instinct. I refer here to Lawrence's publication

34 See Letters Nos. 146, 147, 148.
35 For the prospectus of this scheme, see *C.B.*, I, 348–49.

of *Lady Chatterley's Lover*. The story of this venture is so well known that there is no need to go into the details at this time. What the new letters to Koteliansky help to do is to delineate more fully his part in that affair. If Koteliansky was nervous at times, this is understandable, since he had no claim to British citizenship (Koteliansky became a naturalized British subject on 27 November 1929), and had he gotten into difficulty with the authorities, he might very well have been forced to return to Russia, a fate which he doubtless should not have relished. Despite the risk, Lawrence found Koteliansky dependable and willing to help; and the successful distribution of *Lady Chatterley's Lover* in England is, as the letters reveal, in large measure due to Koteliansky.

VI

It is information of this kind that is to be found in these letters, information which is all relevant to the understanding of Lawrence's art and his character. These letters must be read in conjunction with Lawrence's other published correspondence, whenever a complete study of the artist is undertaken; but there are, I think, a number of special advantages in having Lawrence's letters to Koteliansky in a single volume. One of these advantages, as I see it, lies in the kind of unusual autobiographical account that is revealed in the letters taken as a whole. Although it is true that all of Lawrence's letters have an autobiographical quality in them, the letters to Koteliansky are unique in that they are addressed to one person. Because Lawrence addresses his comments to one individual, Koteliansky soon takes on the characteristics of a Lawrence alter ego; and before long, the reader of these letters is involved in a very personal account of Lawrence's own life, an account which covers nearly sixteen years.

The insight into Lawrence's mind provided by the letters to Koteliansky cannot be derived from other sources. Almost at every step we learn what Lawrence is doing, how he feels, what his hopes are. Having just moved to Chesham, for example, Lawrence writes: "I have been very busy whitewashing the upper rooms. This is a delightful cottage, really buried in the country. Already my wife and I go picking blackberries, and find many" (No. 4). Or, take this example: "I am better in health, though this English autumn gives me a cough. This week we have been helping the Murrys to move in to their cottage. We have painted & plastered & distempered & God knows what" (No. 9). Later, from Sussex, Lawrence writes: "The cottage is rather splendid—something monastic about it—severe white walls & oaken furniture—beautiful" (No. 30). After Lawrence goes to Cornwall, we have him saying: "I like being here. I like the rough seas and this bare country, King Arthur's country" (No. 68). There are moments of revulsion: "I feel perfectly hopeless and disgusted with the world here" (No. 101); there are moments of despair: "There is no hope here, my dear Kot—there is no hope in Europe, the sky is too old" (No. 101); there are also moments of resolution: "Hope is a great thing. We are not beaten yet, in spirit, but it is a critical moment. We must pray to the good unknown. I think we shall come out all right, even against so many millions" (No. 104). There is optimism: "We are coming out of it all. We will be happy before long" (No. 105). These are only a few instances of the way in which the letters provide an index to Lawrence's feelings and reveal what manner of man Lawrence was.

"'Tis not a year or two shows us a man," and for this reason the letters to Koteliansky are invaluable; they show us Lawrence in numerous situations and permit us to see how he reacts. We learn how the buoyant enthusiasm of prewar days is metamorphosed into the despair and vehemence of the dark days of the war, into the black loathing of a social order that has the courage to die but lacks the courage to live. Time and time again we see Lawrence's struggle against ill health, a courageous struggle if there ever was one. We can follow Lawrence's creative efforts, too, as he informs Koteliansky about his work, his problems with agents and publishers, his problems with censorship.

I have called this collection of letters "The Quest for *Rananim*" because it is from Kot that Lawrence obtained the name of the Utopian society which he yearned to establish somewhere in the world. *Rananim* seems to have been derived from one of Koteliansky's songs, which he used to sing to Lawrence. The meaning and origin of the word have been the subject of controversy, but K. W. Gransden has supplied some useful suggestions:

The promised land has had many names. Lawrence's name for it was *Rananim*. This is difficult to explain, but it seems probable that Kot may have bestowed it. It may have had something to do with the Hebrew root meaning "rejoice," for it appears from a letter from Lawrence to Kot of January 14th, 1922, that Kot used to amuse Lawrence by chanting a phrase which Lawrence, not quite correctly, transliterates as *"Ranane Sadikhim Sadikhim Badanoi"* "Rejoice, O ye righteous (his) in the Lord": the first verse of Psalm 33). It may also (I owe this suggestion to Mr. J. Leveen) be connected with the word *Ra'annanim*, meaning green, fresh, or flourishing, an adjective (qualifying, again, *sadikhim*, the righteous) found in the fourteenth verse of Psalm 92 (R.V.).[36]

Whatever the meaning of the original word, it is Lawrence's meaning that is significant. The first time that Lawrence uses *Rananim* in his letters to Kot is in Letter No. 26 dated 3 [January] 1915. It is in this letter that we find Lawrence's most enthusiastic proclamation regarding the new society; here also we have the choice of the rising phoenix as the symbol of the new order.[37] Later in Letter No. 34, Lawrence informs Kot that he plans to hammer out his idea of *Rananim* with Bertrand Russell, but there are already hints of disagreement as to the form of the new community: "But they [Russell and the others] say, the island

36 K. W. Gransden, *"Rananim*: D. H. Lawrence's Letters to S. S. Koteliansky," *Twentieth Century*, CLIX (January 1956), 23.

37 Letter No. 26, as I have indicated in the notes that follow it, was surprisingly misdated by Lawrence. It contains a drawing of a phoenix rising from the flames, which became Lawrence's personal symbol. Although I cannot say for certain, I believe that Lawrence's choice of the phoenix as a symbol may be traced to his reading of Mrs. Henry Jenner's book *Christian Symbolism* (London: Methuen and Co. Ltd., 1910). We know from a letter to Gordon Campbell dated ?19 December 1914 that Lawrence was reading Mrs. Jenner's book, which he "liked *very* much [Lawrence's italics]" (*C.L.*, I, 309). If we examine the book we find the following explanation of the symbol of the phoenix: "The *Phoenix*, which after death rose immortal from its ashes, was a popular myth, introduced into Christianity as early as the first Epistle of St. Clement of Rome, the second or third successor of St. Peter. As its special meaning was the resurrection of the dead and its triumph over death (and it is in this sense that St. Clement uses it), it was often associated with the palm tree on Christian sarcophagi, eloquent of that rapturous belief in immortality that is the prevailing characteristic of the catacombs. Representations of it rising triumphantly from its flaming nest and ascending towards the sun are somewhat less common, but the Phoenix in itself was a recognized emblem of the Resurrection of Christ" (p. 150). Opposite page 150 is a reproduction of a "Phoenix Rising from the Flames" taken from a thirteenth-century Bestiary in the Ashmolean Museum, Oxford. There is an unmistakable similarity between this illustration and that drawn by Lawrence for Koteliansky in Letter No. 26.

shall be England, that we shall start our new community in the midst of the old one."

There was little hope for the birth of a new society in the England of 1914, and Lawrence seized on the idea of Florida as the place where eventually it would be possible to feel "a good peace & a good silence, & a freedom to love & to create a new life." To Kot, he writes: "We must begin afresh—we must begin to create a life all together—unanimous. Then we shall be happy. We must be happy. But we shall only be happy if we are creating a life together. We must cease this analysis & introspection & individualism—begin to be free & happy with each other" (No. 67). From Cornwall at this time, Lawrence wrote to J. M. Murry and Katherine Mansfield: "It would be *so splendid* if it could but come off: *such* a lovely place: our *Rananim*" (*C.L.*, I, 440). But the relationship with Murry, as we know, was far from fulfilling these expectations; and before a year had passed Lawrence was looking towards America: "I don't think America is a paradise. But I know I can sell my stories there, and get a connection with publishers. And what I want is for us to have sufficient to go far west, to California or the South Seas, and live apart, away from the world. It is really my old Florida idea—but one must go further west. I hope in the end other people will come, and we can be a little community, a monastery, a school—a little Hesperides of the soul and body. That is what I will do finally" (*C.L.*, I, 497). A few days later, writing to Koteliansky on 12 January 1917, Lawrence again states his intention: "I shall say goodbye to England, forever, and set off in quest of our *Rananim*. Thither, later, you must come" (Letter No. 102).

This is not the place to record all of the references to *Rananim* in Lawrence's letters; the reader will soon become aware of these; nor is this the place to discuss whether Lawrence's ideas about an ideal society were impractical and ill-conceived. Instead, I wish to emphasize that the kind of human relationship which Lawrence envisaged for the inhabitants of *Rananim* existed between Lawrence and Koteliansky. The mutual trust, dependability, generosity, frankness, and integrity which characterized their relationship, judged by any standard, is indeed worthy of admiration. Although Lawrence often despaired over his failure to establish his Utopia, saying: "That *Rananim* of ours, it has sunk out of sight" (No. 251), I think the letters we can read here indicate that the spirit of *Rananim* in fact existed between the two men, and that to a large degree their quest for *Rananim* had been achieved.

Abbreviations

A.H. *The Letters of D. H. Lawrence*, edited and with an Introduction by Aldous Huxley (London: William Heinemann Ltd., 1932).

B. Warren Roberts, *A Bibliography of D. H. Lawrence* (London: Rupert Hart-Davis, 1963).

B.L.G. Beatrice Lady Glenavy, '*Today We Will Only Gossip*' (London: Constable, 1964).

C.B. *D. H. Lawrence: A Composite Biography*, gathered, arranged, and edited by Edward Nehls, 3 vols. (Madison: University of Wisconsin Press, 1957, 1958, 1959).

C.L. *The Collected Letters of D. H. Lawrence*, edited with an Introduction by Harry T. Moore, 2 vols. (New York: Viking Press, 1962).

I.H. Harry T. Moore, *The Intelligent Heart: The Story of D. H. Lawrence* (New York: Farrar, Straus and Young, 1954).

P.R. Harry T. Moore, *Poste Restante: A Lawrence Travel Calendar*, Introduction by Mark Schorer (Berkeley and Los Angeles: University of California Press, 1956).

The Letters

1

[Lancashire]
Wednesday [5 August 1914][1]

Dear Kotiliansky [*sic*],

I just find that my wife did not go up to Hampstead.[2] I think she is at 9 Selwood Terrace, Onslow Gardens, South Kensington.[3] But I shall be back on Saturday & will send you a postcard. Tell Horne not to go to Hampstead.[4]

I am very miserable about the war.[5]

auf wiedersehen

D. H. Lawrence

1 This is apparently the first letter from D. H. Lawrence preserved by S. S. Koteliansky. The address on the envelope, which has also been preserved, reads as follows: S. Kotilianski, Esq.,/Russian Law Bureau,/212 High Holborn,/ London. The walking tour which took Lawrence to Barrow-in-Furness, Lancashire, commenced on 31 July 1914. See *I.H.*, pp. 167–68. Since Lawrence was definitely back in London by 10 August 1914, this first letter to Koteliansky can be accurately dated 5 August 1914.

2 Lawrence and Frieda were married on 13 July 1914. See *I.H.*, p. 165.

3 According to J. M. Murry, the "Lawrences were at this time staying with the Campbells at Selwood Terrace, the house of the homeless, and their tiny drawing-room was [the] chief meeting place" (*The Autobiography of John Middleton Murry: Between Two Worlds* [New York, 1936], pp. 286–87). Gordon and Beatrice Campbell, now Lord and Lady Glenavy, were very good friends of Koteliansky. Gordon Campbell succeeded his father to the peerage in 1931. See *B.L.G.*, pp. 185–86. Beatrice Lady Glenavy makes numerous references to Koteliansky in her book.

4 Horne, whose first name is not mentioned anywhere in the correspondence, was an associate of Koteliansky's at the Russian Law Bureau, where the latter was employed. Horne apparently had some legal training, which Lawrence refers to in Letter No. 155.

5 For Lawrence's recollection of "the famous walk in the Lake district," see Letter No. 250. For the impact on Lawrence of the news of the declaration of war, see his letter to Lady Cynthia Asquith dated ?31 January 1915, published in *C.L.*, I, 309–10.

2 9 SELWOOD TERRACE
South Kensington S.W.
Sunday [9 August 1914]

Dear Kotilianski,

Can you come round tomorrow evening about 8:30, and
meet my wife. I'm sorry we can't ask you to a meal, but the
man of the house has taken away all the knives and forks and
things.

Our telephone number is 2153 Kensington. You might ring us
up and say if you will come. I shall be glad to see you again.

au revoir

D. H. Lawrence

[PS.]
I ask Horne to come also. Is his address 2 Museum
Mansions? This is near S. Kensington Station, off
Onslow Gardens.

---

3 9 SELWOOD TERRACE
[South Kensington] S.W.
[11 August 1914]

Dear Kotilianski,

I wonder if you & Horne would care to meet two little friends
of ours,[1] with us, at the Café Royal tomorrow night
(Wednesday) about 8:45 or 9:00 o'clock. Ring me up—2153
Kensington—& leave a message if I'm not in—

Yrs

D. H. Lawrence

---

1 Katherine Mansfield and J. M. Murry. According to Antony Alpers, Katherine
Mansfield did not meet Koteliansky until she and Murry went to live at "Rose
Tree Cottage, on the Lee, on October 26, 1914" (*Katherine Mansfield: A Biography* [New York, 1953], pp. 203–5).

Bellingdon Lane
Chesham, Bucks
Sunday [23 August 1914]

Dear Kotilianski,

I am a long time telling you our address. I have been very
busy whitewashing the upper rooms. This is a delightful
cottage, really buried in the country. Already my wife and I
go picking blackberries, and find many.

When will you come to see us? Next Sunday we are invited
out to tea & dinner in London, but can't you come one day
in the week—you & Horne? On certain days one may have a
cheap ticket 2/4 return from Baker St. Metropolitan. I believe
one can also have cheap tickets from Marylebone—Gt. Central.
Unfortunately there is only the one bed in the house, or you
might have stayed. But we are writing for another bed.
When you come, bring along with you my play *The
Widowing of Mrs. Holroyd*—my wife wants to amuse
herself by translating it. You come to Chesham Station.—
You may have to change at Chalfont Rd.—I think that's
the junction on the main line. We are 3½ miles from the
station—ask for Elliott's farm at Bellingdon, & we are quite
near—a stone's throw. Tell Horne—I haven't the energy to
write him another letter. We shall be glad to see you & him
again.

Vale

D. H. Lawrence

THE TRIANGLE
Bellingdon Lane
Chesham, Bucks
Wednesday [9 September 1914]

Dear Kotilianski,

I wish you would come & see us on Sunday.—Can you afford 2/4 in railway travelling? I hear from Horne you are on short wages, like the rest of us. He—Horne—is in Blackpool with his wife, is he not?

I was very cross and quite indignant that you didn't turn up the other Sunday. But I understand you didn't feel like it.

Do come on Sunday. The best train leaves Marylebone— Gt. Central—at 9:00 in the morning, and gets here at 9:55. By that train you need not, I think, change at Chalfont Rd. But ask. The next trains are 10:07 and 11:05 from Baker St. Metropolitan.

At Chesham, ask for the way to Bellingdon—it is about 3½ miles here. We are near Elliotts farm—just down a little lane off the highroad. Elliotts farm is on your *right*, & has a red letter box in the gate. The house stands across a field. Immediately past the farm, our lane goes down to the right.

You cannot get astray. Do come, we shall be so glad to see you.

auf wiedersehen

D. H. Lawrence

6 BELLINGDON LANE
Chesham, Bucks
5 October 1914

Dear Kotilianski,

I ought to have written you before. I have been seedy &
forced to stay in bed for a day or two, so I am not aimiable [*sic*].
It is nothing, but I hate to be unwell.

Will you really type-write me my book[1]—which is supposed
to be about Thomas Hardy, but which seems to be about
anything else in the world but that. I have done about 50
pages—re-written them. I must get it typed somehow or other.
Don't do it if it is any trouble—or if it is much trouble, for
it is sure to be some. I should like a duplicate copy also.

When will you come & see us. The Murrys are taking a
cottage two miles away.[2] I think they are coming down to
stay with us for a week, whilst they make preparations. I
should like to see you, & to know how you are. Frieda
looks *so* nice in the shirt with the blue forgetmenots—she
often wears it. Many regards from us—

auf wiedersehen

D. H. Lawrence

[PS.]
Remember me to Horne.—How are things with him.

---

1 The book is *A Study of Thomas Hardy*, which was not published during
Lawrence's lifetime. It appeared in *Phoenix* (New York, 1936). In a letter to
J. B. Pinker dated 5 September 1915, Lawrence writes: "Out of sheer rage I've
begun my book about Thomas Hardy. It will be about anything but Thomas
Hardy, I am afraid—queer stuff—but not bad" (*A.H.*, p. 208). But he was planning
the Hardy book as early as 15 July 1914. See his letter to Edward Marsh, *C.L.*, I,
287. As Lawrence already realized, the book about Hardy was bound to be
"anything else in the world but that" and became instead an attempt to work out
a "philosophy" of existence. Lawrence's struggle to write the book is documented
in the succeeding letters to Koteliansky.

2 See *The Autobiography of John Middleton Murry: Between Two Worlds* (New
York, 1936), p. 304.

7
Chesham, Bucks
8 October 1914

My dear Kot,

We shall be glad to see you & Horne on Sunday. It is as
well you didn't come last week: I was in bed & very disagree-
able. Now I am better & going to be quite cheerful.

I wonder what on earth you'll think of this stuff I want you
to type. It will amuse me to know.[1]

The Murrys will be here on Sunday. They will like meeting
you & Horne in a quieter & more congenial place than the
Café Royal.

We shall expect you any time on Sunday, but don't be very
late. I shall be glad to see you.

auf wiedersehen

D. H. Lawrence

[PS.]
I partly agree about Gertler.[2] It isn't potatoes, it is cooked
onions: *come dice lui*. But Frieda is very fond of him, so take
care.

---

1 *A Study of Thomas Hardy* as Lawrence's letter of 13 October 1914 to Edward
Garnett confirms: "I have been writing my book more or less—very much less—
about Thomas Hardy, I have done a third of it. When this much is typed I shall
send it to Bertram Christian" (*C.L.*, I, 292–93).

2 Mark Gertler (1892–1939), a painter, who was a close friend of Lawrence
and Koteliansky. For biographical details, see *Mark Gertler: Selected Letters*,
edited by Noel Carrington (London, 1965).

8
Chesham, Bucks
14 October 1914]

Dear Kotilianski,

I shan't come to London on Thursday, because I am still
seedy. And Frieda won't come alone. So we shan't see you
this week. But next week we shall most probably come for
a day. Tell Horne *au revoir*.

D. H. L.

BELLINGDON LANE
Chesham, Bucks
Saturday [24 October 1914]

Dear Kot,

I am sorry you have been expecting us & we have not turned
up. I am better in health, though this English autumn gives
me a cough. This week we have been helping the Murrys
to move in to their cottage. We have painted & plastered &
distempered & God knows what. The place is now almost
ready. They move in on Monday.[1] They have been staying
here these 10 days.

Thank you very much for doing the typing. I don't want you
to send the MS. Either I am coming to London early next
week, or you must come here. Could you not come one day
during the week, & stay the night.

O, and a lady in America has sent me a typewriting machine.[2]
It is now on the way from Liverpool. You must tell me all
about it when it comes, & when you come.

If I can't get to London next week, could you come here—
Tuesday or Wed. or Thursday.

Very many regards

D. H. Lawrence

---

1 J. M. Murry has recorded: "On October 26th, 1914, we moved in, without
enthusiasm. It went against the grain to return to a part of the country where
we had lived before.
"Then began three months of fairly close association with the Lawrences, of
which my memories, though extensive, are miserable" (*The Autobiography of
John Middleton Murry: Between Two Worlds* [New York, 1936], p. 305).

2 Amy Lowell (1874–1925), who was an American poetess and critic. In 1914
Lawrence "happened to be in London when Miss [Amy] Lowell was collecting
the material for the imagist anthologies, and was asked by her to contribute to
them" (*C.B.*, I, 236). In a letter to David Garnett, 5 November 1914, Lawrence
writes: "Amy Lowell sent me this typewriter, so I amuse myself typing my
letters" (*C.L.*, I, 294).

10 BELLINGDON LANE
Chesham, Bucks
26 October 1914

Dear Kot,

We are coming to London on Thursday, staying a night—or two nights—with Mrs. Jackson.[1] Ring us up at her house somewhere about tea-time on Thursday—she is at Holly Bush House, Hampstead. Then we will go to some music [*sic*], if possible. I want very much to hear some music. That would be Thursday evening. Tell Horne.

I am looking forward to seeing you. I have not yet shaved.[2] Many greetings from my wife.

Yours

D. H. Lawrence

---

1 Later Mrs. Catherine Carswell, author of *The Savage Pilgrimage* (London, 1932).

2 Lawrence's characteristic beard dates from this time.

BELLINGDON LANE
Chesham, Bucks
31 October 1914

Dear Kot,

I send you some MS.[1] You must tell me more particularly
what you think of it.

When I went down Wardour Street I saw a necklace I
wanted to buy for Frieda. It is in a shop almost at the south
end of Wardour St. near Leicester Square, on the right
hand side going down—S—a second hand jeweller's—a
necklace of lapis lazuli set in little white enamel clasps—
costs 30/–. It hangs up at eye level near the doorway.
I send you a cheque. If you find the necklace, please buy
it me.—round beads of lapis lazuli—you can't mistake it—
marked 30/–

[drawing of necklace]

If you don't find it you can give me back the cheque.

I hope to see you soon again

Many regards from us

D. H. Lawrence

[PS.]
mind you endorse the cheque just as I have entered it
S. Kotilianski

---

1 *A Study of Thomas Hardy*

BELLINGDON LANE
Chesham, Bucks
5 November 1914

Dear Kot,

The necklace came this morning, much joy in the house. Thank you very much for getting it. Why do you never say whether you like a thing or not? I think it's pretty.

Why does my typewriter print double, have you any idea? You will see I am quite an expert typist, but very slow indeed. I, however, use all my fingers.

My typewriter is a Smith's Premier, No. 2.[1] I think it is a good one, but it distresses me much by printing double. I suppose I tap it wrong.

I don't think Vera Volkhovsky will come on Saturday as she has not written.[2] Will you and Horne come down for the weekend? One of you must sleep at the inn. If Miss Volkhovsky writes to say she is coming, I will let you know, and you will come only for the day, on Sunday.

What do you think of my MSS [*sic*]—have you read it?[3]

Tutti saluti dalla Frieda

Yrs.

D. H. Lawrence

---

1 For further references to this typewriter see Letters Nos. 83 to 87.

2 Frank McShane, *The Life and Work of Ford Madox Ford* (London, 1965), refers to ". . . the Nihilists Sergius Stepniak and Felix Volkhofsky" as being "among the multitude of Russian exiles who flocked to London during the 'nineties of the last century" (p. 16). They were associated with the anarchist journal *The Torch*. Vera Volkhovsky apparently belonged to this group. Madame Stepniak, who was a very close friend of Koteliansky, is mentioned by Lawrence in Letter No. 111. A number of letters in Russian from Madame Stepniak to Kot are preserved in the British Museum in the *Koteliansky Papers*.

3 *A Study of Thomas Hardy*

---

13 BELLINGDON [LANE]
Chesham, Bucks
Sunday [8 November 1914]

Dear Kot,

Horne & his wife & Lewis came today.[1] Lewis made me very depressed because of the war. He [*sic*] is much nicer.

Horne says he will probably come next Sunday. So if you would rather come alone, choose one of the days in the week when you can get a cheap ticket—Tuesday, I think—& come down & stay a night. Decide for yourself.

You should have sent me your long foolish letter, as you call it. It is very weak to write a letter & then not to send it.

Write & say when you will come—any time—

Regards from Frieda & me.

D. H. Lawrence

---

1 Lewis was "an engineer . . . from the Vickers-Maxim works at Spezia" (*I.H.*, p. 163). Also see *C.L.*, I, 282.

---

14 BELLINGDON LANE
Chesham, Bucks
11 November 1914

My dear Kot,

But why this curtness? What ails you? Are you cross or offended, or have you got a "bad mood"—which is it?

Why can't you come down? Why are you so silly? Why don't you say what's amiss? Is it Slatkowsky,[1] or Horne, or just yourself?

If I replied to you in your own terms, I should send you a letter like this:

Bellingdon Lane
Chesham
Bucks
11 Nov. 1914

My dear Kot,

?

Kindest regards from Frieda

Yours Sincerely

D. H. Lawrence

Enquire of Horne if he is coming at the week-end, & if
he is not, you come then. And please tell me what's amiss,
and don't be a chump—

au revoir

D. H. Lawrence

---

1 Koteliansky's employer at the Russian Law Bureau.

15
Chesham, Bucks
undated]

Caro mio,

Ti aspetto Domenicà—tanto piacere vederti.[1]

D. H. Lawrence

1

Dear Friend,

I'll see you on Sunday—so much pleasure to see you [translation].

BELLINGDON LANE
Chesham, Bucks
18 November 1914

Dear Kot,

We may be coming up to London this week-end—Frieda *must* see the dentist. If he gives us an appointment for Saturday, as I have written to ask him to do, we shall be down till Monday. I want very much to go to the National Gallery, and, on a fine day, to the Zoo.

I hope you don't mind my tirades of Sunday. Don't say you will never abuse people any more. It is so nice when you abuse people. But don't avoid everybody, and annihilate him straight off. You must give yourself to people more, & take them as they are.

The Murrys said yesterday how much they like you. They want you to come to their Christmas party. You must come here at Christmas.

I have qualms when I think of you typing my MS. I am afraid you hate it, and I had no right to foist it on you. I am sorry. But then you don't do anything, do you, otherwise?

I have written my war poem, which everybody will think bosh. What do you think of my MS?

Tante belle cose from Frieda and me.

a rivederti—[*sic*]

D. H. Lawrence

17 BELLINGDON [LANE
Chesham, Bucks
27 November 1914]

Dear Kot,

We expect you on Saturday—stay till Monday. If it is perfectly easy will you bring my tooth-brush which I left in
Horne's bedroom. If it is any trouble at all, don't bother—it
is of no matter. You'll see the Murry's [*sic*] tomorrow.

Love

D. H. Lawrence

[PS.]
Excuse the postcard¹—it is the only one I've got

[PPS.]
Come early tomorrow afternoon

---

1 The postcard has on it the following note crossed out by Lawrence:

111 ARTHUR STREET
Chelsea SW.
October 3, 1914

Dear Sir,

Will you kindly send me some particulars of the two cottages you advertise

---

18 [BELLINGDON LANE
Chesham, Bucks
30 November 1914]

[Dear Kot,]

Arrive Baker St. at 11:43—I shall go straight to Hornes.
Frieda sees dentist in Harley St. at 12:15. She'll go there
direct. Gertler will ring up Law Bureau tomorrow afternoon
to tell us about going to see his studio. We'd like to go
Sunday afternoon to tea.

auf weidersehen

D. H. Lawrence

BELLINGDON LANE
[Chesham, Bucks]
Thursday [3 December 1914]

Dear Kot,

I am most probably going to Nottingham with Frieda after all. I don't think she wants to go alone.

You musn't judge her lightly. There is another quality in woman that you do not know, so you can't estimate it. You don't know that a woman is not a man with different sex. She is a different world. You do not understand that enough. Your world is all of one hemisphere.

We laugh at you for your pennyworth of good deeds which were stolen from you.

Do please get my typing done. If I can send it in, I may get a little money for it.

I thank you for getting Frieda into a good state of mind. She says it was absolutely the result of seeing how utterly wrong you were when you talked to her. So beware. Nevertheless things are very good again.

I am working *frightfully* hard—re-writing my novel.[1]

I shall see you very soon, even if I go to Nottingham—whence we return Wednesday night.

Love from us

D. H. Lawrence

[PS.]
Don't tumble out of the attic into the cellar. By the way, the wind blew our attic window clean out—such a wind

---

1 *The Rainbow*. See *B.*, pp. 27–28. Lawrence refers to re-writing *The Rainbow* in a letter to Amy Lowell dated 18 December 1914. See *C.L.*, I, 298.

20
Chesham, Bucks
5 December 1914

Dear Kot,

I send you the last of the MS.[1] Tell me if you get it all right.
I am going to Nottingham till Wednesday. But probably next
week we shall be coming to London for a day or two, with
the Murrys, staying in Campbell's house—he is in Ireland.
I'll let you know.

The weather is hideous. I've got a headache. Frieda shakes
her fist in your direction. I hope you are still happy.

Many regards from us.

Yours

D. H. Lawrence

---

1 The MS is that of the Hardy book but the "last of the MS" refers only to that
portion which Koteliansky was typing. Writing to Amy Lowell on 18 December
1914, Lawrence says: "My wife and I we type away at my book on Thomas Hardy,
which has turned out as a sort of Story of My Heart, or a *Confessio Fidei*: which
I must write again, still another time: and for which the critics will plainly beat
me, as a Russian friend says" (*C.L.*, I, 298). The "Russian friend" is, of course,
Koteliansky.

---

21 RIPLEY—DERBYSHIRE
Wednesday [9 December 1914]

Dear Kot,

We are going back to Bellingdon tonight—tomorrow we go to Garnetts for two days.[1] We shall come to tea with you tomorrow, if we may. No, rather you come to us, at half past four, in the Green Room in Piccadilly Circus. Garnett is taking us to the theatre in the evening—has booked for us I believe.—Frieda saw her husband—he was very dull—affected—quarrelsome—nothing decided. But we'll tell you tomorrow.

Love from us

D. H. Lawrence

---

1 See Lawrence's letter to David Garnett dated ?9 December 1914 in *C.L.*, I, 297.

---

22 RIPLEY—DERBYSHIRE
Wednesday [9 December 1914]

Dear Kot,

We have missed our train so cannot go to Chesham. We shall come down tomorrow straight to London, arriving at Marylebone at 3:00 o'clock. The dentist was making an appointment for Frieda, writing to Chesham. I have asked him to ring you up & leave the time with you, so don't be surprised if he calls you up—Mr. Campkin. If you aren't busy, come to the station to meet us, will you? If you are busy, then Green Tea Room at 4:30.

Love

D. H. Lawrence

18

BELLINGDON [LANE]
Chesham, Bucks
Thursday [17 December 1914]

Dear Kot,

Please will you come down to stay with us next *Wednesday.*
I am so busy writing my novel, & Frieda wants you to come
& help her to prepare for our party, which is on the Thursday—Christmas Eve. We look forward to it immensely—to
your coming to stay with us. Do please try to come on
Wednesday.

How are you? You must be quite jolly when you come—but
it doesn't matter, if you're sad we'll "plainly beat you."[1]

Vale!

D. H. Lawrence

[PS.]
I must call you—what is it—Shimiel—Schmuel—it ends in
"el" like all the Angels—Chamuel, Jophiel, Ladkiel, Uriel,
Gabriel.

---

1 A characteristic Koteliansky expression. See J. M. Murry's letter to Beatrice
Lady Glenavy in *B.L.G.*, p. 191, for Kot's use of "plainly."

---

24 BELLINGDON LANE
Chesham, Bucks
Monday [21 December 1914]

Dear Kot,

We are expecting you on Wednesday. Let us know what train, & I'll come with the [?] tub.¹ And please bring two flasks of Chianti such as you had at Horne's for your Jewish supper. I send you ten shillings in this letter.

I must ask you please not to buy things to bring with you. It spoils my pleasure when you spend your money, because you are poor. Really, I feel a disappointment when you spend money, or when we occasion you to spend your money. Don't do it.

I've got a head that is so heavy it even makes my heart heavy. Gertler is here, very sad. We are going to tea with him.

But I look forward very much to Wednesday & Thursday. Come during the daylight on Wednesday if you can.

mia stretta di mano

D. H. Lawrence

[PS.]
I can only get 6/– in paper money so I send that.

---

1 Probably a tub for carrying things conveniently as the two men walked the three and a half miles to Lawrence's cottage from the station.

---

25 BELLINGDON [LANE]
Chesham, Bucks
[21 December 1914]

I am a dunderheaded donkey—here is the postal order for
the two flasks of Chianti I want you to bring.

D. H. Lawrence

[PS.]
Such as we had at your Jewish Cosher [*sic*] Supper at Horne's

26

BELLINGDON [LANE]
Chesham, Bucks
3 [January] 1915 [1]

Dear Kot,

I was sorry you did not sleep when you got back to the Bureau. But we laughed at you in your letter nevertheless.

What about *Rananim?* Oh, but we are going. We are going to found an *Order of the Knights of Rananim.* The motto is "Fier" or the Latin equivalent. The badge is so: an eagle, or phoenix argent, rising from a flaming nest of scarlet, on a black background.

[large drawing of phoenix]

and our flag, the blazing, ten-pointed star, scarlet on a black background.

[small drawing of flag]

The Murrys will tell you when is their party—perhaps next Saturday, perhaps the one following. Please buy for me *Chapman's* translation of *Homer.* It is published for 1/– in Everyman's Library, I think: or, in two volumes, for 1/– each, in some other little edition. A bookseller will tell you.

We look forward to seeing you. Remember *Rananim.*

auf wiedersehen

D. H. Lawrence

[PS.]
Regards from Frieda

---

1 This letter was dated by Lawrence 3 December 1915. On 3 December 1915, Lawrence was living at 1 Byron Villas, Hampstead. See his letter to Lady Ottoline Morrell written on that date, published in *C.L.*, I, 392–93. The *Rananim* idea was uppermost in Lawrence's mind in January 1915. See Lawrence's letter to W. E. Hopkins dated 18 January 1915 in which he says: "We will also talk of my pet scheme. I want to gather together about twenty souls and sail away from this world of war and squalor and found a little colony where there shall be no money but a sort of communism as far as necessaries of life go, and some real decency. It is to be a colony built up on the real decency which is in each member of the community. A community which is established upon the assumption of goodness in the members, instead of the assumption of badness.

"What do you think of it? I think it should be quite feasible. We keep brooding the idea—I and some friends" (*C.L.*, I, 307).

Lawrence's reference to the Murrys' party also helps to place the letter in January 1915; see Letter No. 27.

The Christmas of 1914 was a memorable one for the Lawrences. Frieda recalls it: "Christmas came. We made the cottage splendid with holly and mistletoe, we cooked and boiled, roasted and baked. Campbell and Koteliansky and the Murrys came, and Gertler and the Cannans. We had a gay feast.

"We danced on the shaky floor. Gilbert with uplifted head sang: 'I feel, I feel like an eagle in the sky.' Koteliansky sang soulfully his Hebrew song: 'Ranani Sadekim Badanoi'" (*Not I, But the Wind* [New York, 1934], p. 81).

Lawrence's views of *Rananim* were further elaborated in a letter to Lady Ottoline Morrell dated 1 February 1915; see *C.L.*, I, 311–12.

---

27 BELLINGDON LANE
Chesham, Bucks
7 January 1915

Dear Kot,

Don't be so absurd, asking why I don't want to invite you to the Murrys party. Of course I want to invite you—& it's not a question of inviting, you are plainly coming. But the party *isn't* on Saturday—it is postponed to an indefinite date—probably till the 23rd

We—Gilbert & Mary[1] & Myself—have done a little Schnitzler play—20 minutes—in readiness. It is funny.

I am writing to Viola Meynell[2] to say perhaps after all we will go to her cottage in Sussex, if we may. I am feeling seedy here, and I don't like this place. The Meynells are kinder. Probably we shall go. I shall let you know. At any rate you will come & see us before long. I will let you know that also. Frieda is not cross. She jumps at the thought of leaving Bellingdon. You would come just the same to Sussex.

sia bene—a rivederti [*sic*]

D. H. Lawrence

---

1 Gilbert and Mary Cannan.

2 Daughter of Wilfred and Alice Meynell who lent the Lawrences their cottage in Greatham, Pulborough. See Lawrence's letter to A. W. McLeod dated 5 January 1915 and Moore's comments in *I.H.*, pp. 179–80.

---

28 [BELLINGDON LANE
Chesham, Bucks
9 January 1915]

Dear Kot,

Do come tomorrow. I've got a cold & can't go out, so shall be glad to see you. We are thinking of moving to Sussex—come & be told about it.

D. H. L.

---

29 [BELLINGDON LANE
Chesham, Bucks
20 January 1915]

We are having rather a rush in London.—Coming up Thursday to lunch with Lady Ottoline[1]—tea with Garnett—then to the Eders.[2] But I shall ring you up from the Eders & we'll make an arrangement. You must come to Campbells—you must know him. Frieda sends warm regards—

Vale

D. H. Lawrence

[PS. in Frieda's hand]
I would have written before—
Love, Frieda[3]

---

1 Lady Ottoline Morrell. See her recollections of Lawrence in *Memoirs of Lady Ottoline Morrell* (New York, 1954), pp. 274–78 *et passim*.

2 Dr. David Eder and Mrs. Eder. "As a pioneer of Freud's theories in England, Dr. Eder found *Sons and Lovers* of great interest and in 1914, the year after the book appeared, became a friend of its author. He was the brother-in-law of Dr. Barbara Low and uncle of Ivy Low-Litvinov" (*C.L.*, I, xxxvi).

3 Frieda Lawrence on occasion did write to Koteliansky. Her letters are also preserved among the *Koteliansky Papers* in the British Museum. The letters (23 in all) date from 9 February 1915 and appear sporadically until 26 January 1930; these are now published in *Frieda Lawrence: The Memoirs and Correspondence*, edited by E. W. Tedlock, Jr. (First American Edition; New York, 1964).

GREATHAM, PULBOROUGH
Sussex
Sunday [24 January 1915]

My Dear Kot,

We got here safely last night, after a wonderful long drive
in the Motor Car [sic] through deep snow, & between narrow
hedges, & pale winter darkness. The Meynells are very nice—
but all return to London tomorrow. The cottage is rather
splendid—something monastic about it—severe white walls &
oaken furniture—beautiful. And there is bathroom & all.
And the country is very fine—Meynell owns a nice piece.

But the cottage is not yet quite finished—there are many
things to do in the way of furnishing and so on. But this is
really a place with beauty of character.

I hope you saw and liked Campbell; you must tell me what
you talked about, & how it was. Please be friends with him. I
shall ask you to come & see us here before long. I wish
you did not spend so much money on us. I plainly hate it.
Frieda likes the Meynells, but is a bit frightened of the cloistral
severity of this place. I must say I love it. Frieda sends warm
regards.

a rivederti—sia bene [sic]

D. H. Lawrence

31 [London
Undated]

Dear Kot,

Here am I, for the night—come up in a motor car with ono of
the Meynells—staying with Horne—returning tomorrow
early. We want to have a meeting at your house tonight.
Lady Ottoline may come.

au revoir

D. H. Lawrence

[PS.]
Come to the Imperial Restaurant—just at the back of South
Kensington Station—through the Arcade & round to the
right—just near—the address is Alfred Place West

[drawing showing directions to restaurant]

---

32 GREATHAM, PULBOROUGH
Sussex
Thursday [28 January 1915]

Dear Kot,

Will you come down on Saturday—write & tell us the train.
I think only Viola Meynell will be here. I will walk down to
meet you—*but come in the daylight.*

Don't bring anything—I do dislike it when you buy things to
bring.

I shan't write a letter because I am very busy.

au revoir

D. H. Lawrence

33
Sussex
Monday [1 February 1915]

My dear Kot,

We were disappointed not to see you—the country is so
beautiful, & you will like this cottage.

If you go to Glasgow, will you see my elder sister, who
lives there, & take her my love? She is a queer creature, she
loves me very much, though. And she is sad up there, &
rather poor. They have a little dairy shop (she is not beautiful
either).

Mrs. S. King
5 Harley St.
Ibrox
Glasgow

is the address. I shall tell her perhaps you will see her. She
has one little girl of about five, Margaret, my niece, of whom I
am very fond. If you took the mother & child out to tea
one day, to some pleasant restaurant, it would be a nice thing.

When are you going to Glasgow? We have had today Lady
Ottoline Morrell down for the day—I like her very much.
You must meet her. You will like her.

I shall after all send you some requests, you see. Send us
one or two boxes, will you—round ones

[sketches of boxes]

We expect you in about a fortnight, seeing you are free
then.

Herzliche Greïsse

D. H. Lawrence

[PS.]
Look after the Murrys a bit—their condition is I think
crucial.

34

GREATHAM, PULBOROUGH
Sussex
Friday [?5 February 1915]

Mein Lieber Kot,

Thank you very much for sending the wooden-box list. Get
me one or two of 11, 12, & 13 flat shape, & one or two
6, 7, 8 tall shape—I would like six flat ones and three or
four tall ones.

I keep wondering when you will go to Glasgow, if ever. It
will be an experience for you.

I have got into the stride of my novel,[1] & am working
gallantly. But I doubt I shall be too late for spring publication.
However, I don't care. What is the use of giving books to
the swinish public in its present state.

I continue to love this place. This long room with its untouched beams is not so very severe—beautiful, I think it. You
are sure to like it. Lady Ottoline says that on her estate are
some monkish buildings she is eager to make into a cottage
for me & Frieda.

I have got a new birth of life since I came down here. Those
five months since the war have been my time in the sepulchre.
Do you remember coming down to Barrow-in-Furness &
finding war declared? I shall never forget those months in
Bucks—five months & every moment dead, dead as a corpse
in its grave clothes. It is a ghastly thing to remember. Now
I feel the waking up, & the thrill in my limbs, & the
wind blows ripples on my blood as it rushes against the
house from the sea, full of germination and quickening.

Tomorrow Lady Ottoline is coming again & bringing Bertrand
Russell—the Philosophic-Mathematics man—a Fellow of
Cambridge University FRS—Earl Russell's brother.[2] We are
going to struggle with my Island idea—*Rananim*. But they
say, the island shall be England, that we shall start our new
community in the midst of the old one, as a seed falls among
the roots of the parent. Only wait, and we will remove
mountains & set them in the midst of the sea.

You will let us know when you can come down.

This week they have killed Hilda's brother at the war. She came running in as if she were shot "Oh Mum, my poor brother's killed at the war—" I feel so bitter against the war altogether, I could wring the neck of humanity for it.

Mais—nous verrons.

je te serre la main

D. H. Lawrence

[PS.]
I will take you to Lady Ottoline's later.[3]

---

1 *The Rainbow*

2 According to Harry T. Moore, Lawrence's letters to Russell began 12 February 1915. "Their hectic friendship," writes Moore, "which endured for about a year, was one of the most dramatic and interesting friendships of Lawrence's life" (*I.H.*, p. 182). Russell's mass of personal papers (150,000 items), including typewritten copies of his letters from D. H. Lawrence, was purchased in April 1968 by McMaster University in Hamilton, Ontario. The correspondence between the two men is to be found in *D. H. Lawrence's Letters to Bertrand Russell*, edited by Harry T. Moore (New York, 1948). See Warren Roberts' notes on this volume in *B.*, pp. 173–74. Bertrand Russell's opinion of Lawrence may be read in *C.B.*, I, 282–84.

3 According to a note from Lady Ottoline Morrell to Kot, the date of Kot's introduction to her was 15 February 1915. The note is preserved in the *Koteliansky Papers* in the British Museum.

GREATHAM, PULBOROUGH
Sussex
Monday [22 February 1915]

My dear Kot,

You are a great donkey, & your letters to Frieda are
ridiculous.—Why the hell do you make such a palaver to her?
She was cross with me—at such times she is indignant with
you for your imagined adoration (as she puts it) of me.
You are an ass to make so many postures & humilities & so
forth about it. Next time, for God's sake write—"My dear
Frieda—Thank you for your letter—*e basta.*"

And if you're going to come & see us, why for Heaven's sake
don't you come—fidgetting & fuming & stirring & preparing
& communing with yourself & reading the portents—it
is preposterous. If you are coming, come, & have done. If
you have anything to say, say it, & have done. But *don't*
be so queasy & uneasy & important—oh damn. Plainly
I do not like you.

Murry is here—I don't know when he is going away. It is
possible Barbara Low[1] may come this week-end. There is still
room for you if you'll come. But I suppose you'd rather come
when we are alone. I will let you know if Barbara is coming.
If she is not, then fidget no more, but come on Saturday.
If she is coming, then you please yourself.

We shall be in London on March 6th. I am going to Cambridge
for the week-end.[2] Now I hope you'll be in a good & careless
state of soul after this abuse. Be *careless,* damn it—not so
careful.

auf wiedersehen

D. H. Lawrence

---

1 Barbara Low, an "Early Freudian psychoanalyst in England. Friend of Lawrence from 1914 . . . sister-in-law of Dr. David Eder . . . author of *Psycho-Analysis:
A Brief Outline of the Freudian Theory* [1920]" (*C.B.*, I, 521).

2 Saturday, 6 March 1915, and Sunday, 7 March 1915. See Lawrence's letters to
Russell dated 26 February 1915 and 2 March 1915 in *C.L.*, I, 323–24, 327–28; see
also Lawrence's letter to Barbara Low dated [19 February 1915] in *C.B.*, I,
274–75.

36 GREATHAM, PULBOROUGH
[Sussex
25 February 1915, postmark]

Katharine[1] came back from Paris this morning—I think they have gone to Bucks. Murry returned to London last night, to meet her.

We shall have no visitors whatsoever this week-end, so that you will find us quite by ourselves if you come. Come over the bridge in Pulboro [*sic*] to Cold Waltham, & I will walk down to meet you on the way, if you let me know your train. We stay next week with Barbara.

D. H. L.

---

1 Lawrence almost invariably spells "Katherine" as "Katharine."

---

37 GREATHAM, PULBOROUGH
[Sussex
?1 March 1915]

My dear Kot,

We've both got influenza & are in bed. If I'm better I may go straight to Cambridge on Saturday, but Frieda certainly can't turn out. We've had this influenza now a week—it got better, & now is worse again. How I hate it! We are disappointed of our town visit—

D. H. Lawrence

GREATHAM, PULBOROUGH
Sussex
Wednesday [10 March 1915]

My dear Kot,

According to my time table there is a bad train leaving
Victoria 1 : 42, arr. Pulborough 3 : 40. It is a slow brute of
a train, but you won't mind. If London Bridge is better, you
leave there 1 : 50—L.B. & S.C. Station. You may have to
change at Horsham—just ask.

You come out of the station & down to the high road, then
turn to the left. You will see the bridge in the meadows. When
you come to the Swan Hôtel, you cross the bridge, which is
just on your right, & come straight forward. I shall meet
you before you get to Cold Waltham Church. If I don't,
in Cold Waltham is a public house—"The Labouring Man."
Next to that is an old house below the level of the road.
At the end of the land of this house is a path going across
the fields on your left. Take that. It crosses the railway
& brings you to our road. Turn to the left again & you
come straight to Greatham. At the red house in Greatham
turn to the right down the lane & the first house is ours.
So—a blind man could walk here without asking a question.

If nothing happens, I shall meet you in or about Cold
Waltham, on the main road.

Will you bring please two boxes like the largest you sent
last time—with sliding lids.

[sketch]

Frieda thanks you for the chocolates. She says—like Barbara [1]
& her wasps—that "cats' tongues" was Freudian on your
part. She says, however, peace must now be declared on both
sides.

Don't be gloomy, neither defiant of all the governments
and all the Fates: prison, Siberia, and the hangmans noose.
But just come in a good & spring-like mood, with a

"*Courage mon ami le diable est mort.*" So we will have a good time. I look forward to seeing you here.

Yours

D. H. Lawrence

[PS.]

We will paint more boxes on Saturday, shall we?—like Christmas

[PPS.]

The *Smart Set*, in case you haven't got it, is John Adams Thayer Corporation, 452 Fifth Avenue, New York.

---

¹ Barbara Low

---

39 GREATHAM, PULBOROUGH
[Sussex]
Thursday [11 March 1915]

Dear Kot,

Please bring a few tubes of Rowney's Elementary Water Colour paints—or Reeves—but better Rowneys—they are about 2ᵈ each.

> 2 tubes Chinese White
> 1 ” Emerald Green
> 1 ” Crimson Lake
> 1 ” Prussian blue

also a couple of penny pencils, one HB one B.

We look forward to having you here.

Bring a 1/– pot of Crosse & Blackwells Bloater Paste.

Mind you are jolly.

D. H. L.

[PS.]

Bring me 2 packets ordinary envelopes. Don't be cross with all these commissions. I'll meet you as near Pulboro [*sic*] as possible

40 GREATHAM, PULBOROUGH
Sussex
Friday [19 March 1915]

My dear Kot,

We are coming to London tomorrow, arrive Victoria 1:52. I have asked Murry to meet us at the station. Will you also be there? Because I don't know what we shall do, exactly, tomorrow. On Sunday we must stay a good deal with Barbara.[1] Tomorrow we are free of her.

You know Katharine has again fled to Paris?[2] Murry once more gloomy.

I hope you are well & cheerful. Buck up or I shall shove you under a bus as a reward for melancholy.

à demain

D. H. Lawrence

---

1 Barbara Low.
2 Katherine Mansfield returned to Paris on 18 March 1915. See *Journal of Katherine Mansfield*, edited by J. Middleton Murry (London, 1954), p. 79.

---

41 GREATHAM, PULBOROUGH
Sussex
Wednesday [?24 March 1915]

My dear Kot,

I am very glad you are quite happy again. Soon it will be your turn to shove me off a bus.

Next week Bertrand Russell wants to come, from Thursday to Saturday. Would you be sad if I asked you to come on Saturday, when we have got rid of him? Barbara also asked if she might come for Easter. Now don't be cross, & say you don't like her. I *do* rather like her. You must like her too—& have a honeymoon in the Garden Suburb.

34

There is a train from Victoria at 10:20 (I believe) on
Saturday morning. Barbara will probably come by that.
Do please be nice, & come with her. Be a good soul.

Gilbert & Mary Cannan are here. I rather love them. There is
real good—power for good—in Gilbert. I am not very well.
It is that which affects me—nothing else.

We *will* have a walk, given a fine Easter. We will set out on
Saturday. I want us really to be happy then. So come & be
nice. I get depressed by the sense of evil in the world.

auf weidersehen

D. H. Lawrence

---

42 GREATHAM, PULBOROUGH
Sussex
Wednesday [31 March 1915]

My dear Kot,

You are commissioned please to bring two bottles of Chianti
as at Christmas. We are having a dinner on Sunday evening—
all the hosts of Midian present.

You will come either by the train leaving Victoria at 10:20
or by the 1:42. Bring Barbara & be nice to her.

Perhaps on Monday we will set out on a walk & go to
Chichester. It will be nice. Mind you are jolly. If I can, I
will walk down to meet you—you won't take a carriage,
will you? But come over Cold Waltham, not the same way
you went last time. Bertrand Russell may be here—he goes
away on Saturday.

au revoir, mon cher

D. H. Lawrence

[PS.]
Don't bring anything but Chianti—& for that I pay you.

GREATHAM, PULBOROUGH
Sussex
Thursday [?8 April 1915]

My dear Kot,

Barbara has just gone. I like her, but she gets on my nerves
with her eternal: "but *do* you think"—"but, look here,
isn't it rather that—." I want to say: "For Gods sake woman,
stop haggling." And she is so deprecating, & so persistent.
Oh God! But—*basta!*

I must tell you, *caro mio*, that I liked you very much while you
were here. You must continue to be patient with me.

But you positively *must not* be so inert. You are getting
simply a monolith. You *must* rouse yourself. You *must* do
something—anything. Really it is a disgrace to be as inert as
you are. Really, it is unforgivable. Write for the papers,
do anything, but don't continue in this negation.

I think I shall send you my philosophy to type again for me.
I have begun it again.[1] I will not tell them the people this
time that they are angels in disguise. Curse them, I will tell
them they are dogs and swine, bloodsuckers.

I will send you the *Idiot* to read.

Will you type my philosophy again?—one copy only this
time, on common paper? I shall have to get it done somewhere
or other. But if the burden on you, monolith, is too great,
then refuse.

I have been fighting the powers of darkness lately. Still they
prevail with me. But I have more or less got my head out of
the inferno, my body will follow later. How one has to struggle,
really, to overcome this cursed blackness. It would do me
so much good if I could kill a few people.

Is Katharine at home, or have you heard from her? And how
is Murry? I will write to him. I feel all right again towards
him. My spleen has worked itself off.

I am still in bed with my cold. It is a sort of cold in my inside—like a sore throat in one's stomach. Do you understand? I am going to stay in bed till it is better. Thank God Barbara isn't here to nag at me—poor thing.

My dear Kot, now that the spring has come, *do* rouse up, & *don't* be sad & inert. It is so terrible to be such a weight upon the face of the earth. But you were almost all right this time you were here. Next time you must come when nobody else is here.

Frieda sends her love, with mine. I am reading the Dostoevsky letters. What an amazing person he was—a pure introvert, a purely disintegrating will—there was not a grain of the passion of love within him—all the passion of hate, of evil. Yet a great man. It has become, I think, now, a supreme wickedness to set up a Christ-worship as Dostoevsky did: it is the outcome of an evil will, disguising itself in terms of love.

But he is a great man & I have the greatest admiration for him. I even feel a sort of subterranean love for him. But he never, never wanted anybody to love him, to come close to him. He exerted repelling influence on everybody.

Write to me soon.

Yrs.

D. H. Lawrence

---

1 The "philosophy" referred to here is the second version of what started off as the book about Hardy mentioned in Letters Nos. 6 and 20. In a letter to Mary Cannan dated 24 February 1915, Lawrence explained his intention to re-write the Hardy book: "The book I wrote—mostly philosophicalish, slightly about Hardy —I want to rewrite and publish in pamphlets" (*C.L.*, I, 323). In a letter to Bertrand Russell dated 26 February 1915, Lawrence says he "used to call it [the Hardy book] *Le Gai Savaire*" and adds: "I now want to rewrite this stuff, and make it as good as I can, and publish it in pamphlets, weekly or fortnightly, and so start a campaign for this freer life" (*C.L.*, I, 324).

---

44 GREATHAM, PULBOROUGH
Sussex
Saturday [?10 April 1915]

My dear Kot,

I send you the first Chapter of my philosophy¹ so that you
can get on with it when you like. Positively² I know how to
do it now. Positively I shall say what I like, very nicely.
Don't be skeptical of it. I wish I could think of a nice title—
like *Morgenrot* in German—or—I don't know.

I got up today, this afternoon—very limp & weed-like. I
wrote to Eder all my symptoms & my ailments—he must
cure me.

> "I am weary in heart & head, in hands & feet
> And surely more than all things sleep were sweet,
> Than all things, save the unconquerable desire
> Which who so knoweth shall not faint nor tire."

I am so limp I would recite Swinburne.³ That is a sign of
great maudlin.

Vado in letto. Buona notte, amico

D. H. Lawrence

[PS.]
On this sort of paper, one copy—don't bore yourself to
death doing it—plenty of time.

---

1 This would be the first chapter of the second version of Lawrence's philosophy
cited above. Lawrence sent Koteliansky some more of his new MS on 20 April
1915 as the next letter indicates.

2 "Positively," like "plainly," was an expression often used by Koteliansky.

3 When composing these lines, Lawrence probably recalled the second stanza
from Swinburne's "The Garden of Proserpine":

> I am tired of tears and laughter,
>   And men that laugh and weep;
> Of what may come hereafter
>   For men that sow to reap:
> I am weary of days and hours
> Blown buds of barren flowers,
> Desires and dreams and powers
>   And everything but sleep.

45 GREATHAM, PULBOROUGH
Sussex
Tuesday [20 April 1915]

My dear Kot,

Thank you very much for the typewriting. Soon you will be
as accomplished a typist as our dear Viola.

I have not sent you any more MS. because I am very slow,
& I thought you wanted to be *lentissimo* yourself. Herewith
I forward a little more—enough to keep you from idleness
and mischief.

I am at last, after swallowing various concoctions, really
beginning to be better. I am "on the mend," as they say.

We have had another influx of visitors: David Garnett &
Francis Birrell turned up the other day—Saturday.[1] I like
David, but Birrell I have come to detest. These horrible
little frowsty people, men lovers of men, they give me such
a sense of corruption, almost putrescence, that I dream of
beetles. It is abominable. To escape from visitors, I must
go to Italy again. Madame Sowerby has been down—&
McQueen—& God knows who.[2]

Probably we shall not have the Lady Ottoline cottage.[3]
In my soul, I shall be glad. I would rather take some little
place & be by myself. We will look out for some tiny
place on the sea, not too far off, shall we. I must write to the
Murrys about it.

But why don't they write to us? It is their turn. Nevertheless
I will write tomorrow.

I don't know when I shall come to London. But I am beginning to get unstuck from this place. There is too great a
danger from invasion from the other houses. I cannot stand
the perpetual wash of forced visitors, under the door. So
be ready for news of our decamping: how & whither I
don't as yet know: but decamp I will before very long.

Thank heaven we shall get out of the Lady Ottoline cottage.
I cannot have such a place like a log on my ankle. God

protects me, & keeps me free. Let us think of some place to which we can betake ourselves.

I have promised to go to Scotland in the Summer. We might stay there for a while.

I feel we shall be seeing you before long. I feel I am like a swallow getting my wings ready for flight.

Frieda sends her love. She will write directly. Love from me.

D. H. Lawrence

---

1 David Garnett's recollection of this visit may be read in *C.B.*, I, 299–302.

2 Madame Sowerby was probably the wife of Richardson Sowerby. See *C.B.*, III, 355. Harry T. Moore identifies McQueen as "a photographer." See *I.H.*, p. 191.

3 Lady Ottoline Morrell had offered Lawrence a cottage on her Garsington estate in Oxfordshire. Lawrence and Frieda often visited and stayed at Garsington Manor. See Lady Ottoline Morrell's recollections in *C.B.*, I, 308–09, published originally in *The Nation and Athenaeum*, Vol. XLVI, No. 25 (22 March 1930), pp. 859–60.

---

46 GREATHAM, PULBOROUGH
Sussex
Friday [?30 April 1915]

My dear Kot,

Did I ever thank you for the collars & shirt? The shirt you should *not* have sent. One day I shall send you a pair of spectacles, & make you wear them, in retaliation. But thank you very much for the collars. I feel like a winged Mercury in them—the wings slipped down to my neck, supporting the Adam's Apple.

We are coming to London next week. I am going to be a bankrupt, because I can't and won't pay the £150 divorce costs.[1] I don't care a damn.

Horne writes he is going to France, to be a bus-driver. I wish I could drive a bus, I'd go as well. He wants us to see him before he goes.

"Onward through shot & shell
Onward thy charge to hell
Lorry & bus as well
Chauffeur & stoker——"2

We might come up on Wednesday—but prefer Thursday
or Friday. We shall stay in a room in a street behind the
National Gallery, which a man called Proctor will lend us.
Then we are on our own.

Frieda wants a coat & skirt. If you would see your tailor, &
ask him if he could do her one, at once, & how much it
would be—an ordinary navy blue coat & skirt—& how many
tryings on, it might all be settled while we are up. We shall
stay four or five days. Say we will pay him *at once*: we will.

So *au revoir*

D. H. Lawrence

---

1 "On May 28, 1914 an event of explosive importance to Lawrence and Frieda
occurred in London. In the Probate, Divorce, and Admiralty Division of the
High Court of Justice, Mr. Justice Bargrave Deane declared that in the case of
'Weekley v. Weekley and Lawrence,' the nisi decree was final" (*I.H.*, p. 163).
Writing to Bertrand Russell on Thursday ?29 April 1915, Lawrence says, "They
are going to make me a bankrupt because I can't—and won't—pay the £150 of the
divorce costs. I wouldn't pay them if I were a millionaire—I would rather go to
prison" (*C.L.*, I, 335).

2 These verses appear to be a parody of the following lines in Tennyson's "The
Charge of the Light Brigade":

> Cannon to the right of them,
> Cannon to the left of them,
> Cannon in front of them
>   Volley'd and thunder'd;
> Storm'd at with shot and shell,
> Boldly they rode and well,
> Into the jaws of Death
> Into the mouth of Hell
>   Rode the six hundred.

47
Sussex
3 May 1915

My dear Kot,

We shall come up to town either on Friday or on Saturday. I am not quite sure.

I am sorry your eyes are bad. I think it is your liver, which is sluggish, which makes them bad. Take some ordinary medicine, effervescing salts or anything, for the liver. And don't bother about the type-writing—I will get it done outside somewhere. I don't want you to trouble with it, particularly when your eyes are not good.

Does Katharine depress you. Her letters are as jarring as the sound of a saw.

au revoir

D. H. Lawrence

48
Thursday [6 May 1915]

My dear Kot,

We go to London tomorrow afternoon, but I don't know the
train. If you come round to 18 Whitcomb St. Pall Mall at
about 6:00 I think we shall be there. Basil Proctor is the
host—a young architect.

Today I walked here from Greatham—very beautiful. I hope
you weren't seedy.

Yrs.

D. H. Lawrence

[PS.]
Proctor—Gerrard 198. Ring up Eder's for Frieda. 32, Well
Walk, Mrs. Dolly Radford.[1]

---

1 "A poet, as her husband Ernest was, Dollie Radford often befriended the
Lawrences, and took them in when they were forced out of Cornwall in October,
1917" (*C.L.*, I, l).

GREATHAM, PULBOROUGH
Sussex
19 May 1915

My dear Kot,

Thank you very much for Soloviev.[1]—He is interesting, very
—but he never says anything he wants to say. He makes a
rare mess, fiddling about with orthodox Christianity.
Dostoevsky made the same mess.

There is no news from here, except that we applied too late for
the rooms in Hampstead. They were too small. Friends are
looking for another place for Frieda, also in Hampstead.
Probably she will go & stay alone in them for some time, if
she gets them. She spends her time thinking herself a wronged,
injured & aggrieved person, because of the children, &
because she is a German. I am angry & bored. I wish she
would have her rooms in Hampstead & leave me alone.

For Whitsun, Viola is staying in this house, & Ivy Low:[2]
so we are full up in such an unwelcome fashion. Never mind—
I stay here only three weeks more. Meanwhile my mornings
are occupied in teaching Mary Saleeby.[3] I am typing my
philosophy myself.[4] When I read it in comparison with
Soloviev, I am proud of my cleverness.

I hope your eyes are getting better. Tell me any news of
Murry or yourself. The country is *very* beautiful. I am happy
when I am gardening over at Rackham Cottage—only then.
But then I am quite happy, with the plants.

I hope you are well. Let me hear from you.

Yours

D. H. Lawrence

---

1 Vladimir Solovyov (1853–1900) was a Russian philosopher. Koteliansky
may have sent Lawrence Solovyov's book, *War, Progress and the End of History:
Including a Short History of the Antichrist*, translated from the Russian by Alexander Bakshy, with a biographical notice by Dr. Hagberg Wright (London, 1915).

The translation, however, might have been Solovyov's *War and Christianity from the Russian Point of View, Three Conversations*, with an Introduction by Stephen Graham (London, 1915). Both are translations of the same work by Solovyov.

2 Ivy Low "visited Lawrence and Frieda in Italy in 1914; the following year she married the future Soviet Foreign Commissar and Ambassador. Author of several novels, Mme Litvinov was the niece of Barbara Low and was related by marriage to Dr. M. D. Eder" (*C.L.*, I, xlv). Lawrence refers to Mme Litvinov's husband in Letter No. 250.

3 See the account of Lawrence's teaching by his pupil Dr. Mary Saleeby Fisher in *C.B.*, I, 303–04, which in part reads "The thing I most enjoyed about Lawrence's teaching was that he taught me some very good songs."

4 It is not known whether this reference is to a continuation of the MS that Koteliansky typed, or whether it is to a third version to which Lawrence refers as *Morgenrot* in his letter to Lady Ottoline Morrell. See the undated letter in *A.H.*, p. 237.
There are no letters from Lawrence to Koteliansky between 19 May 1915 and 22 July 1915, but in a letter to Lady Ottoline Morrell dated [?12 July 1915] Lawrence says: "As for my philosophy, I shall write it again."
It is very probable that some of these attempts, as has been suggested, were later incorporated as parts of "The Crown." See Keith Sagar, *The Art of D. H. Lawrence* (Cambridge, 1966), p. 40.

50

GREATHAM, PULBOROUGH
[Sussex]
Thursday [22 July 1915]

My dear Kot,

Forgive my not having answered your letter sooner.[1] Even now I don't know how to answer it. My feelings are confused & suffering under various sorts of shocks in one direction & another. I hope you will not mind if we leave it for a while, this question of a relationship between us, until I am settled & dependable. Then I will answer your letter.

Yours

D. H. Lawrence

---

1 A break in Lawrence's relations with Koteliansky seems to have occurred during the latter part of May 1915 but I have been unable to discover any material which might help us to understand what happened. When the Lawrences moved to Hampstead in early August 1915, Koteliansky was once again closely associated with Lawrence, as the succeeding letters indicate.

1 BYRON VILLAS
Vale-of-Health
Hampstead [London]
Monday [23 August 1915]

My dear Kot,

Would you mind coming on Thursday instead of on Tuesday evening? Frieda is still in bed with her cold, which has developed into a bad one. I am sorry to change the day, please forgive me. But it would not be so well if you brought your friends when Frieda was laid up.

You take the tube to Hampstead station, from thence walk straight up the hill to the Heath, & continue straight on, past the pond, along the Spaniards Road, a little way, till you come to the public house called Jack Straw's Castle. Across the road from this the path drops down the Heath straight into the Vale of Health, & the road winding to the right leads you to Byron Villas.[1] I hope you will like our flat—I think you will.

Murry just mentioned something about the translating of my book into Russian.[2] I should like that very much. Was that the scheme you meant? I should be very proud to see myself in Russian, & not to understand a single word.

I have been to see a man this afternoon who talks of producing my play in Edinborough [*sic*] and Glasgow & Manchester.[3] That will be rather good fun, seeing what the thing looks like on the stage. We shall probably have to go to Nottingham next week for rehearsals—perhaps.

What a funny life—none of these things seem really to belong to me, & yet I am in them.

Goodbye till Thursday

D. H. Lawrence

---

1 Lawrence's ability to supply directions has often been a boon to those who have undertaken to trace his footsteps. A recent example of such tracing has been published by Armin Arnold. See "In the Footsteps of D. H. Lawrence in Switzerland: Some New Biographical Material," *Texas Studies in Language and Literature*, III (1961), 184–88.

2 *The Rainbow*, which was banned in England. A Russian translation of *The Rainbow* did not appear until 1925. See *B.*, p. 313.

3 *The Widowing of Mrs. Holroyd* (New York, 1914). For publication and production histories, see *B.*, pp. 24–25.

---

52 1 BYRON VILLAS
Vale-of-Health
Hampstead, London
7 October 1915

My dear Kot,

Will you send a copy of the *Signature*[1] to each of the following three, from whom I have received subscriptions:

      1. The Misses Fairfield
        "Fairliehope"
2/6   Chatham Close
        Erskine Hill
        Golders Green N.W.

      2. Dr. Margaret Hogarth
2/6   3 Albany Terrace
        Regents Park N.W.

      3. Mr. Roth Esq.
        Orchestrelle Coy.
2/6   Aeolean Hall
        New Bond St.

Also I have received subscriptions from the following, to whom I have *sent* the *Signature*.[2]

      1. Clifford Bax Esq.
2/6   1 The Bishops Avenue
        East Finchley N

      2. J. F. Cannan Esq.
2/6   92 Furness Rd.
        Willesden N.W.

2/6

3. Mark Gertler
Penn Studio
Rudall Crescent
Hampstead

2/6

4. Mrs. Anna Hepburn
49 Downshire Hill
Hampstead

2/6

5. A. Brackenbury Esq.
14a Downshire Hill
Hampstead

2/6

6. Leonard Smith Esq.
The Vicarage
Cholesbury
Tring
Herts

Also I have a p.c. from Jones & Evans Bookshop, 77 Queen St., Cheapside E.C. saying they want to subscribe for 3 copies, & asking for particulars. I refer them to Fisher St. & ask them to send 7/6.

When there are letters addressed to me at Fisher St., please open them unless they are marked "private."

When you come to Murry's tonight, please bring for me 6 copies of the *Signature*, in their envelopes.

Yours

D. H. Lawrence

---

1 The little magazine which was started in September 1915 by Lawrence and Murry, with Koteliansky as business manager. Only three numbers appeared. For Lawrence's account of the initial plans to issue the *Signature*, see his letter to Bertrand Russell dated 5 September 1915 in *C.B.*, I, 321. For Lawrence's later recollections of the project see "Note to the Crown" at the beginning of *Reflections on the Death of a Porcupine* (Philadelphia, 1925); Murry's recollections are reprinted in *C.B.*, I, 322–25.

2 It is not known how many subscribers there ultimately were. A large number of letters from subscribers requesting the *Signature* have been preserved among the *Koteliansky Papers* in the British Museum. The names of the subscribers in Letter No. 52 and in subsequent letters testify to the lively interest that the

Signature aroused at the time. In addition to the names included in the letters, there is preserved in the *Koteliansky Papers* a separate list of names. Near the top of the list, in Koteliansky's handwriting, is the note "28 Sept. from D. H. L." and below the following names obviously in Lawrence's handwriting:

18th	Mrs. Dollie Radford 32 Well Wall [*sic*] Hampstead	23rd	Miss Louis 7 Colehill Gardens Fulham Palace Rd S.W.
21st	Miss L. Reynolds 20 Ifold Rd Redhill Surrey	24th	E. M. Forster Harnham, Monument Green Weybridge Surrey
22nd	E. Collings Esq 18 Ravenslea Rd Balham S.W.	26	Dr. Ernest Jones 69 Portland Court W
22	Miss Mary Phelps 19 Temple Fortune Hill Hendon N.W.	27	Miss Isabel Carswell 43 Moray Place Edinburgh
23	Miss Barbara Low "	28	Drey

53

Vale-of-Health
[Hampstead, London]
Sunday [10 October 1915]

Dear Kot,

Will you put down these names of subscribers, to whom I
have *already* sent copies of the *Signature*.

Lady Lewis
The Grange
Rottingdean, Sussex   5/–
Two copies

Mrs. Poole
Buckless [*sic*] Hard
Beaulieu   2/6
Hants

Mrs. Riviere
10 Nottingham Terrace   2/6
York Gate N.W.

Tomorrow (Monday) at 8 o'clock we are to have a meeting
at Fisher St., for discussion. Will you come? It would be
nice if you were there at 7:30, as Frieda and I want to put
up curtains. Then you could open us the door. We shall
bring a lamp, and oil, and some sticks. Could you bring
just a little bit of coal, enough just to make one fire? I'm
afraid we can't carry so much.

Today we are going to Horne's to tea: but dread the Maisie.[1]
I hope you don't mind my rudeness of the other evening.

Yours

D. H. Lawrence

---

[1] Probably a reference to Horne's wife.

---

1 BYRON VILLAS
Vale-of-Health
Hampstead, London
Monday [11 October 1915]

Dear Kot,

Thank you very much for making the room so nice, & the fire.

Did you not stay to the meeting, because you were busy, or too sorry about Katharine's brother,[1] or because you were offended with me. If you are offended, that is foolish. But you do as you like.

Three people took *Signatures* & paid me 2/6

Percy Peacock Esq.
2 Leighton Gardens
Streatham
S.W.

A. P. Lewis Esq.[2]
19 The Drive
Golders Green
N.W.

T. S. Knowlson Esq.
Meloin Hall
Golders Green Rd.
N.W.

I hope you will keep an account, of the money you have spent, for coal etc. Also I owe you for the teas of the other day. We will have a reckoning.

There is another meeting this day fortnight. I hope you will come to it.

D. H. Lawrence

[PS.]
The printer has not sent me my *Signature* proofs—I wonder why? I write to him now.

---

1 Katherine Mansfield's brother Leslie Heron Beauchamp (1894–1915) was killed on 7 October 1915. See Antony Alpers, *Katherine Mansfield: A Biography* (New York, 1953), pp. 206–12.

2 This may be the Lewis mentioned in note 1 to Letter No. 13.

55 [1 BYRON VILLAS
Vale-of-Health
Hampstead, London
14 October 1915]

Dear Kot,

Please send a copy of the *Signature* to A. Robert Mountsier
Esq.,[1] 36 Guilford St., Russell Square, W.C. but don't enter
him as a subscriber.

Yours

D. H. Lawrence

[PS.]
Also send me, please, by post or by Murry, 4 copies of the
Signature. Also please post one copy to C. P. Sanger Esq.,
50 Oakley St., Chelsea, S.W. I have received his subscription.

D. H. L.

---

1 Later Lawrence's literary agent in New York.

56 [1 BYRON VILLAS
Vale-of-Health
Hampstead, London
?October 1915]

Please send Nos. 1 & 2 to Monroe, Calhouse, Ricketts &
Tchaichowsky—No. 2 to Piccoli and de la Feld.

Miss Harriett Monroe [1] 543 Cass St. Chicago U.S.A.	2/6
Miss W. J. Calhouse 1310 Astor St. Chicago U.S.A.	2/6
Raff Piccoli	2/6
Count de la Feld	2/6
Chas Ricketts Esq. Lansdowne House Lansdowne Rd Holland Park W.	2/6
Miss Vera Tchaichowsky Seven Winds Naphill High Wycombe Bucks	2/6

P.T.O. [please turn over]

Herbert Watson Esq. 13 Holly Mount Hampstead N.W. 2 copies *already sent*	5/–

---

1 Harriet Monroe was an American poet and critic. She was responsible for
founding and editing *Poetry: A Magazine of Verse* in which she published several
of Lawrence's poems. Lawrence met her very briefly in Chicago on 19 March
1924. Harriet Monroe's account of that meeting with Lawrence may be read in
C.B., II, 330.

1 BYRON VILLAS
Vale-of-Health
Hampstead, London
21 October 1915

My dear Kot,

I send you back the letters, so that you can always check
them.[1] I am giving one weeks notice when I pay the rent
today—so that we shall have the Fisher St. rooms only for
one week more, now. Everything comes to an end.

But there will be a meeting at Fisher St. on Monday at 8:00—
come if you can.

I think we are going to try to get to America, Murry & I.
I shall go down about a passport tomorrow. My soul is torn
out of me now: I can't stop here any longer & acquiesce in
this which is the spirit now: I would rather die. I will let
you know what I am doing exactly, & perhaps you will
come up & see us—I'll tell you when.

Yours

D. H. Lawrence

---

1 The letters from subscribers to the *Signature.*

1 BYRON VILLAS
Vale-of-Health
Hampstead, London
29 October 1915

My dear Kot,

I have 2/6 from this man—send him the 3 numbers on Monday:

> Professor H. V. Meredith
> 55 Bryansburn Rd.
> Bangor
> Co. Down
> Ireland

You remember that the tenancy of 12 Fisher St. ends tomorrow: Can you take away all the *Signatures* to the Law Bureau: also let Narodiczky know that he must send the new numbers to *you*.[1]

When we have got something a bit settled, we will have an evening together. At present all is turmoil and unrest.

Yours

D. H. Lawrence

[PS.]
I should also be *very much* obliged if you could carry round to the Bureau the curtains and the carpet out of Fisher St. Then I will come & fetch them.

---

1 Narodiczky was the printer of the *Signature*.

---

59 [1 BYRON VILLAS
Vale-of-Health
Hampstead, London
4 November 1915]

My dear Kot,

Send *Signatures* to these two people, will you? [1]—I expect we shall see you at Brett's studio tomorrow.[2]

Thanks for p.o.'s [postal orders] last night.

D. H. Lawrence

---

1 The MS gives no clue as to the identity of "these two people."

2 The Hon. Dorothy Brett.

---

60 [1 BYRON VILLAS
Vale-of-Health
Hampstead, London
?6 November 1915]

My dear Kot,

How is your head this morning?

Would you go round to Wheeler, at 12 Fisher St., and ask him, will he buy the whole of the *Signature* furniture, as it stands?—and take what he will give. We paid about £3.5.0 for it.

D. H. Lawrence

61 [1 BYRON VILLAS
Vale-of-Health]
Hampstead [London]
Sunday [?7 November 1915]

Dear Kot,

Will you send the 3 numbers of the *Signature* to:

Trevor Walsh Esq
Scott House
West Malling
Kent

I have his 2/6.

If you don't come to see us tonight, don't come till the
end of the week, as we are going away, Monday till Friday.[1]

Greetings

D. H. Lawrence

---

1 In a letter to J. B. Pinker dated 6 November 1915 Lawrence writes: "I am away
from Monday to Thursday of next week. If there is anything to write to me,
address me at Garsington Manor, Near Oxford" (*C.L.*, I, 376). In a letter to
Dollie Radford dated 6 November 1915, Lawrence writes: "We are going on Monday to stay with Lady Ottoline Morrell at Garsington Manor Nr Oxford. We shall
be there till Thursday, when we are home again" (*C.L.*, I, 377).

GARSINGTON MANOR
Oxford
Tuesday [?9 November 1915]

My dear Kot,

We are down here for a day or two.

Pinker—my agent—is making arrangements with Conard—a sort of Tauchnitz publisher in Paris—to publish the *Rainbow* in English there. That would be a good idea.

I wonder if you know Zenaida Vengerova's present address:[1] if you would ask her, could she let me have back the proofs of the novel, which I sent her some time ago, so that Conard could print from them. In that case it would not be necessary to tear a book to pieces.

We shall be back on Friday—come & see us during the weekend. I hope soon we shall be going to Florida.[2]

Many greetings from

D. H. Lawrence

---

1 Unidentified, but an entry in Koteliansky's address book gives the address for Z. A. Vengerova as 97 Gower Street, W.C.1. Nothing is known about these plans for the publication of *The Rainbow*.

2 Florida was hopefully to be the site of *Rananim*.

---

63 [1 BYRON VILLAS
Vale-of-Health]
Hampstead [London]
Monday [22 November 1915]

Thank you very much for the Tchekov:[1] I am very glad to have it. The first story reads *splendidly*: you have done it well. Will you send *Signatures* to:

V. H. Bischoff-Collins Esq.
2 Hurst-Close
Hampstead Garden Suburb

I have his subscription.

When I said 8/– from the Poetry Bookshop, of course I meant 3/–. The man only wants *one* copy—I was thinking three.

Come up again soon.

Yours

D. H. Lawrence

---

1 In all probability the reference is to Chekhov's *The Bet and Other Stories*, translated from the Russian by S. S. Koteliansky and J. M. Murry (London and Dublin, 1915).

64 [1 BYRON VILLAS
Vale-of-Health]
Hampstead [London]
Friday [3 December 1915]

Come on Sunday evening instead of Saturday—will you please.

Yours

D. H. Lawrence

[PS.]

Bring me 2 sets of *Signatures* also, will you.

---

65 103 HAMPSTEAD WAY
Thursday [?23 December 1915]

My dear Kot,

This is a handkerchief for your Christmas.

I want to say to you, please gather your money during these next few months, so you can come to Florida with us. This is serious. Do make some money & save it, & come with us.

Best of greetings for Christmas from both of us.

D. H. Lawrence

[PS. from Frieda]
Dear Kot,
I hope you like the hanky—it looks like the unutterable name of the Lord—I chose it—.

66 c/o MRS. CLARKE[1]
Grosvenor Rd., Ripley
Derbyshire
25 December 1915

My dear Kot,

Will you send copies of the *Signature* to H. Booth, The
Gables, *Swanwick*, Nr. Alfreton, Derbyshire. He says he
sent his 2/6 & never had the book. So enter his name, will
you, & see that the postage is all right.

We are here with all my people—very nice: but it is painful
to go back so into the past. One's people are the past—pure,
without mitigation. And it is so hard to get to the future:
and one *must* look to the future: one must create the future.
That is why we go to Florida: a new life, a new beginning:
the inception of a new epoch.

We are coming down to London on Wednesday evening,
and going on to Cornwall on Thursday morning. I'm afraid
to make any appointments, it is such a rush. But we shall
meet before long.

The Kümmel & the sweets are very good: but the others
don't like Kümmel; it makes them cough. My sister has got
a very beautiful child, a boy, a year old. There is something
lovely about these pure small children. It makes one hate the
cowardly suppressed grown-ups.

I hope you will make up your quarrel with Barbara.[2] I really
like her, & we might as well all remain friends.

auf wiedersehen

D. H. Lawrence

---

1 Lawrence's sister Ada.

2 Barbara Low.

---

67 PORTHCOTHAN
St. Merryn
Padstow, Cornwall
Thursday 30 Dec [1915]

My dear Kot,

We got here tonight—it is splendid—a biggish house with
big clear rooms, & a good housekeeper to look after us. This
is the first move to Florida. Here already one feels a good
peace & a good silence, & a freedom to love & to create a
new life. We must begin afresh—we must begin to create a
life all together—unanimous. Then we shall be happy. We
must be happy. But we shall only be happy if we are creating
a life together. We must cease this analysis & introspection
& individualism—begin to be free & happy with each other.

Tell Murry please to write to me—I have forgotten his
address, but I want to hear from him. Tell him as soon as you
can.

You also write & tell me how things are with you.

Yours

D. H. Lawrence

---

68 PORTHCOTHAN
St. Merryn
Padstow, Cornwall
Thursday [6 January 1916]

My dear Kot,

Well, I am willing to believe that there isn't any Florida—
assez, j'en ai soupé. I am willing to give up people altogether—
they are what they are, why should they be as I want them
to be. It is their affair, not mine: English individualists or not
individualists, it is all the same to me. I give it up. *Je n'en*

peux plus. And the same with the world: it is what it is: what has it to do with me, or I with it? I admit it all: you are right: there's no *rapport.*

There is my intimate art, and my thoughts, as you say. Very good, so be it. It is enough, more than enough, if they will only leave me alone.

As for their world, it is like artificial lights that are blown out—one can only remember it. I can't see it or hear it or feel it any more—it must be all blown out to extinction. There is another world, a sort of rarer reality: a world with thin, clean air and untouched skies, that have not been looked at nor covered with smoke. There is another world, which I prefer. And I don't care about any people, none, so long as they won't try to claim attention from me. The world goes on, the old world, very much like a sordid brawl in last night's café-restaurant: like an ugly thing which one remembers in the morning, but which is non-existent. It is non-existent: their wars & lies and foulnesses: last night's sordidness. What has morning got to do with it.

I like being here. I like the rough seas & this bare country, King Arthur's country, of the flicker of pre-Christian Celtic civilisation. I like it very much.

We are here till March: what then, I neither know nor care. I shall just go where the wind blows me, the wind of my own world. I am not going to urge & constrain any more: there are no people here in this world, to be urged. My dear Kot, it is very nice down here, in Cornwall. Some day you must come & see us.

Yours

D. H. Lawrence

69 [PORTHCOTHAN
St. Merryn
Padstow, Cornwall]
Thursday [27 January 1916]

My dear Kot,

Will you please send me a packet of type-writing paper, like this [I] write on, and also some carbon paper—about eight sheets. We are as usual miles from every shop. I enclose a p.o. for 1/6, which I have in my pocket. It is not enough, I know, but it saves my going to St. Merryn. I will owe you the rest.

Will you please send two sets of *Signatures* to

Miss Amy Lowell
Sevenels [*sic*]
Brookline, Mass.
U.S.A.

also one set to

A. Hathaway Esq.
258 Garden Avenue
Toronto, Canada

I have been in bed this last fortnight, but am getting better. The Murrys write that they are still dancing with happiness. I am doing the proofs of a book of Italian Studies, & am preparing a book of poetry.[1] I am very fond of Cornwall still & Frieda is happy here. You would at last approve: a large house and a very efficient housekeeper.

I had a letter from Gertler. Thank him from me for the books he sent. Tell him I am sorry he is having such a bad time. He must come down here & recuperate when his picture is done. I wish him God-speed with it.

Why don't you write & tell me some news of yourself, oh tacit one! Best greetings from Frieda and from me.

Yours

D. H. Lawrence

---

1 *Twilight in Italy* (London, 1916), and *Amores* (London, 1916).

PORTHCOTHAN
St. Merryn
Padstow, North Cornwall
9 February 1916

My dear Kot,

I never thanked you for the paper, and now I am writing for
some more. Heseltine[1] typed the whole MS. of the poems, &
that used it up. Send me another packet of the same, will you,
and some more carbon paper. The last carbon paper was very
bad, ask if they have some better, will you; I think the blue
is really better.

Will you also send to Philip Heseltine, c/o me, two more
sets of *Signatures*. I will get a postal order this afternoon, and
send it you: for all the things.

I am much better. Maitland Radford came down to see me.[2]
He says that stress on the nerves sets up an inflammation in
the lining of the chest, & the breathing passages and the
stomach, and that I must be very quiet and very warm and
still, and that I musn't think at all about anything. I lay
quite still in bed for two weeks, and kept indoors very quiet
another week, now I can walk out and feel something like
myself again. My whole left side went numb like paralysis.
It is all nerves, Maitland Radford said. Lady Ottoline sent
me a lot of things to swallow, and they are really splendid.
Soon I shall be a Hercules, a Samson.

I was glad to have your letter. It is a good idea to come down.
But leave it about a fortnight longer, because Heseltine & a
young woman are here, & they take up the beds. I think they
will go in about a fortnight's time. Then we should be so
glad to see you & Gertler. You would stay as long as possible
—this idea of hurrying off in two days is absurd. We are in
this house until March 9th: then I suppose we shall find
another place in Cornwall. You must come down, it is so
different from the rest of England. I am afraid Heseltine will
be conscripted.—What about Gertler? We must meet soon
to talk things over: I want to very much. I shall write to
Gertler today—& to you immediately again.

The Murrys continue at a high pitch of bliss. There is no worldly news to tell you. I hope you are cheerful. I look forward to having a talk with you.

Somehow I feel that things are going to happen now—nice things—to us.

Frieda wishes to be remembered to you.

Yours

D. H. Lawrence

---

1 Pseudonym, Peter Warlock. See *C.B.*, I, 346–54.

2 "Son of Ernest and Dollie Radford and husband of Dr. Muriel Radford, Maitland Radford was a writer as well as a physician" (*C.L.*, I, l).

---

71 [PORTHCOTHAN
St. Merryn
Padstow, North Cornwall
15 February 1916]

My dear Kot,

Thank you very much for the paper. I send you a p.o. for
5/–, to pay for it, & for things for which I shall be asking
you shortly. And that bold Frieda asked for Kümmel, for
which I abused her. But I like Kümmel very much. Don't
be jealous of the Ottoline's sendings: they were only vile
essences and extracts and plasmon: but they do one good. I
am much better, but still a sufferer.

If I had the energy I should tirade you about Dostoevsky. He
has lost his spell over me: I was bored rather by the *Possessed*.
The people were not possessed enough to be really interesting:
Stavrogin is a bore. He was only interesting when he bit the
old man's ear. Pyotr Stepanovitch was *nearly* interesting.
The two most interesting are Varvara and Stepan Trofimo-
vitch—their relation was good & subtle. I thought the *Idiot*
far better than *Possessed*, also *Karamazov*.

I could do with Dostoevsky if he did not make all men fallen
angels. We are not angels. It is a tiresome conceit. Men want
to be Sadists, or they don't. If they do, well & good.
There's no need to drag in the fallen angel touch to save
ourselves in our own sight. I am most sick of this divinity-of-
man business. People are *not important:* I insist on it. It
doesn't matter what Stavrogin does, nor whether he lives or
dies. I am quite unmoved when he commits suicide. It is
his affair. It bores me. People are so self-important. Let them
die, silly blighters, fools, and twopenny knaves.

I have sent off to the publishers the MS. of a book of poems.[1]
I am once more in the middle of my philosophy.[2] My dear
Kot, this time at last I have *got* it. Now you would not tell
me, if you read it, that I shall write it again. This time, my
dear Kot, I have put salt on its tail: I've caught the rabbit:
like the old hare in Tartarin.[3] My dear Kot, it is the new word,
at last.

I know you don't believe me, but it doesn't alter it.

My dear Kot, I feel anti-social. I want to blow the wings off these fallen angels. I want to bust 'em up. I feel that everything I do is a shot at these fallen angels of mankind. Wing the brutes. If only one could be a pirate or a brigand nowadays, an outlaw, to rob the angels & hang them on a tree. But long-distance guns has [*sic*] stopped all that jolly game.

We are going to look for another house down here. The wind blows terribly, the house shudders, for all its thick old walls. The sea bursts high in towers of foam. We leave here March 8th. I suppose it will be in the next house that you will come & see us. But come before, come here to this house, if you are ready.

Yours

D. H. Lawrence

---

1 *Amores.*

2 Probably a reference to *Goats and Compasses,* which was announced as Lawrence's "new philosophical work" in the prospectus for "The Rainbow Books and Music." For a reprint of this prospectus, see *C.B.,* I, 348–49. The manuscript of this version of Lawrence's "philosophy" has apparently not survived, but Cecil Gray, who read it, described it as "Lawrence at his very worst: a bombastic, pseudo-mystical, psycho-philosophical treatise dealing largely with homosexuality" (*C.B.,* I, 582).

3 Reference to *Tartarin of Tarascon* (1872) by the French novelist Alphonse Daudet (1840–97).

PORTHCOTHAN
St. Merryn
[Padstow,] N. Cornwall
[19 February 1916]

My dear Kot,

Thank you for the Kümmel and the sherry. It grieves me rather, that we should drink up your few wages.

We haven't found a house yet—it rains so much, we can't go out.

It's a good thing somebody believes in me. I am very frightened of the foulness of the world. One feels as if all the time one were dodging the blind, flying tentacles of an octopus. It is hideous.

I understand Nietzsche's child. But it isn't a child that will represent the third stage:[1] not innocent unconsciousness: but the maximum of fearless adult consciousness, that has the courage even to submit to the unconsciousness of itself.

Many warm greetings

D. H. Lawrence

---

1 A reference to Nietzsche's *Thus Spake Zarathustra*: "Three metamorphoses of the spirit do I designate to you: how the spirit becometh a camel, the camel a lion, and the lion at last a child" (*The Complete Works of Friedrich Nietzsche*, edited by Dr. Oscar Levy, XI [New York, 1964], 25). Also "Innocence is the child, and forgetfulness, a new beginning, a game, a self-rolling wheel, a first movement, a holy Yea" (p. 27).

---

73 PORTHCOTHAN
St. Merryn
[Padstow,] N. Cornwall
25 February 1916

My dear Kot,

We are leaving here on Monday next, to go to Zennor. The address is: "The Tinner's Arms, Zennor, St. Ives, Cornwall."

Zennor is a lovely place far down in Cornwall, towards Lands End: very wild and remote and beautiful. We shall stay for a week in the inn, then I think we shall take a furnished house. There you must come & see us: it will be *much* better than here. The address will always be Zennor. It is a *tiny* place—seven houses.

I go with a strange feeling to Zennor: as if it were in some sort of Promised Land: not territorially, but of the spirit. I feel as if a new heavens & a new earth would come to pass there.

The Murrys will come not [*sic*], till the end of April: they said before, the end of March, but now they put it off for a month, so that the winter may be over, for Katharine's sake. They will, I think, come & live with us.

You will be seeing Heseltine, & talking of the publishing scheme with him.[1] I believe in him, he is one of us. Mind you are nice to him. He is in a very overwrought and over-inflammable state, really.

Here it is very cold. Snow falls, then disappears. But I do wish this black wind would depart again.

I loathe the world outside. How unspeakably foul it is. If only one can sufficiently retire from it, and create a new world, from the spirit. It could be done, with a few people. I think it will come to pass. I think, intrinsically, we can conquer the world. I think, intrinsically, we have conquered the world. I feel victorious, somehow.

But I also feel very shaky, and as if I *must* escape from the contact with this foulness of the world. But I am better in health: only still feel horribly vulnerable & wincing.

The Murrys accused me of being treacherous and not taking them into the publishing scheme. I tell them of course they are included, & they are far more treacherous to me, intrinsically, than ever I shall be to them.

We must add all our strength together, all of us, to win a new world, a new being all together; it is not enough to have being individually, we must have a true being in common.

Yours

D. H. Lawrence

---

1 For details of the publishing scheme called "The Rainbow Books and Music" see the copy of the announcement of the scheme reprinted in *C.B.*, I, 348–49. For further references by Lawrence to the scheme see his letter to J. M. Murry in *C.L.*, I, 434, and the letter dated 15 January 1916 in *C.B.*, I, 354–55. Lawrence's explanation for the failure of the plan was that it had "fallen through, there having been 30 answers to 700 pamphlets" (*C.B.*, I, 383).

---

74 TINNERS ARMS
Zennor
St. Ives, Cornwall
2 March 1916

My dear Kot,

Thank you very much for the Kuprin,[1] which has just come. I
shall read it & tell you how I like it, at once.

I enclose a letter from a man for the *Signature*.

It is very rainy here. We live warmly in the inn—& don't
bother.

I don't want to write the novel of the young Englishman—he
bores me. Forgive me.—Why don't you write your novel of a
Jew: the truth, all of it. *That* would be interesting indeed;
only save yourself from being sentimental.

Yours

D. H. Lawrence

---

[1] A reference to I. A. Kuprin's *The River of Life and Other Stories*, translated by
S. S. Koteliansky and J. M. Murry (Boston, 1916).

Zennor
St. Ives, Cornwall
8 March 1916

My dear Kot,

Thank you very much for the Kuprin. He reads awfully well
—I think you must have translated him well. But I don't
care for him. He is not very significant, I think, and rather
vulgar. The Ribnikov story[1] is the only one that really interests
me: if *only* he could have created a Japanese, it might have
been wonderful. But the Japanese himself is not created:
only his attributes, not *he*. It is a pity.

We have taken a little 2-roomed cottage, for £5 a year.
We are going to furnish it and live like foxes under the hill.
The situation is beautiful, indeed, under the moors, above the
wide sea. *Do, please*, go and help Gertler to pack up our
things to send us: we want them now.

Next to ours is a big cottage, seven rooms, for £16 a year. I
want the Murrys to have that—a little settlement. Wouldn't
it be good?

I suppose you will be seeing Lady Ottoline this week—go &
see her.

We are going to be very very poor. So we must live very
cheaply indeed.

molti saluti buoni

D. H. Lawrence

---

1 The title of the story is "Captain Ribnikov."

HIGHER TREGERTHEN, ZENNOR
St. Ives, Cornwall
28 March 1916

My dear Kot,

I haven't written before because we have hardly had a place to
sit down in. But now the cottage is beginning to be something
like ship-shape. It is a warm and cosy place, with great thick
walls. But the weather is terrible. All yesterday, a solid
blackness over the sea, & masses of snow driving out of it,
and a wind that shook the very earth. Today, happily, the
snow is almost gone & the wind is stiller. What a life!

As for the man who wants the *Signature*, in America, don't
bother with him.

I hear from Katharine this morning that they, she & Jack,
thought of leaving France *yesterday* (Monday), so they
should be in London at least by Wednesday. They don't
know where they will stay, in town. But they will not be
long there: they will come down here to the cottage next door.
I hope to heaven they will get safely across the Channel.

It will be a great blessing when they are safely settled here.
I confidently expect the war to end this year. I expect us all
to be so happy. We have learned some lessons, let us hope,
during these two years of misery, and got rid of a great deal
of spleen. Now let us be happy: if only the war will end.

I don't know quite what sort of Children's books you would
like to translate (was it translation you were thinking of?)
Do you mean the *Robinson Crusoe* type: R. L. Stevenson's
Treasure Island for example. In that list come Captain
Marryatt (very good), R. M. Ballantyne, W. H. Kingston,
Henty, Ralph Boldrewood, Melville—all these are authors.
Then there is the *Little Lord Fauntleroy* type (this was a *very*
popular book), authors Frances Hodgson Burnett, Annie
S. Swan, Mrs. Ewing (oldfashioned & good *Lob-lie-by-the-Fire*
etc.). Then there are the "school book" series—public-school,
like *Tom Brown's Schooldays*.

Do you mean boys' books or girls' books: because they are rather sharply defined? I think our boys' books of adventure are best, like *Treasure Island*, or books by Henty, or Kingston, or Collingwood. I used to *love* them. And if I could get hold of a school library list, I could tell you what books were most popular with my boys. I used to keep the school library.[1] But Barbara Low could *easily* help you here, she is in a school. I think our *boys* [sic] *books* are really rather good, & rather fun to translate into Russian.

Will you, when Mudie's sale comes on, please go in and buy me two copies of my *Trespasser*.[2] They are going at fourpence each. The sale begins April 3rd, I believe—next Monday.

Tell Murry to write me at once: but I will enclose a little note for him.

I hope soon you will come & see us, here in Cornwall. Greetings from Frieda.

Yours

D. H. Lawrence

[PS.]
If you see Gertler, ask him if he knows anything of my pair of brass candlesticks. He has sent only an old copper one, & those brass ones were old family relics.

---

1 This was one of Lawrence's responsibilities at the Davidson Road School in Croydon, where he began teaching in 1908. Lawrence's headmaster at the school, Philip F. T. Smith, recalls "Lawrence assumed quite voluntarily the responsibility for many of the least desired of school routine duties. This included the constant attention bestowed on the details connected with the school library. He used to affirm 'Let them read any rubbish they like as long as they read it at all. They will very soon discard the bad'" (*I.H.*, p. 79).
2 Lawrence's second novel, *The Trespasser*, was published by Duckworth and Co. in 1912.

HIGHER TREGERTHEN
Zennor
St. Ives, Cornwall
Saturday [1 April 1916]

My dear Kot,

We had a telegram from the Murrys yesterday. They say they will be coming down here early next week. I don't know where they are staying, so I enclose their letter to you.

The letter from Fisher St. was from a man wanting to set some of my verses to music.

I am glad you did not go to the Hutchinson's.[1] I think they are bad people. I'm sure you are a social success, but I think it is better not to be one. Better be an unsocial success.

Here it is marvellously beautiful, now the fine weather has come. When we are all settled, you will come down, won't you? I am just beginning to feel really better.

Have you read any good books lately? I seem to have nothing but Greek Translations and Ethnology, in my head. Stories don't interest me very much just now.

Yours

D. H. Lawrence

---

1 Probably Mr. and Mrs. St. John Hutchinson. See note 2 to Letter No. 331. See also *C.B.*, III, 638.

HIGHER TREGERTHEN
Zennor
St. Ives, Cornwall
Sunday [9 April 1916]

My dear Kot,

Thank you very much for the two copies of the *Trespasser*. I must send you a p.o. soon. You sent me back some money a little time since, which I am sure you did not owe me, by any possibility. But I will settle up directly.

The Murrys are here, and we are all very busy getting ready their house. It is rather a nice job, especially when the weather is so beautiful. But we are as yet rather strange and unaccustomed to each other. It is so difficult to reestablish an old footing, after a lapse during which we have all endured a good deal of misery. But I am sure we shall all eventually be happy here.

I am getting really well now, the spring coming back. Soon I shall be like a lion raging after his prey, seeking whom he may devour.

I find Katharine simpler and better, but Murry not much changed in any way.

How are you, and what are you doing? You must be doing something.

Frieda sends her regards.

Yours

D. H. Lawrence

---

79 HIGHER TREGERTHEN
Zennor
St. Ives, Cornwall
24 May 1916

My dear Kot,

It is a long time since I have written to you: but you must not be cross with me. One waits, always expecting the happy miracle to happen, when one will rush to write a jubilaeum: but the occasion never comes.

Gertler told me you were joyous when you heard I was doing a novel.[1] That pleased me. It is a novel wherein I am free. It comes very quickly and I am well satisfied. For the rest, there is no news, except that I have finished correcting the proofs of a little vol. of poetry, which Duckworth will bring out in the early autumn.[2] *The Italian Sketches* will verily *not* be long now.[3]

It is very beautiful here now, with all the flowers out. And we had a great excitement—a Spanish ship on the rocks in the mist on Saturday morning, just below our house. There she still lies, poor thing. They tried to get her off on Saturday evening, but they could not. The hawsers broke as the tugs were pulling, and she had to be left, with her fore deck submerged. I cannot tell you how it made me sad: it seemed a symbol of something, I don't know what. We sat on the cliffs above, watching. And there she lay, in the mist below, with her crew rowing pathetically round, in the small boats. Then they left her alone. She will be a complete wreck.

The Murrys, I think, are going away. They do not like this country, it is too bleak and rocky for them. They want the south side, with trees and gardens and softness. Also the walls of their house are damp. It is a great pity. I love this country, it is big & free. And I love my little cottage. But folk like different things.

I wonder what will happen about compulsion. I suppose they will give me medical exemption.[4] I don't care very much, but I'd rather be left alone.

How are you and what are you doing? Tell me some of your news. Do you think the War is going to end soon?—I do. I wish so very much also that it would. It is enough.

The Murrys want to go to South Cornwall—some 20 miles away. We of course shall stay here.

Greetings from Frieda & from me.

Yours

D. H. Lawrence

---

1 *Women in Love*, which was later circulated in MS; see Letter No. 107. For a full account of the writing of the novel see George Ford, *Double Measure: A Study of the Novels and Stories of D. H. Lawrence* (New York, 1965), pp. 164–68. The novel was not published until 1920. For an outline of the complex publishing history of the novel, see *B.*, pp. 43–46.

2 *Amores.*

3 *Twilight in Italy.*

4 Lawrence's first experience with the medical examination took place on 11 December 1915. Lawrence describes the experience in greater detail in a letter written to Lady Ottoline Morrell on 12 December 1915 (*C.L.*, I, 397).

HIGHER TREGERTHEN
Zennor
St. Ives, Cornwall
12 June 1916

My dear Kot,

I am sorry you had a black mood. What was the cause this time?

I saw in the papers that foreigners—Russians & French—might enlist now. Do you still think of wearing khaki? Oh abominable!

Of course I shall have to report myself soon. I expect I shall be exempted on the score of health. If not, we shall be comrades in arms. I'd rather be comrades in anything else. But I have ceased to bother over these things.

It does not seem to me so monstrously important, what happens. One will live through it all. One is very tough and resistant inside.

The Murrys have taken a house 30 miles away, on the South side. They will probably be moving this week. Then we shall be alone here. But I am very content, really, to be alone. "Every prospect pleases, and only man is vile," as the hymn says.[1] Not that man is vile—only wearying and confining. It is the most weary thing in this life, this being confined by one's fellow man. But then, that is the fault of taking people seriously. Why should one consider them more important than the horses in the field and the dogs about the farm. The importance of each individual human being has dwindled down to nothing in my soul.

What will you do when you have £50 and are a private gentleman? One cannot exist merely by living on one's means.

Did Farbmann [*sic*][2] choose a boy's book to translate into Russian? I must tell you we have a beautiful literature for boys, adventurous and romantic. I can read it now, when all other books seem rather tiresome. Fennimore [*sic*] Cooper is

lovely beyond words *Last of the Mohicans, Deerslayer.*
Do you think they are done into Russian? Then Hermann [*sic*]
Melville's *Moby Dick* (Everyman 1/–) is a *real* masterpiece,
& *very good* is Dana's *Two Years Before the Mast.* These
are books worth preserving in every language. My dear Kot,
translate them at once. Dana's *Two Years* you can get for
6d (Nelsons).

The weather is cold, the country is beautiful. I shrink from
asking you down here to the coast—they make such an
absurd fuss about foreigners. Oh what fools people are.

I hope your black mood has become a rosy one. Send me all
the news—of Horne & Lewis for example.

Many regards from us both.

Yours

D. H. Lawrence

---

1 See "From Greenland's Icy Mountains" in *Hymns* by Bishop Reginald Heber
(1783–1826):

> What though the spicy breezes
> Blow soft o'er Ceylon's isle;
> Though every prospect pleases,
> And only man is vile:
>
> In vain with lavish kindness
> The gifts of God are strown;
> The heathen in his blindness
> Bows down to wood and stone.

2 The first mention of Michael Farbman. See note 1 to Letter No. 108

HIGHER TREGERTHEN
Zennor
St. Ives, Cornwall
Saturday [17 June 1916]

My dear Kot,

If you feel like sending this man a post card & lending him your copy of *The Rainbow*, I wish you would.[1] I don't want to answer these people myself.

The Murrys have gone. I told you I had my paper, ordering me to join the colours on the 28th? Yesterday I had to forward to Murry a similar notice, ordering him to join on the 30th. Our brave boys in Khaki.

There is no news. Remember me to Campbell when you see him.

Many greetings

D. H. Lawrence

---

1 Douglas King-Page, who had written to Lawrence an eloquent plea for a copy of the suppressed novel *The Rainbow*. The letter is now preserved among the *Koteliansky Papers* in the British Museum.

BODMIN
Thursday [29 June 1916]

I spent last night in the barracks here, like a criminal.[1]
Today I have a complete exemption. But—fui!

D. H. Lawrence

---

1 This was Lawrence's second medical examination for military service. See
his letter to Dollie Radford dated Thursday 29 June 1916 (*C.L.*, I, 456).

HIGHER TREGERTHEN
Zennor
St. Ives, Cornwall
4 July 1916

My dear Kot,

I don't know why you send me this cheque:[1] I am sure it
belongs far more to you than to me. It reminds me though
that I want you to get me a black ribbon for a Smith-
Premier No. 2 type-writer. I will send another 2/6—I don't
know how much they are. I have finished my novel—except
for a bit that can be done any time. I am going to type it
out myself—or try to.

At present I am working in the hay, helping the farmer.[2]
That makes me happy.

You must, if they are really going to 'compel' you militarily,
get a job in an office. With your knowledge of English, &
other languages, I am sure they would have every use for
you. Besides, the war is not going to last much longer.
It will end with this year.

But what a mess altogether! I hated my conscription experience. There is a sense of spiritual disaster underlying this
new militarism of England, which is almost unbearable.
When one is there, in barracks, with the new conscripts &
the old soldiers, there is a strange sprightliness, a liveliness,
almost like a slight delirium, and underneath, this sense of
disaster which nobody dares acknowledge. They are not
afraid of Germany, or anything of that: but of their own
souls. They feel something has happened to themselves,
of their own choice, which is wrong. This sense, of having
chosen wrongly, to the last degree, will haunt & pursue
my nation like the Erinnyes pursued Orestes—God save us.

But the war will end this year, and the terror will come upon
us. Then we must keep our heads, & see what we can do.

I am pretty well, because, for some reason, I feel I have
conquered. I felt I conquered, in the barracks experience—

my spirit held its own & even won, over their great collective spirit. I always feel ill when I feel beaten.

Molti saluti buoni

D. H. Lawrence

[PS.]
Go & see D. King-Page: that is amusing.

---

1 The cheque might be related to Douglas King-Page's request for a copy of *The Rainbow*. In his letter to Lawrence (see note 1 to Letter No. 81 above) King-Page had offered to donate one guinea to a charity of Lawrence's choice for the privilege of reading the book. When Kot lent *The Rainbow* to the man, as apparently he did, it is possible that Kot, who knew of Lawrence's poor financial circumstances, suggested that the guinea should be paid to Lawrence. I have no evidence for this conjecture.

2 William Henry Hocking, who was a friend and neighbour of Lawrence in Cornwall. See *I.H.*, p. 232 and *C.B.*, I, 365–67, 384–85, 409–10, 425–28.

HIGHER TREGERTHEN
Zennor
St. Ives, Cornwall
Friday [7 July 1916]

My dear Kot,

Thank you very much for the typewriting ribbon. But it is
just twice *too wide* for my machine, which takes a ribbon
not more than half an inch wide. I have never seen a ribbon
so wide as this. Ought I to *double* it, fold it?—or must I send
it back and have it changed? Please let me know. I enclose
p.o. for 2/6. I know I owe you various small sums for
postage and books.

I hope you will get an interpreter's job—you ought to. I
think also that you will. How queer, if they send you to
Russia!

I am glad to hear of the new book with Duckworth.[1] How
did you like working with Gilbert? What, by the way, is he
doing about his own military service? Is he a conscientious
objector, or what? What do you think of him lately?

I know Katharine is coming to London. I think—well, she &
Jack are not very happy—they make some sort of a contract
whereby each of them is free. She also talks of going to
Denmark! But don't mention to her that I have told you
anything. She has so many reserves.—But really, I think she
& Jack have worn out anything that was between them. I
like her better than him. He was rather horrid when he was
here.

But it wearies me in my soul, this constant breaking with
people.—I hope Katharine will keep steady, and quiet. She
needs to be quiet, to learn to live alone, & without external
stimulant.

I shall be glad if you can get a decent job and leave the dirty Bureau & the obscene Slat.[2] It has lasted long enough.

Yours

D. H. Lawrence

---

1 Probably a reference to *The House with the Mezzanine and Other Stories* by A. P. Chekhov, translated by S. S. Koteliansky and Gilbert Cannan (New York, 1917).

2 The Russian Law Bureau where Koteliansky worked; Slatkowsky was Koteliansky's employer.

---

85 HIGHER TREGERTHEN
Zennor
St. Ives, Cornwall
10 July 1916

My dear Kot,

I send you here the typewriting ribbon. I am very sorry to give you so much trouble—I do hope you aren't cursing it.

You sound gloomy in your letter. I suppose it is the army. Don't bother, I feel sure they will give you a decent job, which you will like.

When you see Katharine, tell her to write to us and send us all the news: we are thinking of her, up in London.—You are quite right about her wanderings—she wants to run away from herself—but also from Murry, which complicates matters. I don't know what the upshot will be, how it will end between him & her. To settle that point, of her connection with M., a small sojourn in Denmark might be useful. After that, I do wish she could learn to be still—and alone.

Yours

D. H. Lawrence

Zennor
St. Ives, Cornwall
Monday [17 July 1916]

My dear Kot,

I am so sorry to trouble you again about the type-writer ribbon. The new one has come *this morning*, but it is exactly like the last. I can't possibly put it on my machine. And as it arrived without a word to say who sent it, or anything like that, I am at a loss.

My machine is L. C. Smith & Bros. Number 2. Perhaps I am wrong in calling it a Smith Premier. It takes a ribbon exactly half an inch wide. What then am I to do with a ribbon one-inch wide? All I want is an ordinary half-inch black ribbon. Can you solve the mystery for me?

Have you any news yet? The weather is bad here, & I am feeling sick: which is all my news. I had a mere note from Katharine at Garsington, to say she is back in Mylor today, & will we go & stay. But I am not keen on it.

Barbara is coming to see us in August. Have you seen her lately?

Yours

D. H. Lawrence

[PS.]
Why did you send back the 2/6? I know I owe it you

87
Zennor
St. Ives, Cornwall
Tuesday [1 August 1916]

My dear Kot,

Many thanks for the ribbon. This is perfect. I suppose all
the mistakes came from saying "Smith Premier." I am very
sorry.

We have been for the week-end to Mylor. The Murrys have a
pretty little villa there—he loves it—Katharine does not care
for it. He, as you will know, is declared fit for service at
home & abroad, & will be called up on Oct. 1st. He is in a
bad state, dreading it & hating it, & only hoping to get a
job. How devilish this all is!

Let me know when you have some news. Tell me also, if you
cannot get the 2/6 back, & I will send it.

Yours

D. H. Lawrence

HIGHER TREGERTHEN
Zennor
St. Ives, Cornwall
30 August 1916

My dear Kot,

Do not mind if my letters are far between. I have wondered
very often how things are going with you. But I believe, no
steps have been taken as yet with regard to Russians in
England, have they? Write and give me all your news.
Tell me also about Gilbert Cannan & Gertler, and Murry. I
suppose Murry has got his job in the Home Office. He sent
me his book from London.[1] But I am weary, & I don't
want him to write to me any more—at least at present. I don't
know what Katharine is going to do—and don't care. They
weary me, truly.

We had Barbara here. I do really like her. There is something
fierce & courageous in her which wins one's respect. Now we
are alone. It is sad, but the world seems wider & freer when
one is alone.

I am typing away at my novel, to get it done.[2] I often think of
you, & how you laboured at the typing for me, two years
ago. I know you hated it. I hope that things will so go,
that you get some *real* work to do & *have* to do it: that you
have to work *hard*, at something worth doing. It is terrible
to have so much inertia as you have.

With greetings from Frieda

D. H. Lawrence

---

1 Murry's book was *Fyodor Dostoevsky: A Critical Study* (London, 1916).
See Lawrence's letter to Murry dated 28 August 1916 in *C.L.*, I, 469–70.

2 Lawrence had by now gotten used to the machine. Writing to Amy Lowell
on 23 August 1916, he says: "I am busy typing out a new novel, to be called
Women in Love. Every day I bless you for the gift of the typewriter. It runs so
glibly, & has at last become a true confrère. I take so unkindly to any sort of
machinery. But now I & the typewriter have sworn a Blutbruderschaft" (*C.B.*,
I, 389–90).

HIGHER TREGERTHEN
Zennor
St. Ives, Cornwall
Monday [4 September 1916]

My dear Kot,

Both your letters came this morning. Your "Dostoevsky evening" gives me a queer contraction of the heart. It frightens me. When I think of London, the Café Royal[1]—you actually there, and Katharine—terror overcomes me, and I take to my heels, and hide myself in a bush. It is a real feeling of horror. I dare not come to London, for my life. It is like walking into some horrible gas, which tears one's lungs. Really—*Delenda est Carthago.*

I don't believe they will conscript you, in the end. For some reason, I think they will leave alone the Jews & the Russians. Surely they have got their mouths as full of conscripted England, as they can chew. I must say I hate mankind— talking of hatred, I have got a perfect androphobia. When I see people in the distance, walking along the path through the fields to Zennor, I want to crouch in the bushes and shoot them silently with invisible arrows of death. I think truly the only righteousness is the destruction of mankind, as in Sodom. Fire & brimstone should fall down.

But I don't want even to hate them. I only want to be in another world than they. Here, it is almost as if one lived on a star, there is a great space of sky and sea in front, in spirit one can circle in space and have the joy of pure motion. But they creep in, the obstructions, the people, like bugs they creep invidiously in, and they are too many to crush. I see them—fat men in white flannel trousers—*pères de famille*—and the *familles*—passing along the field-path and looking at the scenery. Oh, if one could but have a great box of insect powder, and shake it over them, in the heavens, and exterminate them. Only to clear and cleanse and purify the beautiful earth, and give room for some truth and pure living.

Perhaps after all we shall prevail over the creeping multitudes. The weather will soon wash them back from these coasts. If only the war ended, you could come & stay here. *Devise some job* that will let you out of that Bureau.

Write and tell me what Katharine is doing in London: also Jack. I wrote to him very disagreeably, & said I wanted him to leave me alone entirely. But I feel myself relenting, & a little sorrow coming over my heart.

The heather is all in blossom: there are very many black-berries, heavy on the briars: We got some mushrooms on the cliffs yesterday, small and round in the close grass: the sea was very beautiful, dark, dark blue, with heavy white foam swinging at the rocks. If only one had the world *to oneself!* If only there were not more than one hundred people in Great Britain!—all the rest clear space, grass & trees & stone! Where is our *Rananim?* If only we had had the courage to find it & create it, two years ago. Perhaps it is not utterly too late.

I'm glad you are not going to Garsington. The place is very bad, really. Don't say anything to the Murrys, of what I say. I think he and she should ultimately stick together—but there is so much in their mutual relationship that must pass away first. Oh, dear, how weary things make one.

Greetings from Frieda & me.

D. H. Lawrence

---

1 A reference to the incident in which Katherine Mansfield rescued a copy of Lawrence's *Amores* "which the anti-Lawrence crew in the Café Royal were making fun of" (*I.H.*, p. 216). See Murry's account of the incident in *C.B.*, I, 399, also note 340 by Warren Roberts in *C.B.*, I, 586.

HIGHER TREGERTHEN
Zennor
St. Ives, Cornwall
12 September 1916

My dear Kot,

Now you have some news, and do not tell me. Why are you leaving the Bureau, and what are you going to do? Is it merely that you have had enough Slatkovsky, or is it something better?[1]

Frieda is coming to London on Saturday, & staying for several days with Dollie Radford, 32 Well Walk, Hampstead. You can always ring her up there. Do not trouble about Saturday. Ring her up on Sunday morning & make an appointment.

We heard from Katharine that she is staying in Brett's studio.

Tell me about your new move.

Yours

D. H. Lawrence

---

1 This appears to be about the time that Koteliansky ceased to work at the Russian Law Bureau in High Holborn. There is no hint as to the nature of his new employment.

HIGHER TREGERTHEN
Zennor
St. Ives, Cornwall
15 October 1916

My dear Kot,

How is the world going with you? Don't take any notice of
the Murrys & what they say & do. There is something in them
both you have liked, & therefore you like still. What you hate
was always there. People are not homogeneous or even co-
herent. They are dual and opposite. We know the bad things
about each other, all of us, pretty thoroughly by now. And
they aren't interesting, even though they are true. Murry is
a toad—all right. With the toad in him I will have nothing
to do any more. If there is a decent creature in him also, and
that comes forth, then we will accept that and be thankful. I
refuse to see people as unified Godheads any more. They are
this & that, different and opposing things, without any very
complete identity. Individuality & personality bores me. There
is a world I want and seek. Wherever I find a bit of it, I am
glad, it goes to make my desired world. So if there is a bit of
what to me is true and real in Murry, I am glad of that bit, and
all the rest of himself he can take elsewhere. That is how I feel
about him, & about people in general. As individuals, they bore
me. As pieces of dirt containing bits of true metal, I can
accept them.

It has rained heavens hard, and blown great guns, here, for a
long time. Today it is better. I feel fairly well. I have felt sick
about the world. Now I hardly care. I believe we shall see
changes. I believe we shall be able to set our hands to the re-
making of the world, before very long. For this that is, will
fall to pieces very soon. We can set to to build up a new
world of man in a little time, believe me. So be ready—like
the Virgins with the lamps. *Nil desperandum*—this world
can go, there shall be another, we will shape its beginnings at
least.

With *saluti buoni*

D. H. Lawrence

HIGHER TREGERTHEN
Zennor
St. Ives, Cornwall
7 November 1916

My dear Kot,

I must tell you we laugh at you when you are in your bad
moods, and see the world with a clear eye, and try to rebuke
yourself that the eye which sees is wrong, not the world that
is seen. My dear Kot, if only you would accept what your
eye tells you; that people and the world *are* foul and obscene,
that their life *is* a complication of ghastly trickery, then you
would be free: because that is the *truth*. The world is quite as
bad as you have ever seen it in your worst and most lucid
moments; and *even worse*. Accept the fact baldly and callously,
and you are a free man. Say "No-no, men are good creatures,
'tis I who am bad,"—and you are the slave to a coward's
self-delusion. The world *is* bad, bad beyond bearing. So reject
it, spit it out, trample on it, and have done with it in your
soul. Then you will be strong & free. Meanwhile, making
these false efforts to see good in all, you become imprisoned
in a lie.

Though everybody says the war will go on for ever, yet I
think that this particular war will not last *very* much longer.
While it lasts, we are more or less trapped. When it is over,
we can clear out of *this* world, for ever. I tell you my
Rananim, my Florida idea, was the true one. Only the *people*
were wrong. But to go to *Rananim without* the people is
right, for me, & ultimately, I hope, for you.

I have done with the Murries [*sic*], both, for ever—so help
me god. So I have with Lady Ottoline and all the rest. And
now I am glad & free.

Now we must wait for the wheel of events to turn on a little,
so that we can escape out into the open, to the *Rananim*.
That is all.

Yours

D. H. Lawrence

[PS. in Frieda's hand]
Your picture of your terrible visitors was most vivid.

HIGHER TREGERTHEN
Zennor
St. Ives, Cornwall
Monday 20 November 1916

My dear Kot,

Mendel & the Baedeker came this morning:[1] many thanks for
them. I looked into *Mendel*. It is, as Gertler says, journalism:
statement, without creation. This is very sickening. If Gilbert
had taken Gertler's story and *re-created* it into art, *good*. But
to set down all these statements is a vulgarising of life itself.

The Baedeker is *very* nice: I love its plans and maps and pano-
ramas. We have been such Romans today, on the strength of
it. Would God we were all in Italy, or somewhere sunny
and war-less.

I think I shall come up to London for a few days before
Christmas, to see a doctor, and to get my eyes re-tested, and
so on. I shall be glad to see you again. Today[2] I have sent
off the MS. of my new novel *Women in Love*. Can I tell you
how thankful I am to have the thing done, and out of the
house!—But I have a great respect for this new book. I think
it is a great book—though no doubt I shall share the opinion
with nobody.—Whether the book will ever get published, I
do not know—and don't greatly care. It seems such a
desecration of oneself to give it to the extant world.

You must let me pay you for the Baedeker—please tell me how
much it cost. I too have got a little money again, so, as far as
that goes, am a free man. Please tell me how much the
Baedeker cost. A thousand thanks for getting it.

I think I am the opposite of Gertler—my work nearly kills me.
I feel I shall be a new man now this book is done, strong and
adventurous.—Say to Gertler I will write to him in a day
or two.—Oh, I *don't* like *Mendel*.

I hope you will like Miss Andrews[3]—the American—if
Gertler forgets the address, it is 131 Cheyne Walk, Chelsea—
and Mountsier is a *very nice fellow*.

Yrs

D. H. Lawrence

---

1 *Mendel* (London 1916) was a novel written by Gilbert Cannan. For details see the
"Appendix" in *Mark Gertler: Selected Letters,* edited by Noel Carrington
(London, 1965), pp. 253–56. Karl Baedeker (1801–59) was a German printer and
publisher who became famous for a series of guidebooks. Lawrence here refers
to Baedeker's guidebook to Italy.

2 For a discussion concerning the date of the completion of *Women in Love,* see
Edward Nehls's note 340 in *C.B.,* I, 586. Although this letter has been dated 21
November 1916 by Moore (see *C.L.,* I, 484–85), in view of Lawrence's letter to
Dollie Radford dated 23 November 1916, in which Lawrence writes "I have
finished and sent in my novel *Women in Love*" (*C.B.,* I, 405), I think it safe to
assign the date 20 November 1916. November 21, in any case, was a Tuesday;
and Lawrence has written Monday on his letter.

3 Esther Andrews, an American journalist who visited the Lawrences in Cornwall
in 1916–17. See "The Lawrence Circle," *C.B.,* I, 511.

HIGHER TREGERTHEN
Zennor
St. Ives, Cornwall
Saturday [25] November 1916[1]

My dear Kot,

We sent the *Mendel* back straight to Gertler, as no doubt he told you. I only looked it through: could not read it.

Now I am not doing any work, we need books to read. I enclose ten shillings, with which will you pay yourself for all I owe you, *including postage*. With what remains, will you get me any of these books I put down: Zola: *L'Assommoir* or *Nana*; Fennimore [*sic*] Cooper: *Last of the Mohicans* & *Pathfinder*; Hermann [*sic*] Melville: *Omoo* or *Typee* (preferably *Typee*); Captain Marryatt: *Peter Simple* or *Jacob Faithful* or *Poor Jack*; D'Annunzio: *L'Innocente* (in Italian)—also an Italian dictionary. My dear Kot, some of these books are done at sixpence or sevenpence, some are in *Everyman*, some you might find second hand—Zola at 1/–, for sure. Buy them as cheap as you can—and send me just a couple at a time—and keep a *strict* account for yourself, postage as well, and tell me when my ten shillings is spent.

This is a kind of interval in my life, like a sleep. One only wanders through the dim short days, and reads, and cooks, and looks across at the sea. I feel as if I also were hibernating, like the snakes and the dormice.—I saw a most beautiful brindled adder, in the spring, coiled up asleep with her head on her shoulder. She did not hear me till I was very near. Then she must have felt my motion, for she lifted her head like a queen to look, then turned and moved slowly and with delicate pride into the bushes. She often comes into my mind again, and I think I see her asleep in the sun, like a Princess of the fairy world. It is queer, the intimation of other worlds, which one catches.

I shall come to London when the energy comes upon me. We shall meet like exiles returned—it seems so long since we saw each other.

D. H. Lawrence

---

1 In *C.L.*, I, 485, Harry T. Moore dates this letter [?23 November 1916]. Assuming that Lawrence would likely not be mistaken as to the day of the week, I have dated this letter 25 November 1916, since Lawrence's MS clearly reads Saturday 23 November 1916.

HIGHER TREGERTHEN
Zennor
St. Ives, Cornwall
1 December 1916

My dear Kot,

We got the letter with the photograph,[1] also the second letter
about books. The portrait has really something of you—quite
true. But it has indeed none of your good looks. It makes you
uglier. It is you in your bad & hopeless moods. I don't
really like it. But don't tell Gertler. There is still a youthful
and foolish warmth about you, which is perhaps the nicest
part, and this is left out on the photo. You are here, the old old
old *Jew*, who ought to hasten into oblivion. But there is a
young & clumsy uncouth human being, not a Jew at all, a
sort of heavy colt, which I should paint if *I* painted your
portrait.

About books—it grieves me to have to pay 6/– for a dictionary
—yet one needs a decent one. But I *can't* pay 5/– for
L'Innocente. There is a shop in Charing Cross Rd., rather
far up, which is a Libreria Italiana and Espagnol—it only has
Italian and Spanish books, do see what they can do for you.
If there is no cheap *Innocente*, buy some other book—
D'Annunzio or Matilde Serao or Grazia Deledda—I have
read *Fuoco, Vergine Delle Rocche*, and *Trionfo della Morté*—of
D'Annunzio.

It will be a great boon if S.[2] goes to Russia—we might have
a very free and simple time at 212[3]—But I suppose the old
landlord will *never* clear out. And he is impossible.

I know you don't mind looking for the books. Find that
Italian shop.

Post-rush

D. H. L.

---

1 This photograph was of a portrait of Koteliansky painted by Mark Gertler.
It is reproduced in *Mark Gertler: Selected Letters*, edited by Noel Carrington
(London, 1965), opposite p. 144.

2 Slatkowsky.

3 212 High Holborn, London, E.C., the address of the Russian Law Bureau.

[HIGHER TREGERTHEN]
Zennor
St. Ives, Cornwall
Monday [4 December 1916]

My dear Kot,

The books came today—a great pleasure. The dictionary is
one of the "faithful friend" sort. Do borrow me an Italian
book, if you can. But you spent all the money, & now I owe
you for the Baedeker & the postage. Never mind, when I
have read these books, I will send money for more. For the
present we sail on gaily.

With many thanks.

D. H. Lawrence

97 [HIGHER TREGERTHEN
Zennor
St. Ives, Cornwall
Before 12 December 1916]¹

My dear Kot,

Thank you very much for the Italian books. I will not keep them too long—Frieda rushes in, as usual.—It is the merest chance we might go to Guildford for a week or two.—But it is quite near London, we should see you. I am sure Sl[atkowsky] won't go to Russia. We shall certainly come to London in January. I wonder if this new government will worry you.² All is vile.

D. H. Lawrence

1 Lawrence's letter appears at the end of Frieda's letter to Koteliansky. The latter is dated by E. W. Tedlock, Jr., "Before 12 December 1916"; see *Frieda Lawrence: The Memoirs and Correspondence* (New York, 1964), pp. 207–08.

2 Probably a reference to the government of Great Britain under Lloyd George, who became Prime Minister in December 1916. As an alien living in England, Koteliansky would be anxious about his status under a new government.

98 [HIGHER TREGERTHEN]
Zennor
St. Ives, Cornwall
Friday [15 December 1916]

My dear Kot,

Thank you for the little Dostoevsky book.¹ I have only read Murry's Introduction, and Dostoevsky's "Dream of a Queer Fellow." Both stink in my nostrils. I call it offal, putrid stuff. Dostoevsky is big & putrid, here, Murry is a small stinker, emitting the same kind of stink. How is it that these foul-living people ooze with such loving words. "Love thy neighbour as thyself"—well & good, if you'll hate thy neighbour as thyself. I can't do with this creed based on self-love, even when the self-love is extended to cover the whole of humanity.—No, when he was *preaching*, Dostoevsky

was a rotten little stinker. In his art he is bound to confess
himself lusting in hate & torture. But his 'credo'—!—My
God, what filth!

And Murry, *not being an artist*, but only a little ego, is a
little muckspout, and there is an end of it. I never said he was
honest: I said we *had* liked him & therefore we still liked
him. But one can mend one's ways. I have liked him and I
don't like him any more. *Basta!* As for his novel[2]—I read it
in MS. and thought it merely words, words. It is the kind of
wriggling self-abuse which I can't make head or tail of. But
then, as Murry says, I am not clever enough.—Enough
enough—I have had filth in my mouth. Now I spit it out.

We have read the *Cavalleria Rusticana*:[3] a veritable blood-
pudding of *passion*! It is not at all good, only, in some odd
way, comical, as the portentous tragic Italian is always comical.

I don't want too much Varvara when we are in town.[4]

I heard from Campbell.[5] It's about time he made a fresh
start somewhere. He's worn his legs to stumps trotting in an
old round. *Basta!* That's a great word.

I have just read *Deerslayer*.[6] What an exquisite novel. Oh,
English novels, at their best, are the best in the world.

I don't want to hear you talk for a fortnight about Murry.
Five minutes, then not a moment more. Stink bores me, as
well as oppresses me.

Yours

D. H. Lawrence

---

1 F. M. Dostoevsky's *Pages from the Journal of an Author*, translated by S. S.
Koteliansky and J. Middleton Murry (London, 1916).

2 Probably J. M. Murry's *Still Life* (London, 1916).

3 By Giovanni Verga, later translated into English by Lawrence in *Cavalleria
Rusticana and Other Stories* (London, 1928).

4 Varvara is the Russian equivalent for Barbara; here the reference is to Barbara
Low.

5 Gordon Campbell.

6 By James Fenimore Cooper. See Lawrence's essay "Fenimore Cooper's
Leatherstocking Novels" in *Studies in Classic American Literature* (New York,
1964), pp. 60–63.

---

99 [HIGHER TREGERTHEN]
Zennor
St. Ives, Cornwall
18 December 1916

My dear Kot,

Many thanks for thinking about publishing my book in
Russia.[1] I should like it to be done. Unfortunately there is no
spare MS.—one must go to America—but one might be
made. I have written to Pinker about it, & asked him to
ring you up. He is my literary agent: J. B. Pinker, Talbot
House, Arundel St., Strand, W.C. He would arrange with
you, & get a type-copy made. He has the MS. now. I hope
this will come off: It would be a real pleasure.

With many thanks, & greetings

D. H. Lawrence

---

1 *Women in Love.*

[HIGHER TREGERTHEN]
Zennor
St. Ives, Cornwall
23 December 1916

My dear Kot,

Thank you so much for thinking about the Russian translation
of the novel. I hope it will come off.

I send you a tiny little paper-knife of blue agate. It is a
curious stone that loses colour when exposed to light. It is a
fragment of Cornwall itself, as the stone is found here.

One doesn't feel very Christmassy. For some reason, I am sad
at heart, and very heavy-spirited. But next Christmas we shall
be happy, really doing something and happy.

With love from both of us.

D. H. Lawrence

[HIGHER TREGERTHEN]
Zennor
St. Ives, Cornwall
8 January 1917

My dear Kot,

I ought to have written to you before. I got your letter, & the little money order from America—which I have lost: not that it matters, it wasn't much.

There isn't any news, except that I feel perfectly hopeless and disgusted with the world here. My dear Kot, when we can but set sail for our *Rananim*, we shall have our first day of happiness. But it will come one day—before very long. I shall go to America when I can—& try to find a place—& you will come on. That is the living dream. We will have our *Rananim* yet.

I think my novel won't get published in England: it is just as well it shouldn't. Perhaps I shall be able to lend you another copy of the MS—but you will read the one Pinker sends you for Russia. Has it come yet.

There is no hope here, my dear Kot—there is no hope in Europe, the sky is too old. But we will find a new sky, & pitch our tents under that.

D. H. Lawrence

[HIGHER TREGERTHEN]
Zennor
St. Ives, Cornwall
Friday [12 January 1917]

My dear Kot,

Thank you very much for the offer of the £10. If I need it, I shall ask you for it. Meanwhile, if my plans come off, I shall make Pinker supply me, if I can.

It is true, I must go away. At the present moment, I am trying to get passports for America. If these come all right, then we shall sail for New York next month, I hope. I shall say goodbye to England, forever, and set off in quest of our *Rananim*. Thither, later, you must come. For the present I only want to get to the U.S.A.

It seems nobody will publish the novel *Women in Love*. It is just as well—why cast the pearls before irredeemable swine.

Don't tell anybody about the American project. It is, like so many of our plans, a secret. But I hope we can go—I do hope so. We should see you first.

Love from both

D. H. Lawrence

[HIGHER TREGERTHEN]
Zennor
St. Ives, Cornwall
19 January 1917

My dear Kot,

It is a trying and difficult life. But I shall see that Pinker
gets the MS. next *Tuesday* or *Wednesday,* and then I shall
ask him to type off two or more copies, so that I can keep
one by me. You shall have yours for Russia very shortly:
about a week's time. Just be patient for one moment.

I don't seem to get any nearer to passports for America. If
you see Campbell, you might ask him, if he can tell me what it
is necessary for me to do to get these passports renewed
now. I want to go to New York as soon as ever I can,
and I am afraid it will be rather difficult. I wonder if Campbell
could help me. Shall I write to him.

It has been snowy all the week here, very cold. I don't like it.
And I can't live in England any more. It oppresses one's
lungs, one cannot breathe. Wait, only wait for our *Rananim.*
It shall come quite soon now.

Yes, I have decided I shall ask you for the £10 as soon as ever
I need it. I count it a reserve store, to fall back on in any
moment of urgency. It is very nice to feel it behind me.

What is all this that happens in Russia now: about the Duma
& the resignations? Is there anything behind it, do you know?

Now I *do want* something nice to happen.

It doesn't seem much good offering the novel to the English
public: really.

D. H. Lawrence

[HIGHER TREGERTHEN]
Zennor
St. Ives, Cornwall
Friday 9 February 1917

My dear Kot,

Your letter to Frieda came today. I meant to have written
you before. Pinker has got the MS, and has put it out to be
typed. He is having two copies made, one for you, one for
me, so that I can always keep by me a spare MS. I should
think it ought to be done very soon.

We have not heard yet about passports. Everything seems to
have gone to pot in the world. And still I hope—hope to get
away, hope that America won't come in, hope we can find
our *Rananim*, hope they won't conscript you in any way.
Hope is a great thing. We are not beaten yet, in spirit, but
it is a critical moment. We must pray to the good unknown.
I think we shall come out all right, even against so many
millions.

Campbell wrote today: yes, he is quite friendly. I have written
to Gertler. I would write to poor Gilbert & Mary, but I
feel I could do no good.[1] As for the rest, they are gone,
like the leaves of last autumn. The Ott., the Murries [*sic*]—
they are gone into the ground. Only for poor Katharine &
her lies I feel rather sorry. They are such self-responsible
lies. But then, pity is worse than useless. I move no more
upon the basis of feeling sorry for anybody.

I should like the novel to be published in Russia. Certainly
it won't come out here—not as long as the war lasts: but I am
just as well content. I have got together my final book of
poems.[2] It seems like my last work for the old world. The
next must be for something new.—I want you to read the
novel.

I am pretty well in health—so is Frieda—though the weather
is most devilish cold. We shall all come to our *Rananim*
before many years are out—only believe me—an Isle of the
Blest, here on earth. But the first thing is to cut clear of the
old world—burn one's boats: if only one could.

I shall let you know as soon as there is any news of us: and you do likewise for yourself. They will not conscript you.

The world is at an end.

D. H. Lawrence

1 Gilbert and Mary Cannan, who were later divorced.
2 *Look! We Have Come Through!* (London, 1917).

105   [HIGHER TREGERTHEN]
Zennor
St. Ives, Cornwall
12 March 1917

My dear Kot,

I believe it was your turn to write. At any rate I have been expecting a letter from you this long while. What is happening to you now? What is happening in Russia? Is the world coming to an end?

They wouldn't let me go to America. I will go one day. Meanwhile I content myself at Zennor. I have done some peace articles—called "The Reality of Peace." [1] I wonder if anybody will publish them. They are very good, & beautiful. I have heard nothing from Pinker about the MS. of the novel. What about your copy?—But everything seems to have gone to pot.

Now I am going to garden. I believe we are really going to be pinched for food. But we are going to see the end of the war soon. Anything to have that. I will become even a little thinner than I am, if only the war will end.—It will end soon. It is *virtually* over. We are coming out of it all. We will be happy before long. I send you back the Italian books. Alas, I have wearied of passion and eroticism and sex perversions, so that though we have read through these books, I end with a feeling of weariness and a slight nausea against things Italian.

I *do* wish peace would come quickly. You might then come down here and help me to dig gardens. You would be happy here. I only want the war to end now.

Have you got any news? I have none. I was seedy these last weeks, but I feel better again, and am sure we shall soon have peace and some happiness, even if there is not quite enough for us to eat. Tell me news of yourself, and of other people. I *do* hope Gertler is better. His letter was so painful I couldn't write about it. And the news of Gilbert was nasty—something sordid & putrid—We want to get into something new. But very soon now, we will. Is there any news of Murry? I have not heard from either of them for many months, which is as it should be. I have really a disillusion from [*sic*] them.

Oh, do get me a gardening book *Culture of Profitable Vegetables in Small Gardens* by Sutton & Sons—6ᵈ.

You will think I only write when I want something. But it isn't so.

The spring is coming quickly, the birds whistle their best, the lambs are full of spirits, they hold a Panatheneia under the windows of the house. They are *very* jolly when the sun shines. It shone so beautifully today. I have been painting a picture of the death of Procris, which fills me with great delight.—I wish you could come down for a time—do you think you might manage it? If only the war stopped, you would certainly come.

What do you do with yourself nowadays, tell me that.

I should think you could get the little sixpenny gardening book anywhere.

Thank Mr. Shearman [2] very heartily on my account, for the books.

I wish you could come here for a few weeks. Warm greetings from Frieda.

D. H. Lawrence

[PS.]

I send you *Moby Dick*, because I have two copies, and it is a book I like *very* much.

---

1 The publication history of these "Essays" is given by Warren Roberts in *B.*, p. 255. See in particular items C45, C46, C48, C50.

2 Montague Shearman was the "Son of a Judge of the King's Bench and a friend of Gordon Campbell and Mark Gertler . . . a notable patron of the arts" (*C.L.*, I, liii).

[HIGHER TREGERTHEN]
Zennor
St. Ives, Cornwall
1 April 1917

My dear Kot,

You saw Frieda on her visit—otherwise I should have written
sooner to thank you for the gardening book. Your elation over
Russia, has it come back, or do you feel still despondent? I
am very sick with the state here. The new Military Service
still makes me liable to be pestered again. But I am resolved
this time. If they bother me, I will go to prison. I *will not
be compelled*: that is the whole of my feeling. I should very
much like to do something to get a better government. This
Parliament must be kicked out: it is a disgusting fraud. It is
time we had a living representative government here. How
can we tolerate such a grunting *schweinerei*? I think I must
come to London soon and see a few people.

I believe Austin Harrison is going to publish some essays of
mine, called "The Reality of Peace," in the *English Review*.
I hope he will. It may start a new feeling among people. It
is time now that there was something new. It is quite time.

You will have got the complete MS of the novel by now. I
want you to tell me if you like it to the end. Don't hurry
about Russia. I always believe in giving things time. If
Gertler likes to read the MS, lend it to him: or to Campbell,
if you are keeping it long enough.

I am busy gardening: breaking up a little field to set vegetables.
It is hard work & I wish I had you here to utilise some of
your spare force. But we drive slowly ahead. I wish I could feel
real occasion for my coming to London. But I don't see that
it is any use contemplating it, for the moment.

Frieda greets you.[1]

D. H. Lawrence

---

[1] Appended to Lawrence's letter is the following postscript in Frieda's hand:
"How is your poor suicide Russian? Has your new hat recovered from the snow-
storm on the bus? I was *disgusted* to find Ernst [*sic*] who poses as the tragic
figure to the children takes Gladys (some coarse girl) out to dinner, flirts with her,
but keeps of course the last respectability—Lord I was so furious—but then he is
both things, but the children are different, thank God!
"My love to you.
"Frieda"

[HIGHER TREGERTHEN]
Zennor
St. Ives, Cornwall
4 April 1917

My dear Kot,

I was out when Carrington's telegram came, and Frieda answered it.[1] I don't really want anybody else to read the MS.—I don't very much want even Carrington to have it. But it is all right, since Frieda wired yes. Let her have it on the stipulation she shows *nobody else*: and if Campbell & Gertler have read it, then *don't let it go any further*. You know that the Ottoline threatens me with law-suits: I feel she would go any length to do me damage in this affair. I feel that these people, all the Ott. crowd, are full of malice against me. Altogether I feel bad about that novel, and I will not publish it now. I *know* it is a good book. But my god, to have all these *canaille* already grunting over it is more than I can bear. I feel awfully raw against the whole show. I will show the MS to *nobody* absolutely any more: so please help to protect me in this.

Don't say anything to hurt Carrington's feelings: don't tell her I would rather she *hadn't* seen the MS., since things have happened as they have.

I cannot cannot cannot [*sic*] bear the feeling of all these *canaille* yapping and snapping at me—they are too disgusting and insufferable. *Why* did I give myself away to them—Otts & Murries [*sic*] etc!—

D. H. Lawrence

---

1 Dora (Dorothy) Carrington was Mark Gertler's fiancée. See "The Lawrence Circle," *C.B.*, I, 514. See also Gertler's letters to Carrington, as she was usually called, in *Mark Gertler: Selected Letters*, edited by Noel Carrington (London, 1965).

c/o MRS. CLARKE
Grosvenor Rd.
Ripley, nr. Derby
Monday [16 April 1917]

My dear Kot,

I shall come down to London from Nottingham on Thursday,
arrive Marylebone at 1:12—so that I should be at Acacia Rd.
at about 1:30. I do hope I shan't be a nuisance to Mrs.
Farbman.[1] My regards to her, and I am very sensible of her
kindness in letting me stay in her house. Don't bother about
lunch on Thursday, for me.—I stay here till Wednesday—
stay Wed. night in Nottingham—then come on.

Dollie Radford is getting copies made of the *Peace Articles*. I
hate the Midlands.

D. H. Lawrence

---

1 In *B.L.G.* Beatrice Lady Glenavy says of the Farbman family: "After the death
of Katherine's brother [see note 1 to Letter No. 54], she and Murry left Acacia
Road. A Russian journalist, Michael Farbman, and his wife and daughter took
the house [No. 5 Acacia Road, St. John's Wood, London], and Kot went to
live with them. When a few years later, the Farbman family went away Kot
kept on the house and lived there till his death in 1955" (p. 89).

HERMITAGE
Thursday [26 April 1917]

My dear Kot,

I got here all right last night:[1] am feeling almost quite well. Tomorrow I am going back to Cornwall.

I shall think about the Russian question when I am at home. But for the time, I feel I can't bother about anything. It is spring, let us not worry at all about anything whatsoever.

I was very glad to stay with you. I feel that everything is working itself out, and we will all have a happy time, in the end. As for the others, vile ones, Campbells and Murrys etc, they are being carried their own separate way to their own separate end. It is as if the Current of life was dividing now, and carrying some definitely one way, others definitely in a quite different direction. And the Murrys Campbells etc, the whole crew, are being borne off away from me, but you and I, we bob about tipsily like two vessels in the same stream. But we shall get our clear direction soon.

D. H. Lawrence

---

1 Lawrence arrived at Hermitage on Wednesday 25 April 1917; hence the letter to Kot must have been written on Thursday 26 April 1917. See Lawrence's letter to Catherine Carswell dated 28 April 1917 in *I.H.*, p. 231, which is not included in *C.L.*

110
Zennor
St. Ives [Cornwall]
Tuesday [?1 May 1917]¹

My dear Kot,

I got your telegram yesterday about Gorki's paper.² Write &
tell me what it means exactly—I shall be only too glad to
contribute anything I can.

I feel that our chiefest hope for the future is Russia. When
I think of the young new country there, I love it inordinately.
It is the place of hope. We must go, sooner or (a little) later.
But let us go gently. I feel a violent change would be the
death of me. *Toujours doucement*, as the nuns say.—I am
working in the garden.—We will go to Russia. Send me a
Berlitz grammar book, I will begin to learn the language—
religiously. And when Farbman comes back, we will scheme—
and perhaps you will come down here for a few weeks.
*Nuova speranza—la Russia.—Please send me a grammar
book.*

Greet Mrs. Farbman from me—*di cuore.* I must learn her real
name—Sonia—what else? I hate the word "*Mrs.*"—and
"*Mr.*"

It is most beautiful weather & gardening makes me happy.

D. H. L.

---

1 On the basis of internal evidence, I have placed this letter before No. 111,
which is dated 11 May 1917. In the first place, the telegram appears to have been
jubilant and, in the second place, Lawrence is asking for Mrs. Farbman's "real"
name. In No. 111, Lawrence refers to "unfathomable depths of gloom in your
last letter," so we must conclude that Koteliansky wrote *after* sending the telegram.
Also in No. 111, Lawrence now familiarly greets Mrs. Farbman as Sonia Issayevna
and sends greetings to the Farbman daughter, "Gita," as well.

Letter No. 110 could, of course, have been dated 8 May 1917, but to do so would
not allow sufficient time for the exchange of letters which is implied in No. 111.

2 K. W. Gransden says: "In April 1917, Maxim Gorki was organizing and co-
editing the paper *New Life.* Kot obtained various messages from British Liberal
and Socialist thinkers greeting the revolution and offering statements of Britain's
war-aims.... Kot... supplied Gorki with messages from Wells, Lord Bryce,
Lord Loreburn, Arnold Bennett and a number of Socialist M.P.'s" ("*Rananim*:
D. H. Lawrence's Letters to S. S. Koteliansky," *Twentieth Century*, CLIX
[January 1956], p. 27). Among the *Koteliansky Papers* in the British Museum are
various documents related to these activities.

111 [HIGHER TREGERTHEN]
Zennor
St. Ives, Cornwall
Friday 11 May 1917

My dear Kot,

I read unfathomable depths of gloom in your last letter, and concluded, alas, that the wrong things were happening in Russia. Was that what cast you down so deep? Never mind, Russia is bound to run wrong at the first, but she will pull out all right. As for me, I sincerely hope she will conclude a separate peace. Anything to end the war.—But tell me what news there *really* is, from Petrograd.—In the meantime, I keep my belief in Russia intact, until such time as I am forced to relinquish it: for it is the only country where I can plant my hopes. America is a stink-pot in my nostrils, after having been the land of the future for me.

Frieda is a good deal better at last. She has been quite seedy. I am pretty well. I felt the effects of my London upset—still feel them a bit.—We are alone in Tregerthen. Esther Andrews[1] has gone back to London. Philip Heseltine has taken a bungalow about two miles away, but we see little or nothing of him. I sit looking towards the North West [*sic*], and wondering what next. This is the interregnum in my kingdom.

The weather is very hot and lovely. I go about in a silky shirt you gave me, & a pair of trousers, and nothing else. Today I have been cutting blackthorn & gorse to make a fence to keep the lambs out of my garden. I loathe lambs, those symbols of Christian meekness. They are the stupidest, most persistent, greediest little beasts in the whole animal kingdom. Really, I suspect Jesus of having had *very little* to do with sheep, that he could call himself the Lamb of God. I would truly rather be the little pig of God, the little pigs are infinitely gayer and more delicate in soul.—My garden is very beautiful, in rows. But the filthy lambs have eaten off my broad beans. The salads are all grown, and the scarlet runners are just ready for the sprint.

Remember me in the nicest possible way to Sonia Issayevna, also to Gita [*sic*].² Tell me what news there is. I cannot write or do anything, but wait for a new start from somewhere.—If only the war would end! But don't be downcast—nothing in the outer world is worth being downcast about.—Remember me to Madame Stepniak.³—I have heard nothing of Campbell or Fothrell—but tell me about Biddie⁴ the child.

affectionately

D. H. Lawrence

---

1 American journalist who visited the Lawrences in Cornwall and at Mountain Cottage, she was a friend of Robert Mountsier, Lawrence's American literary agent in New York (1916–1923).

2 See note 1 to Letter No. 108. Lawrence later writes "Gita" as "Ghita."

3 According to Beatrice Lady Glenavy, "the widow of a leader of the Russian Revolutionary Party, who wrote under the name of 'Stepniak'" (*B.L.G.*, pp. 103–04). See note 2 to Letter No. 12. See also Lawrence's letter to Mrs. S. A. Hopkin in *A.H.*, p. 405.

4 Campbell is Gordon Campbell; Fothrell was Netty Fothrell, a beautiful young woman who developed an admiration for Gordon Campbell in 1917; Biddie was Lady Beatrice Glenavy's little girl, who had just had an operation for appendicitis.

[HIGHER TREGERTHEN]
Zennor
St. Ives, Cornwall
3 July 1917

My dear Kot,

I was glad to hear of Farbman's safe return, and to have
hopeful news of Russia. Russia seems to me now the positive
pole of the world's spiritual energy, and America the negative
pole. But we shall see how things work out. Meanwhile
everything looks dreary enough, and I do not feel at all
happy. But *ça passera.*

How can I write for any Russian audience!—the contact is not
established. How can the current flow when there is no connection? As for England, it is quite hopeless.

I wrote & told Pinker I must soon have more money. He does
not answer. Probably he does not want to advance any more.
Tant pis pour lui—I am just as well satisfied. My relations
with that little *parvenu* snob of a *procureur* of books were
always strained, best have them broken.—As for money, I
have got plenty to go on with, & more will come.

There is no actual news at all. I feel you in a bad mood. I
am not in a good one. I would read Béranger if I had got a
copy of him.

> "O Richard, O mon roi
> Tout le monde l'abandonne—"

though who Richard is, is a puzzle.

Why humanity has hated Jews, I have come to the conclusion,
is that the Jews have always taken religion—since the great
days, that is—and used it for their own personal & private
gratification, as if it were a thing administered to their own
importance & well-being & conceit. This is the slave trick
of the Jews—they use the great religious consciousness as a
trick of personal conceit. This is abominable. With them, the
conscious ego is the absolute, and God is a name they flatter
themselves with.—When they have learned again pure

reverence to the Holy Spirit, then they will be free, and not slaves before men. Now, a Jew cringes before men, and takes God as a Christian takes whiskey, for his own self-indulgence.

This is the conclusion to the last conversation—an exhortation to the unflinching adherence to the Spirit. I am preaching at you, Kot, because you are "near the mark,"—but let us trust to the invisible spirit, not to ourselves and our own ridiculous universality of Knowledge.

At any rate, don't be cross.

D. H. Lawrence

113 [HIGHER TREGERTHEN]
Zennor
St. Ives, Cornwall
23 September 1917

My dear Kot,

I was thinking about you several times these last few days.—
You should never mind my onslaughts: go on as if they hadn't
taken place: why answer them, they're no better for it.

Please unlearn all the social lessons. I have learnt to be unsocial entirely, a single thing to myself. I hate being squashed
into humanity, like a strawberry boiled with all the other
strawberries into jam. God above, leave me single and separate
and unthinkably distinguished from all the rest: let me be a
paradisal being, but *never* a human being: let it be true when
I say '*homo sum, humani omnis a me alienum puto.*' Henceforth
I deal in single, sheer beings—nothing human, only the
star-singleness of paradisal souls.

This is the latest sort of swank: also tone.

The summer has gone quickly. We have been all the time here.
Frieda had a bad attack of neuritis in her leg, in July. She is
well again now. I am pretty well. We have had nobody to see
us since Esther Andrews was here in the spring: that is,
nobody to stay. There is a young fellow Gray,[1] once friend
of Heseltine, has taken a house about four miles further on,
down the Coast. He comes occasionally, occasionally we go
to him. I like him. He is music. Then there is a rather dreadful Starr,[2] with a Lady Mary Starr, half-caste she. We try
to get out of seeing them.—Murry wrote me once or twice—but
it fell off again. Katharine wrote once or twice—that too falls
off again. The past is past. So little of it has survived into the
present.—I am fond of the people at the farm.

I am finishing correcting proofs of a book of poems which
Chatto & Windus are bringing out next month.[3] I have written
into its final form that philosophy which you once painfully &
laboriously typed out, when we were in Bucks, and you were
in the Bureau.[4] I always remember you said "Yes, but you
will write it again."—I have written it four times since then.

Now it is done: even it is in the hands of my friend Pinker. But I have no fear that anybody will publish it.—Now I am doing a set of Essays on *The Mystic Import of American Literature*.[5] I hope the title doesn't seem ludicrous: perhaps I shall find a better.—These were begun in the hopes of making money: for money is a shy bird.—But I am afraid they have already passed beyond all price. It is a pity.

I think this is all the news, as news goes. We have had fine gardens full of vegetables: I have worked like a laborer through corn and hay harvest: corn yet remains to be carried in. There has been a curious subtle mystic invisibleness in the days, a beauty that is not in the eyes. Mystically, the world does not exist to me any more: nor wars nor publishings nor Gertlers nor Ottolines: I have lost it all, somehow. There is another world of reality, actual and mystical at once, not the world of the Whole, but the world of the essential now, here, immediate, a strange actual hereabouts, no before and after to strive with: not worth it.

I wonder when we shall see you again. Everything seems strange, as having passed beyond.—Remember me very kindly to Mrs. Farbman & Gita, also to Mr. Farbman. Where did they go to, for the seaside?

Frieda will write to you.

D. H. Lawrence

---

1 Cecil Gray (1895–1951), a "Scottish writer on music and composer. Friend and neighbor of Lawrence in Cornwall (1917). In late 1917, Lawrences temporarily housed in mother's flat at 13b, Earl's Court Sq., London, S.W. In 1915, settled in London and in 1919 edited with Philip Heseltine *The Sackbut*, a progressive, critical journal" (*C.B.*, I, 518).

2 Meridith Starr, author of *The Future of the Novel* (London, 1921). See *C.B.*, I, note 390, p. 589.

3 *Look! We Have Come Through!* (London, 1917).

4 This would be the work which Lawrence described in his letter to J. B. Pinker, dated 30 August 1917, as follows: "I will send you on the MS. of *At the Gates* in a day or two. On second thoughts, I send it at once. You will see it is based upon the more superficial *Reality of Peace*. But *this* is pure metaphysics, especially later on: and perfectly sound metaphysics, that will stand the attacks of technical philosophers. Bits of it that might be very unpopular, I might leave out" (*A.H.*,

p. 414). What happened to the manuscript of *At the Gates* is still a mystery, although it is known that the manuscript was still in Pinker's hands as late as 6 February 1920. See *The Frieda Lawrence Collection of D. H. Lawrence Manuscripts: A Descriptive Bibliography*, edited by E. W. Tedlock, Jr. (Albuquerque, N.M., 1948), p. 89.

5 Later published as *Studies in Classic American Literature* (New York, 1923). For publication history see Warren Roberts, *B.*, pp. 62–64. Also see Armin Arnold's "Introduction" to *D. H. Lawrence: The Symbolic Meaning: The Uncollected Versions of "Studies in Classic American Literature*," with a Preface by Harry T. Moore (New York, 1964), pp. 1–11.

---

114 CHAPEL FARM COTTAGE
Hermitage
nr Newbury, Berks
Wednesday [19 December 1917]

We got here yesterday [1]—snow everywhere, and sharp frost: very cold but very pretty. The cottage is nice—I wait to hear from my sister [2]—perhaps she will write direct to you.

Greet the Farbmans kindly from me.

D. H. Lawrence

---

1 Lawrence was suspected of espionage and ordered to leave Cornwall by 15 October 1917. In a letter to Lady Cynthia Asquith dated 12 October 1917, he says: "The police have suddenly descended on the house, searched it, and delivered us a notice to leave the area of Cornwall, by Monday next. So on Monday we shall be in London" (*C.L.*, I, 527). In a letter to J. B. Pinker written from Hermitage dated 18 December 1917, Lawrence says: "We have come down here for a fortnight or so" (*C.L.*, I, 534). By 29 December 1917, Lawrence was at his sister's place in the Midlands; see *C.L.*, I, 535. Since the letter to Koteliansky anticipates the visit to the Midlands, I have assigned to Letter No. 114 the date 19 December 1917.

2 Mrs. Clarke, Lawrence's sister Ada.

CHAPEL FARM COTTAGE
Hermitage
nr Newbury, Berks
Thursday [20 December 1917]

My dear Kot,

My sister says she arrives at Marylebone Great Central at
5:40 on Sunday, in the evening. She wants to go straight on to
Waterloo to catch the 6:40 train to Portsmouth. According
to my timetable, however, there is no 6:40 on Sunday to
Portsmouth, only a 7:00 o'clock train. I have written her to
this effect. If my time table is right, she will take the seven
train.

You will go straight across by the Bakerloo, I suppose.

She says you are to look for a tallish thin woman with dark
furs, in a pale bluey-grey long coat.—I'm sure you will
know each other. I described to her your villainous appearance.

Thank you very much for meeting her.

It is *very* cold here. I wish the world were nicer.

D. H. Lawrence

116   [CHAPEL FARM COTTAGE]
Hermitage
[nr. Newbury, Berks]
Wednesday [26 December 1917]

Thanks so much for going to Marylebone to my sister. She
told me you were there.

We are going to the Midlands on *Friday*—address there—

> c/o Mrs. Clarke,
> Grosvenor Rd.,
> Ripley,
> nr. Derby.

We shall stay about a week, then come back here, I think.
But we will see you as we cross London on our return. Let
me hear from you.—No news from Gertler. When do the
Farbmans return?

D. H. L.

17 c/o MRS. CLARKE
Grosvenor Rd.
Ripley, nr. Derby
Saturday [29 December 1917]

My dear Kot,

Here we are in the snowy Midlands—very queer. I think we
shall stay till next Thursday. We are going to look for a
cottage near here—Derbyshire is beautiful—and it will be
near my sister.—She made us laugh very much about your
one eye-glass, your pseudo-monocle, and your serious outgaze,
and the relief you evidenced in fleeing.—

We shall look for a cottage, and have our goods sent from
Cornwall. That will take five or six weeks. We shall return to
Hermitage, I think, for the meantime. The war will end by
the summer. Then we will really go to Russia, & leave our
cottage to my sister. It is a good arrangement.

When do the Farbman's [*sic*] return? If they are not back on
Thursday, could we stay one night with you? If they are
returning before then, don't mention it to them.

See you next week

D. H. Lawrence

118 c/o MRS. CLARKE
Grosvenor Rd.,
Ripley, nr. Derby
1 January 1918

My dear Kot,

If the Farbmans are back, we shall not trouble you. Perhaps we shall not stay in London: perhaps we shall stay a couple of nights in the rooms of a man called Collins.[1]

We shan't come to London before Friday, and it may be not till Saturday. I shall let you know. We will have an evening meeting.

I heard from Gertler—*peu de chose*. We'll all meet if I am in town.

May the New Year make us all happier.

D. H. Lawrence

[PS.]
All good greetings to Mr. & Mrs. Farbman.

---

1 Vere Henry Graz Collins, who "as a member of the staff of Oxford University Press, suggested that [Lawrence] write *Movements in European History*, which the Press first published in 1921 with Lawrence using the *nom de plume* of Lawrence H. Davison" (*C.L.*, I, xxxiii). See Lawrence's reference to Vere H. Collins in a letter to Lady Ottoline Morrell dated [?22 December 1915] in *C.L.*, I, 402. For Collins' account of his relations with Lawrence, see *C.B.*, I, 470–72.

CHAPEL FARM COTTAGE
Hermitage
nr Newbury [Berks]
Sunday [20 January 1918]

My dear Kot,

I alas am seedy, & Frieda not very well.—But this will pass.

About the money, I shall be glad to ask for it when the hour comes—but not yet.

About the cottage in Cornwall—I think the Woolfs might have it.[1] For how long a time do they want it? And do they share the house in Richmond? I wonder if they would care to change houses.—Gray said he would like to go to Tregerthen instead of to his Bosigran[2]—which is some 4 miles further on. If he persists, the Woolfs might have his Bosigran, a much better house.—Do they want to take a servant, do you know? And when do they want to go?

I am afraid peace won't come without the great Bacchanalia you mention. And god knows when the people will be worked up to this.—But it *will* come. It is *en route*.

As for myself, I sit in bed and look at the trees and learn songs from a book & wait for the Judgment Day—there is not much more to be said for me.

Perhaps we shall be in town again soon—everything is in flux like a pot that is vigorously stirred.—It might be possible for us to stay awhile in the Woolfs house—I think Frieda wants to be nearer London.

Hope I shall be out again soon. Remember me very kindly to Sonya Issayevna, and to Grisha the Odessa villain[3]—why has he always got his villain face on now, even when he is not acting?

D. H. Lawrence

---

1 Leonard and Virginia Woolf.

2 The name of Cecil Gray's cottage in Cornwall.

3 Mr. and Mrs. Michael Farbman.

---

120 CHAPEL FARM COTTAGE
Hermitage
nr. Newbury, Berks
Saturday 16 February 1918

My dear Kot,

Your last was a very desperate letter, in a quiet way. It's a
good deal how I feel myself. The damned show goes on and
on, grinding like a coffee-mill, till one feels one will burst
with the madness of it. But do you know I believe it will go
on for quite a long while yet. Only a cataclysm will stop it—
and a cataclysm is quite a long way off, I believe.

We are rather in a tight corner just now, what with money &
houselessness. But nothing serious. We shan't come to London.
Probably we shall get rooms in this village, for such time as
Dollie Radford is here. It doesn't seem much to matter, so
long as one gets through the days.

I wish you had got a type-writing machine now, I should
ask you again to do some typing for me, as before, in those
fatal first months of the war, when most wearily you pegged
through a hundred pages of philosophy. Alas, the bureau—
alas, Slatkowsky. Alas, that one cannot hang a wreath of thin
cheap sausages over the mantel-piece of his room in 212, in
memoriam. Well, one blot is under the earth instead of upon
it—which is a blessing.[1]

So you and Farbman are setting up another Russian Lawless
Bureau at No. 5. I see it coming—another bureau—history
repeating itself.—Why this break-up of the family circle?
Alas, and nothing but alas, everywhere.

I have had a sore throat for such a long time now, that I am
getting thoroughly tired of it. Oh my dear, dear Kot, why
didn't we go to our *Rananim*! What a weak-kneed lot we
were, not to bring it off. I do so want something nice—a
bit of a pleasant world somewhere—nothing but the corner of
a cemetery seems to offer—& I might find a Slat[kowsky]
there first.[2]

130

You grumble at me for not writing, but you never answered my last letter. Even now it is your turn to write to me.

Remember me to the grim & grizzly Grisha.

D. H. Lawrence

---

1 A reference to Slatkowsky's death.

2 "... I might find a slab there first" (*C.L.*, I, 540) is an inaccurate transcription, as is "Shutkowsky" for Slatkowsky.

---

21 [CHAPEL FARM COTTAGE]
Hermitage
[nr. Newbury, Berks]
Wednesday [20 February 1918]

My dear Kot,

Will you be good, & get for me Edgar Allan Poe's *Tales of Mystery & Imagination*, out of the Everyman's Library, and send the book to me by return—I think it is 1/6 now. I am in the middle of an essay on Edgar Allan, and have lost my copy.

I got your letter. Yes, I know the Ot. is very nice, somewhere. I once was *very* fond of her—and I am still, in a way. But she is like someone who has died: and I cannot wish to call her from the grave. She is good and, in a way, I love her, as I love someone who is dead. But not for life.

I too am sick of world builders—à la Lansbury.[1] I want their world smashed up, not set up—all the world smashed up. These Lansbury & Bertie Russell world-builders are only *preventers* of everything, the negators of life.—I'm afraid there will be noise for a long while yet.

D. H. Lawrence

---

1 Probably a reference to George Lansbury (1859–1940) who edited the *Daily Herald* (1919–22) "written for the most part by young middle-class intellectuals. Some of them, such as William Mellor and G. D. H. Cole, had already been socialists before the war. Others—Siegfried Sassoon, Osbert Sitwell, W. J. Turner—had become radicals as the result of their wartime experiences" (A. J. P. Taylor, *English History, 1914–45* [Oxford, 1966], p. 142). What Lawrence's connection with Lansbury and his group was, if any, is not known.

[CHAPEL FARM COTTAGE]
Hermitage
nr. Newbury, Berks
Thursday [21 February 1918]

My dear Kot,

I didn't tell you about the pennilessness because
(1) You are a gentleman of strictly limited means, and
(2) —much too ready to dissipate those limited means in
which case
(3) —you are a stranger in a strange and not very friendly
land, with no prospect but to bay the moon.

But thank you very much, though it is really a blow to me,
to diminish your capital.[1] We will bay the moon together,
when it comes to that.

If I came to London for a few days, in a week or a fortnights'
time, could you put me up? I would bring food—what I
could.—Beaumont, in Charing Cross Rd., *might* be doing
the novel—in which case I should have to discuss with him.[2]

Spy round, and see if there isn't a typewriter anywhere. It
would be good for you to do something, and a great blessing
for me. Out of these *Essays on American Classical Literature*
I might even make some money—if you typed them for me—
in which case we could all say Pfui! to the moon.

I have such a desire, that after the war, we should all go together to some nice place, and be really happy for a bit—
insouciant, *sans souci* & all that—perhaps in Italy—Gertler
& Shearman & Campbell & Frieda & you & me—& anybody
else that seemed particularly nice—& Gertler to be weaned
from the paint brush—and we'll cook for ourselves, and row
in a boat, & make excursions, and talk, & be quite happy for
a while: in the Abruzzi, for example.—Shearman sent me
£10, in a very decent way.[3]—I told him about this post-war
plan. Let us have our *Rananim* for a month or two, if we
can't for ever.—One must have something to look forward to.
And the only way is to get out of the world.

Eder is going with a commission in a fortnight to prospect
Palestine for Zion. I wish they'd give *me* Palestine—I'd
Zionise it into a *Rananim*. Zion might be *so* good—save
for the Zionists.

Have you sent me the Poe? I hope it'll come tomorrow.

mila saluti cari

D. H. Lawrence

---

1 A reference to the fact that Koteliansky had sent Lawrence £10. In a letter to
Mark Gertler dated 21 February 1918, Lawrence says: "Thanks very much for
your letter and the help from Shearman. I must say Shearman is very decent—much
better than Eddie [Marsh]. But Kot went and sent me also £10 when you told him,
though really I don't want to take his money, when he has *no* prospects. But
perhaps things will clear up" (*C.L.*, I, 542).

2 Cyril W. Beaumont, who later published Lawrence's book of poems called
Bay in November 1919. The press was located at 75 Charing Cross Road. See
B., p. 39. The novel referred to here is *Women in Love*.

3 Lawrence apparently forgot about this loan, when in April 1928 Shearman
asked for a complimentary copy of *Lady Chatterley's Lover*. See Letter No. 299.

HERMITAGE
nr. Newbury, Berks
c/o Mrs. Lowe
Monday [?25 February 1918][1]

My dear Kot,

I send you the first part of the essays. I am afraid there is much more to follow.

It troubles me that I have made so many alterations, you will have difficulty in reading.

In the first essay, I have made little marginal headings. Don't type these. We must consider whether to write them small in the margin of your typed MS when it is done:—so that it should be printed in small fount marginal headings. Decide that for me—help me.

Oh, my dear Kot, these essays are a weariness to me. I know they are really very good. You may not be in tune for them, so they may bore you. But do read them through *very* carefully for me, before you type them. And then, if you see anything that would be best left out, from the publishing point of view, do leave it out. I very much want to sell these essays. I know how good they are in substance. Yet I know it will be difficult to get them accepted. I want to make them acceptable to a publisher, if it is in any way possible. So go through them carefully as if you were an editor, will you.

I send you type-paper. Do me *two* copies will you—one carbon.

Tomorrow Dollie Radford comes here with the madman,[2] so we go to rooms in the village: c/o Mrs. Lowe.

I *might* come to London at the weekend—Friday or Saturday. Could you do with me for a brief day or two.

I am so grateful to you for this typing work. We *must* sell these essays if we can.

D. H. L.

[PS.]

I underlined the little marginal headings in the first essay.
Don't type them.

---

1 The date of this letter (*C.L.*, I, 594–95) is given by Moore as ?29 September
1919. Since Lawrence was revising the essays on American literature again in
1919, Moore's date is a plausible one. There are, however, cogent reasons for
assigning the letter to 1918. The previous letter, No. 122, makes a reference to having the essays typed, and Letter No. 123 follows this up with more references to
typing. But Moore's letter dated ?24 September 1919 refers to copying "three
of the American essays" (*C.L.*, I, 594), and says "Your handwriting is so nice
and plain" (p. 594). If Koteliansky had agreed to write the essays in longhand,
Lawrence would not be sending him "type-paper," and referring again to "this
typing work," as he does in Letters Nos. 123 and 125. In addition, if we read
Lawrence's letter to Huebsch dated 30 September 1919, in which he says: "I
shall send you the MS. of the American essays as soon as this railway strike
ends—I expect this week" (*C.L.*, I, 596), it is highly unlikely that on the previous
day Lawrence would have written to Koteliansky, "I *might* come to London at
the weekend—Friday or Saturday," without mentioning the railway strike.

2 According to Moore, "'The madman' refers to Dollie Radford's husband,
Ernest, who was mentally incapacitated" (*C.L.*, I, 595).

CHAPEL FARM COTTAGE
Hermitage
nr Newbury, Berks
Thursday [?28 February 1918]

My dear Kot,

I got back here last night[1]—very tired. I had your telephone message from Collins—saw Beaumont. He says he himself would not have anything to do with the publishing—but gave me estimates from another man. It would cost about £375 to do the book—an enormous sum. He suggests selling at a guinea a copy, by subscription—says it could be made to pay. I am bored.

I have a kind of belief we shall make some money with the *American Essays*. And when I have money, if ever I do, you will have money too. We'll take courage.

I like being at Acacia Rd. without Mrs. Donald[2]—it is fun. Thank you very much for doing for me so well.

Don't get despairing—I really think we have come to the bottom of things. We'll start to rise up just now, see if we don't.

Let me hear from you. Remind Gertler to ask Ottoline about the book.[3]

D. H. L.

---

1 The reference to Beaumont in this letter places it after 21 February 1918 but before 8 March 1918. Writing to Lady Cynthia Asquith on the latter date, Lawrence refers several times to Beaumont. See *C.L.*, I, 544–45.

2 Mrs. Donald Carswell, i.e. Catherine Carswell.

3 Probably a MS book of poems, as the next letter (No. 125) suggests.

25

My dear Kot,

Thank you very much for the MS. which has come today. I know you hate typing. Tell me the moment you have had enough—don't for the Lord's sake go on when you're sick of it.

We're going to Derbyshire after Easter to look for a house. Gertler says you will come & see us there—as he is off to Garsington. Margaret Radford is coming here—so we shan't stay. The Midlands is the place where we will *really* meet—as we first met in the North. London & the south is wrong for us.

Why don't you write, you owe me a letter.

Ask Gertler if he would ask Ottoline if she would be so good as to have posted to me here the bundle of MS. she kept for me. A man worries me to give him some poems[1]—& I might root out a few from the old books—& make a trifle of money.

Rien de nouveau, in our world. Write to me. And if you would like to run down for a few days before Easter, *do.*

D. H. Lawrence

[PS.]
I don't believe Mrs. Eder will come this week-end. Won't you come?

---

1 Probably Beaumont.

---

126 [CHAPEL FARM COTTAGE]
Hermitage
[nr. Newbury, Berks]
Thursday [?21 March 1918]

My dear Kot,

We've had a wire from Mrs. Eder and she's *not* coming.[1]
I've got a feeling that I wish you'd come for a day or two.
We've got *plenty* of *food* for the moment—a haul.

Come Saturday—1:40 Paddington—change at Reading &
Newbury. I will meet you at *Hermitage* station at 4:50.

Let me have a line by return, that you will come.

D. H. Lawrence

---

1 Mrs. Eder was planning to visit the Lawrences from the 22nd to 25th of March
1918. See Lawrence's letter to Mark Gertler dated ?16 March 1918 in *C.L.*, I,
548.

27 [CHAPEL FARM COTTAGE]
Hermitage
[nr. Newbury, Berks]
Saturday [?30 March 1918]

My dear Kot,

Please don't have any qualms about the MS. I am very grateful for what you have done, & only sorry to think of your
having slaved at it. The rest I will do myself one day. What
you have done will be a good lift to start with. Don't think
about it again—& don't curse me for having let you in for
this unpleasant job, in the first place.

I shall be thankful if you get telegrams again from Russia, &
are a man of business. You will be much happier.

We are staying on here till a week or so after Easter—
Margaret Radford will be here; & then, I think we shall go
to the Midlands, where I hope you will be able to come.

I will tell you if there is any change in this. Let me know
about your telegrams.

D. H. Lawrence

_____

28 [CHAPEL FARM COTTAGE]
Hermitage
[nr. Newbury, Berks]
Wednesday [3 April 1918]

Thanks for the MS which came today.—I am going to the
Midlands on Saturday, but shall probably be back in a week—
going to look at a place—shall let you know what turns up.

D. H. L.

CHAPEL FARM COTTAGE
Hermitage
nr Newbury, Berks
19 April 1918

My dear Kot,

I heard from my sister today that she has taken a house for us
in Derbyshire, furnished, and we can go in on May 1st. So I
suppose we shall be soon moving from here.—I saw the place
last week—it is a very nice situation—and a very pleasant
little bungalow, with grounds—a croquet lawn: we can play
croquet. It looks over a steep valley—something like the
memorable Westmorland where we first met.[1]

There is no news other than this—except it is very nastily
cold. You have promised to come & see us in Derbyshire—
when we get settled down you must keep your promise.

Let me know how you are, and the Farbmans.

Greetings from both

D. H. L.

[PS.]
Tell Gertler I'll write him directly.

---

1 A reference to the walking tour in the summer of 1914.

MOUNTAIN COTTAGE
Middleton-by-Wirksworth
Derby
Thursday [?20 June 1918]

My dear Kot,

Many thanks for the cheque¹—I shan't use it if I can help it—because what if your bank broke, what should we all do?

No, I haven't any news. It is true my cursing *mood* isn't my only mood: but my cursing *news* is my only news. I have finished up all the things I am writing at present—have a complete blank in front of me—feel very desperate, and ready for anything, good or bad. I think something critical will happen this month—finally critical. If it doesn't I shall bust. Arabella² is here—been here a week—stays another week, I suppose. She is very nice. We were over in my native place for a day or two—queer—I can accept it again—no longer have to fight it at all. We get a lot of the old people—people of my pre-London days—to see us. Arabella is the first from the South.—You said you were coming. But perhaps the hour isn't due yet. You'll come before the summer is over.

Are the Farbmans still at Eastbourne—& you alone with Fox?³ You must have an abnormal *static* power—I should have gone mad long since. Aren't you afraid of becoming one day rooted and immovable, like a graven stone, or a wooden image? I think a bomb will have to fall *very* near to you, or you'll metamorphose into a sort of rock.—But it needs a great effort to bear up against these days. Write again soon.

Frieda greets you.

D. H. L.

---

1 The cheque for £10 is dated 19 June 1918. Lawrence never cashed it. It is preserved among the *Koteliansky Papers* in the British Museum. The cheque indicates Kot's willingness to give Lawrence financial assistance.

2 Identified by Moore as Dorothy Yorke. "An American friend of the Lawrences and Richard Aldington, 'Arabella' came from Reading, Pa., but lived many years on the Continent" (*C.L.*, I, lv–lvi).

3 According to Beatrice Lady Glenavy, the name of a dog which belonged to the Farbmans. For some fascinating details of "the most exceptional dog in London," see *B.L.G.*, p. 89.

MOUNTAIN COTTAGE
Middleton-by-Wirksworth
Derby
2 July 1918

My dear Kot,

I wrote to Gertler thinking we might see the Ott. again—
then we should have come to London for a bit. But I got such
a stupid answer from him—vague and conditional like Mr.
Balfour discussing peace terms. To Hell with Ott. & the
whole Ottlerie—what am I doing temporising with them.

Now why don't you come here. Plainly and simply, why don't
you come here for a time. You said you would—so just do it.
If you don't want to report yourself to the police, well,
don't. Arabella didn't & she is American. She just came &
stayed her two weeks and took no notice. You could do the
same, if it is the reporting which irks you.

There isn't any news—everybody seems immersed in the most
hopeless stupidity & vacuous misery—I have no patience, and
no hope from such spiritless *Canaille.* But I don't care. I do
verily believe the war is going to fizzle out—though what
next, I don't know,—nor how we are going to live. It is the
end of the tether—and what when the tether breaks, God
knows: it even may not break, and we shall strangle ourselves.

Never mind, I don't care. We'll just hang on while we can.
Do really uproot yourself and come and stay here for a bit.
It's a case of move or perish: so move.

I am still hanging on in the hope that I need not use your
cheque. The meeting that decides the money from the Literary
Fund is on the 10th. I hope the dogs and swine will have
sufficient fear of God in their hearts: *fear,* that is the only
thing that will do them any good: fear of the wrath of the
Lord.

We are alone, save for my little nephew—who is only three
years old, & therefore quite decent. Next week my sister
may be here for two or three days—no more—but that need
not prevent your coming.

Gertler's letter made me mad. What in the name of hell do I care about the Ott's queases and qualms.

Now then stir yourself & take a train.

D. H. L.

[PS.]
Frieda greets you, & will be glad to see you.
I had another letter from Lewis which I ignored.

MOUNTAIN COTTAGE
Middleton-by-Wirksworth
Derby
12 July 1918

My dear Kot,

I got a miserable £50 from that dirty Royal Literary Fund [1]—
so I shall not need your £10 for the moment. I send you the
cheque back. You can't be offended, because I'm afraid that in
a few month's time, I shall be asking you for it again.

I can't come to London. Really, I haven't the energy. But
you should really stir yourself, and come here. The people
at the police station at Wirksworth are the most aimiable [*sic*]
on earth.—We shall be quite alone for the next fortnight.
Rouse yourself up—it will be so good for you.

I haven't any news—have you? Do take a trip up here, it is
necessary for you.

D. H. L.

---

1 This was Lawrence's second grant from the Royal Literary Fund. He received
£50 in October 1914. See his letter to Catherine Carswell dated 21 October
1914 in *C.L.*, I, 293. For a recent history of the Royal Literary Fund, see the
Times Literary Supplement (21 March 1968), p. 300.

[MOUNTAIN COTTAGE]
Middleton-by-Wirksworth
Thursday [?25 July 1918]

My dear Kot,

Are you still living, & can you still speak? I'm sure I feel
about as bad as you do, altogether.

Will you still be in No. 5 next month—and if we wanted to
come for a few days, would it be feasible? Frieda will be seeing
her children—I don't know exactly when. But we just *might*
want to come in a week's time—might: probably it will not
be for a month.

Oh my dear Kot, for these months & years of slow execution
we suffer, I *should* like my revenge on the world. Are we
really quite impotent, all of us? *Quoi faire?—che fare?*—Can't
you answer?

D. H. Lawrence

134 [MOUNTAIN COTTAGE]
Middleton-by-Wirksworth
Tuesday [30 July 1918]

My dear Kot,

The coming to London depended on other people.—My
aunt & uncle, whom I have not seen for 6 years, are coming
here next week for a day or two.—But then Frieda wants to
come immediately to London to see her children. So we might
come on Friday week—Aug 9th is it?—or more probably the
Monday following—Aug. 12th. Would that do?—As for
gas etc, they won't matter.

Like you, I hate the reformers worst, and their nauseous
Morrellity. But I count them my worst enemies, and want my
revenge on them first. *Ça ira.*

Frieda thanks you for your invitation, & is pleased to come to
the Cave.[1]

Where is Gertler?—still Ottling?

D. H. L.

---

1 The designation for Koteliansky's residence at No. 5 Acacia Road, St. John's
Wood, London, from which he seldom stirred.

35 [MOUNTAIN COTTAGE]
Middleton-by-Wirksworth
Derby
Tuesday 6 August [1918]

My dear Kot,

I expect we shall come next Monday—12th. I will let you know exactly. We will bring our rations—don't get much in.

I am quite thankful that you have got to scrub etc.—we might find you inseparably glued to a chair.

à bientôt

D. H. Lawrence

---

36 [MOUNTAIN COTTAGE]
Middleton-by-Wirksworth
Derby
Friday [9 August 1918]

My dear Kot,

We shall come on Monday, *Deo Volenti*—arriving St. Pancras 3:37. It seems very strange to be coming to London—I can hardly believe it will happen. But I am glad to come.

My uncle & aunt are here. He is interesting—my aunt bores me a bit.

Will you be alone in the house, or will the Farbmans be there? I should like to see Mrs. Farbman—& Farbman. I hope they'll come.

If my uncle & aunt should come to London on Wednesday night, just for a night—do you think we could put them up? Perhaps we might, if the Farbmans are not there.

I will bring what food I can. We shall be glad to see you, and talk out all things.

D. H. L.

137

Hermitage
nr. Newbury, Berks
Friday [23 August 1918]

My dear Kot,

We got our train & got here all right.

We were very happy in Acacia—stay on there, I think
probably we shall come again later—then we will make a
proper arrangement.

The plums are out of the garden—I picked them from the
tree last evening. I hope they'll arrive nicely. They are not
many, alas—but share them with Sophie Isaayevna [*sic*] &
Ghita.

Frieda left tooth brushes & tooth-paste, and the little black
nail-brush, in the bathroom. Send them to us, will you.
On Monday we go to

>   "The Vicarage,
>   Upper Lydbrook,
>   Ross-on-Wye,
>   Herefordshire."

I feel we shall meet again soon.

D. H. L.

[PS.]
Have asked Arabella to send *The Rainbow*. Let me know if
she did.

38 THE VICARAGE
Upper Lydbrook
Ross-on-Wye, Herefordshire
27 August 1918

My dear Kot,

We got here yesterday—rather lovely—in the Forest of
Dean—a real forest—The Carswells very nice but depressed.
Margaret Radford was horrible.—Everywhere a nasty sense of
sordid despair. You, my dear Kot, are a tower of strength—a
real tower of strength to us both—and a solitary tower
in the land, at that. We must meet again soon. Thank you
for the boots etc.[1]

Frieda quite loves you since open enmity is avowed.

We go back to Middleton Saturday or Monday.

D. H. L.

---

1 This is one of the many kindnesses that Koteliansky tactfully bestowed on
Lawrence in the latter's time of need.

[MOUNTAIN COTTAGE]
Middleton-by-Wirksworth
Wednesday [?18 September 1918]

My dear Kot,

I am thinking I shall never be able to sit at Middleton this
winter. If I don't do something I shall burst or go cracked.
I *must* move.

Now would it be all right if we came to you—not as guests—
but as Campbell would have come—just to share expenses, all
expenses? I will get money somehow. We would probably
come in two weeks time—and stay some weeks, at least.—
I want to know Robert Smillie & Snowden & Mary
Macarther & Margaret Bondfield.¹ I must find somebody to
bring me to them. It is no good, one cannot wait for things
to happen. One must actually move.

I got notice to go & be medically examined once more. I
sent it back. They replied with their usual insolence. I must
go on the 26th.² It infuriates me to such a degree, that I
feel I will not go.—One must have one's *own* back—oh,
thoroughly.

Grisha was a wise man, to go.³—Did Sonia get *The Rainbow*?
I sent it to her.

As for Russia, it must go through as it is going. Nothing but
a real smelting down is any good for her: no matter how
horrible it seems. You, who are an ultra-conscious Jew, can't
bear the chaos. But chaos is necessary for Russia. Russia will
be all right—righter, in the end, than these old stiff senile
nations of the West.

I don't think chaos is any good for England. England is too
old. She'll either have to be *wise*, and recover her decency—
or we may as well all join Eder in Jerusalem.

Well, my dear Kot, I am at the end of my line. I had rather be
hanged or put in prison than endure any more. So now I

shall move actively, personally, do what I can. I am a *desperado* [Editor's italics].

D. H. L.

[PS.]
Is Campbell back? I was a bit disgusted with him last time.— But I must see him again, if only to abuse him.—How is Gertler?—Did Murry fetch his books? Tell me about them.

---

1 Enid C. Hilton recalls some of these people as working "for the women's cause" in Nottingham. She says: "Meetings were held in our small town [Eastwood] and there was much enthusiasm, many fights and some really productive effort. Kier Hardy [*sic*] stayed with us, Ramsey [*sic*] MacDonald, Philip Snowden, Edward Carpenter, Margaret Bondfield—many others" (*C.B.*, I, 135).

2 According to Moore "On September 26 [1918] Lawrence reported for medical examination in a big schoolroom in Derby" (*I.H.*, p. 244).

3 Reference is obscure, but in Letter No. 143, the remark "I would like to hear Grisha, by now, on 'America'," suggests that Farbman may have gone to the United States.

---

140 [Originating address probably
London
Prior to 11 November 1918]

[The first part of this letter is missing. Ed.] . . . to be peace
soon. So be damned to all jobs and jobbers.

Frieda has a bad cold & throat—Maitland Radford says she
must stay in bed.—She won't be able to go out for some days.
So we can't go to Mrs. Farbman on Wednesday. I have
written to Richmond to say so.[1] When Frieda is well enough
we shall move down to 66 Adelaide Rd. N.W.3.—it is near
Chalk Farm station.[2] But if there is peace we shall go back
to Middleton in about a fortnight's time.[3]

I don't care about anything, if there is peace.

See you one evening.

D. H. L.

---

1 Richmond might have been where the Farbmans moved after leaving St.
John's Wood.

2 There is no record of Lawrence's residence at this address; however, see *P.R.*,
pp. 50–51.

3 He was back at Middleton as early as 6 December 1918. See his letter to Herbert
Farjeon in *C.L.*, I, 567. Lawrence spent Christmas, 1918, at his sister's place in
Ripley. See his letter to Katherine Mansfield dated 27 December 1918 in *C.L.*, I,
571.

MOUNTAIN COTTAGE
Middleton-by-Wirksworth
Derby
22 December 1918

My dear Kot,

Frieda told me you had influenza. I hope it is better by now, and that you are prepared for laying waste to various Christmas preparations for feasting. I too have got a bad cold, and feel like crawling into a deep hole to hide there. The weather is very dark and bad. I have been going to Eastwood to a friend, who has now died.[1] "Christmas comes but once a year.—And that is once too often, dear." We are going to my sister's on Christmas Day, if ever I get so far, which I probably shan't.

For news, there is none. I wrote four little essays for the *Times*, and sent them in, but have heard nothing at all of them.[2] It is not likely they will come to anything.—I wish I need never write another line of any sort, for publication, in my life. I've had enough. If only I had a small income, I'd chuck writing altogether. I'm really sick of it. The necessity to earn something is all that drives me—& then I earn nothing, so I might as well keep still. Well, there's a Carol for you.

Greet me very kindly to Sophie Issayevna & to Ghita, and I hope Ghita will have a good & festive time. Send me some news of you. It is four years since the Bucks cottage Christmas—my God, what wrecks we are! Nevertheless, all good wishes.

D. H. L.

---

1 Not identified.

2 Lawrence's essays on *Education*; see *C.L.*, I, 568. The "Essays" were published posthumously in *Phoenix* (New York, 1936).

[MOUNTAIN COTTAGE]
Middleton-by-Wirksworth
Derby
1 January 1919

My dear Kot,

I got your letter this morning: a deep snowy morning, very
still and isolated—the first day of the year. I do hope it will
be a new start of a new time for us. I do want to get out, to
get across into something freer and more active.

Yes, do give me a little New Year gift, but nothing extrava-
gant and solemn. I should like a book—or perhaps two
books, to read. One depends on reading here: and the more I
live, the more I respect the good genuine books of mankind.
I should like, from the Everyman Library

Bates'—*Naturalist on the Amazon*	1/9
Scheffel—*Ekkehard: A Tale of the 10th Century*	1/9

The first I want because I intend someday to go to South
America—to Peru or Ecuador, not the Amazon. But I know
Bates is good. The second I want because he will help me
with my *European History*,[1] & because I began him once and
never had a chance to finish him.—I don't like the more
expensive bindings of Everyman—only the ordinary pre-war
1/– sort, now 1/9, I believe.

About money, I got £10 from Harrison for two essays,[2]
which I circumvented from Pinker's clutches, so please don't
lend me anything yet. Later on, if I am cornered, I will
ask you. I am doing the history—it will take about a month
or six weeks, I suppose.—If Shearman likes to send me a little,
well and good: but don't bother him.

Tell Gertler that Cynthia Asquith has the play and is seeing to
it.[3] She has some part in some new theatrical concern. I
suppose it is Bennetts. Tell Gertler also that Bibesco,[4] the
buffoon-prince, was approached last year on my behalf. He
said he would rather help me to publish my work than give
money direct. He had the MS of the novel, returned it
without a word, and did nothing. So that, although these

buffoon-princes have money and pretensions, they are just like the Bennetts and Wellses and Selfridges and Lyons of this world—or even the Howard de Waldens—they will only pay for their own puffing-up. Tell Gertler that there is nothing doing in the Bennett-Bibesco quarter. Pah! So much the better.

We hear from Germany. My brother-in-law, Edgar Jaffé, a rich Jew & Professor, is Minister of Finance for Bavaria. From Frieda's mother also news that she has money for her. Between the Minister of Finance and the *gute Schwiegermutter* we may find a solution of this money difficulty—perhaps—& perhaps not.

I still have some sort of hope of our *Rananim*: the last hope.

My sister gave me a bottle of gin. I drink the New Year to you.

D. H. L.

[PS.]
The *Times* sent me back my little essays on *Education*: "Very interesting, but too deep, rather matter for a book than for a supplement."

---

1 Lawrence was already "struggling with a European History for Schools" (*C.L.*, I, 567) as early as 6 December 1918. The idea for the book dates back to the summer of 1918. See Lawrence's letter to Cecil Gray dated 3 July 1918: "The Oxford Press said I might do a school book, of European History" (*C.L.*, I, 561). Further notes are to be found in *B.*, pp. 48–51, 339.

2 A reference to the essays on American literature. The "two essays" would be "Spirit of Place" and "Benjamin Franklin." See *B.*, pp. 256–58.

3 Probably *Touch and Go*.

4 "Prince Antoine Bibesco who married Elizabeth Asquith" (*Mark Gertler: Selected Letters*, edited by Noel Carrington [London, 1965], p. 168). See Moore's note in *C.L.*, I, 576.

MOUNTAIN COTTAGE
Middleton-by-Wirksworth
Derby
6 January 1919

My dear Kot,

Ekkehard & the *Amazon* came today: what nice, happy kind of
books they are to have: they mean such a lot more to one
than Lloyd George or Ottoline Morrell or Middleton Murry.
To me they mean real living mankind—not this squirming
spawn which passes today for man. I should never be a sad
man, whilst it was possible for a real book to come along.

I knew that it was Desmond Mcarthy [*sic*] who had put a
stopper on Prince B., moaning on Ottoline's outraged behalf.
I knew that. And I knew that Prince B. had not the courage
to say a word either to me or to Cynthia Asquith, but
returned the MS.[1] wordless. And I knew that Desmond
Macarthy was quite pleased with himself for having arse-licked
Ottoline and the Prince both at once, both of them being
pretty sound benefactors of Desmond, who rather enjoys
his arse-licking turns. All these things, my dear Kot, I knew
and know: in fact I know very many things which I prefer
to leave, like manure, to rot down in my soul, unspoken,
to form the humus of a new germination.

The Rainbow was printed by a Jewish publisher called Huebsch,
in New York.[2] Then the suppression came on, and he dared
not bring it out. It still lies, no doubt, on Huebsch's hands. I
had one copy—a paltry looking black book, rather like a
text-book, with several pages of the English edition omitted
in it. You have illusions, my dear Kot, about my being able
to make money by my writing. Whilst President Wilson coos
and preens in New York, whilst Ottoline stinks in Garsington,
whilst Clemenceau spouts in France, whilst Murry "Dostys"
and you "Rimbaud," I am not worth a penny: nay, even
whilst Katharine attaches a purple Cashmere shawl in
drapery behind her arms, and whilst Campbell says "Ireland."
And the world will end before these things cease. So an end,
my dear Kot, to those illusions of prosperity which I am to

find through some *good* new journal here, or through some puff in the U.S.A.

I would like to hear Grisha, by now, on "America."

Here we are deep in snow, very white and strange, beautiful, not very cold, but the roads difficult. I am working away at the history: hope to get it done soon enough to save my situation: otherwise I shall come to you for £10. I will not ask the Prince for anything—not I.

I suppose we shall all be struggling for passports soon. The moment it becomes possible, I shall leave England. I don't care where I go, so long as I can turn my back on it for good. Nor do I care what I do in the future, so long as I can just walk away.

Remember me very nicely to Sonia & to Ghita: also to Gertler. When I can get as far as Matlock I shall buy you a tiny thing as a memento of bad times—they have been pretty bad times, these four years, haven't they? *Chi lo sa?*—We may come to reckon them as having been good.

Vale

D. H. L.

---

1 *Women in Love.*

2 B. W. Huebsch, "head of the publishing firm that bore his name ... brought out the first American edition of *The Rainbow* in 1917" (*C.L.*, I, xl–xli).

144

My dear Kot,

Rather a blow to hear of you going into the War Office.[1] It *does* go against one's grain. If I had any capital you should share it. I am going to get about £10 from Cornwall, after selling up there, so I shall manage till the *History* is done: two more chapters now, & then revision.[2] Barbara told you about the Stanley Unwin. I loathe returning to my vomit: going back to old work. And it won't mean more than £15. Still, I'll have a shot at it.[3]

I am interested and a bit amused to know how the War Office works out in you. Tell me. And tell Campbell to come up here and see me for a day or two. Really, that man should shift—I like Murry as the benevolent patron of us all: tra-la-la!

I'm awfully mad and rampageous inside myself, but just hold my nose down and grind on at the history etc. Blast the world, blast it, it is soft-rotten, & if one takes a step one goes head over heels in soft-rottenness.

Very kind regards to Sonia. Grisha will find a way of some sort. Send me news.

D. H. L.

---

1 I have thus far been unable to trace any record of Koteliansky's service in the War Office, although the suggestion here of such service is unmistakable. The Ministry of Defence (London) has informed me that "the negative result cannot conclusively confirm that he [Koteliansky] did not serve at all, because it seems that some records have been destroyed."

2 This is a clue to the accurate dating of this letter. Writing to Catherine Carswell on 23 January 1919, Lawrence says: "Meanwhile I am finishing my *European History*, for the Oxford Press: have only one more chapter" (*C.L.*, I, 577).

3 Stanley Unwin was interested in publishing Lawrence's essays "On Education," which the *Times* had rejected. In a letter to Catherine Carswell dated 23 January 1919, Lawrence says: "Barbara [Low] saw the essays—showed them to Stanley Unwin, who wants me to write as much again, and he will publish in a little book, and give me £15 down" (*C.L.*, I, 576–77). Nothing seems to have come of this plan.

MOUNTAIN COTTAGE
Middleton-by-Wirksworth
Derby
8 February 1919

My dear Kot,

I wrote you straight away, some time ago, & congratulated
you on your heroism, and asked you to come and stay with
us a bit. Frieda enclosed a note also. Did you never receive
that letter? I wondered why you did not answer.

I have at the present moment got £20;—£5 from Harrison &
£15 from selling up in Cornwall. So I must send back your
cheque, for I fear to imagine myself richer than I am. If I
thought I had thirty pounds to lash out with, heaven knows
what I might do. Sufficient unto the day is the good thereof.

I read about London in the newspaper—and am not thrilled.
What a great nation we are! If the tube stops running, the
commonwealth collapses. *Basta!* Here it is terribly frozen
and snowy. I have been in bed for a week with a cold. But
am much better. The sun shines, but the windows are covered
with very magnificent ice flowers, so we are observed as if
in a frozen under-sea.

There isn't anything really to say. I hear the Derby railway
men are anticipating a strike.

"Strike while the iron's hot, boys"

I often wonder about Grisha, how he is getting on. Remember
me nicely to Sonia & Ghita. It is so cold, one could almost
speak Russian.

Vale

D. H. L.

[c/o MRS. CLARKE
Grosvenor Road
Ripley, Derbyshire]
Wednesday [?19 February 1919]¹

My dear Kot,

Thank you for all the things—don't send so much. Tea
sweets & honey came today. Today for the first time I have
food—not only accursed milk—also for the first time sit
up in bed & write this—so shall soon be better—get out of
bed for ½ hour next Sunday.—Am very weary & a little
downhearted however—the world seems so nasty ahead of
one. Will write again. Hope to see you before long.

D. H. L.

[PS. in Frieda's hand]
I will write tomorrow all about him.—It is cheering to have
you there.
F.

---

1 The date of this letter has been difficult to establish with any degree of certainty.
Letters Nos. 146–151 have no dates except days of the week, and the biographers
of Lawrence provide very little information about Lawrence's crucial illness
during the flu epidemic of 1919. The sequence Letters Nos. 146–151 is bound in
by 8 February 1919, on the one hand, and 20 March 1919, on the other. I think it
reasonable to assume that the first letter in the sequence would not likely have been
written before 19 February, since Lawrence was seriously ill; but it might have
been written as late as 26 February. I would, however, argue for the earlier date,
since it is unlikely that Koteliansky would have been ignorant of Lawrence's
illness for more than two weeks.

For some more information on this period in Lawrence's life, see *P.R.*, pp.
52–53.

---

47 [c/o MRS. CLARKE
Grosvenor Road]
Ripley [Derbyshire]
Friday [?21 February 1919]

My dear Kot,

Yesterday came the grapefruit—a godsend—they are so good
—one doesn't want to eat, except these.

I am getting better—shall get out of bed on Sunday for $\frac{1}{2}$ hour
—still have the cough & the heart-pains, but not so much.

I am going to the seaside—we want to find a cottage. My
uncle will drive me in his motor car, he says. Do you know
a place?

I think even my soul is recovering. I thought it was cracked
for ever. But no, I shall shake off the world.

Perhaps you will come & stay with us at the seaside—will
you?

I'll write again.

D. H. L.

[PS.]
My uncle has sent 2 champagne—what luxuries.[1]

---

1 "Lawrence's uncle, Herbert Beardsall, kept the Lord Belper public house in
Nottingham" (*C.L.*, I, 580).

---

148 [c/o MRS. CLARKE
Grosvenor Road]
Ripley [Derbyshire]
Saturday [?1 March 1919]

My dear Kot,

The brandy & port came on Wednesday—Frieda says she told you—I'm sorry you didn't know. The brandy is very good and soft. Spare Selfridges.[1]

Tell Sophie Issayevna I shall write to her.—Poor Beatrice, let me know if she lands safely.[2]—Do you go & see Katharine?—I think she's been very ill too.

I shrink from putting my foot out of bed into the world again.

D. H. L.

---

1 A large department store in London.

2 Beatrice Campbell, who probably was making a journey by sea to Ireland. See Letter No. 150.

149 [c/o MRS. CLARKE
Grosvenor Road]
Ripley, Derbyshire
Thursday [?6 March 1919]

My dear Kot,

The grapefruit have come—just as the last were finished. I wonder if Katharine has them—they are such a good fruit.

I am getting better—today I shall try to go downstairs. It is the stairs I fear. But I want to go back to Middleton. Perhaps next Wednesday I can be driven up. I give up the seaside idea: too great a struggle to travel to a new place. Next month we might go to Hermitage—or we may stay at Middleton. Frieda wants to go to Germany as soon as we can —I too want to leave England.—Eder will come this month to Middleton to see me—what if I went to Palestine! I feel I *must* get out or I shall die of soul-suffocation—out of this island. I wonder when one can go.

Murry has asked me to contribute to his *Athenaeum*.[1] That is very nice, & I shall be pleased to have a try at it.

I will write to Pinker soon—it nauseates me, all that business of publishers & publication.

The day is sunny. I must lay fresh hold on life.—Thank you for the fruits.—How do you feel yourself? Are you very bored?

au revoir

D. H. L.

---

1 See Lawrence's letter to Murry in *C.L.*, I, 579.

150 [c/o MRS. CLARKE
Grosvenor Road]
Ripley, Derbyshire
Tuesday [?11 March 1919]

My dear Kot,

I am going to be motored up to Middleton next Sunday.[1]—it
is so shut in here. I go downstairs to tea—but am so tire-
somely feeble, I can't walk.—I suppose in a month we can
go to Hermitage. My sister will go to Middleton with us, she
is the responsible nurse.—Eder is coming—I don't exactly
know when.—I feel as if we never should get out of this
beetle-trap of an island.—but June, you say—I'll look to
June. Murry vaguely asked me to contribute to the
Athenaeum—but he doesn't tell me what he wants, nor when
he wants it.[2] I feel fearfully mistrustful of him—feel sure we
shall be let down. Poor Katharine—I'm afraid she is only
just on the verge of existence. Beatrice wrote to me very
nicely from Ireland—told me about Gordon. Did you see
him this week-end, & what was he like? Beatrice sent me a
pound of butter—a great kindness, for margarine is uneatable.
If ever you *can* get 4 oz. of China tea, do. I hate the black
taste of the other.—But $\frac{1}{4}$th will last me a long time, don't
buy any more.—Of course if I went to Palestine it would only
be for a little while, & as a *pis aller*. Don't become cynical.—Is
there any newspaper news—I daren't read the papers, I
become at once ill.

How reduced we all are—only a few fragments of us left!
The world has walked over us and trodden us very small. I
suppose one day we shall spring up like corn.

Remember me very nicely to Sonia & Ghita. I suppose we'll
have a meeting before long.

D. H. L.

---

1 For the date of Lawrence's return to Middleton, see *P.R.*, p. 53.

2 Lawrence's contribution to the *Athenaeum* was "Whistling of Birds" which
appeared on 11 April 1919 under the pseudonym "Grantorto." See *B.*, p. 257.

51 [c/o MRS. CLARKE
Grosvenor Road]
Ripley, Derbyshire
Friday [?14 March 1919]

My dear Kot,

The grapefruit came. They are at their best now—perfectly
ripe. I am getting stronger. I am feeble now because, the
doctor says, I was run down to start with, & have been
very ill—for two days he said he feared I should not pull
through. But doctors—bah! Anyhow I am nearly myself
again, in my soul if not in my body. I have walked out a
few yards. But it is *so* cold: as cold here as at Middleton.
If the weather is fine we are going to Mountain Cottage on
Sunday.[1]

It would be fun to go to Ireland soon—perhaps we can do it.
The expense deters me a little. We'll see.

My sister goes with us to Middleton. I am not going to be
left to Frieda's tender mercies until I am well again. She really
is a devil—and I feel as if I would part from her for ever—let
her go alone to Germany, while I take another road. For it is
true, I have been bullied by her long enough. I really could
leave her now, without a pang, I believe. The time comes, to
make an end, one way or another. If this illness hasn't been
a lesson to her, it has to me.

Write next to Middleton—I will tell you how we get on.—My
sister also broke her glasses last week—so she cannot laugh
at you. But she borrows mine.

I have been trying to write for the *Athenaeum*. Why is it such a
cold effort to do these things? Have you seen Barbara lately—
she is suddenly very silent.—I *do* wish it would be warm.

D. H. L.

---

1 This would be 16 March 1919.

MOUNTAIN COTTAGE
Middleton-by-Wirksworth
Derby
20 March 1919

My dear Kot,

We came here on Monday—it was sunny then. Tuesday was a
mild sweet morning. Tuesday afternoon it began to snow—it
has snowed ever since—deep and white. My sister Ada is
here, with her little boy Jackie. Ada & Frieda beat the trees,
which are being smashed down by weight of snow, I stare
stupidly out of the window like a sick & dazed monkey.—I
shall have to stay here for another month, as the doctor—the
Parsee—is coming over from Ripley to give me certain
injections for the lungs.[1] At the end of the month I shall
fairly flee to Hermitage.[2]

I had a letter from Horne, who is back from $2\frac{1}{2}$ yrs. in
Salonika, & is in London on leave, not discharged. I wrote
to him, & shall see him if it is easy. If I don't like him I
shan't see him twice.[3]

No news, save snow & blank stupidity—except, oh yes,
Eder came to Ripley last week-end—brought me a bottle of
claret, cake, sweets, & was very nice indeed. He is sailing with
Mrs. Eder & the younger boy on April 3rd. I have promised
to go out to Palestine in September, leaving Frieda in
Germany. In Palestine I am to view the land and write a
Zioniad. What do you think of it?

My sister has given me 10/– for books—I haven't a shred to
read. Get me these four books out of the *Everyman* series,
will you?—they cost 1/9 each, don't they?—that will allow
you to buy one vol. for Ghita—buy her *Swiss Family
Robinson* or Johanna Spyri's *Heidi.*—or Ballantyne's
Ungava—or Collodi's *Pinocchio*—or better still, let her
choose for herself from the *Everyman* list. Anyhow buy
Ghita a volume. 5 books at 1/9 = 8/9. That just leaves
enough for postage. If they cost more than 1/9, leave out
Charles Auchester.—I have to make a scrupulous account, or
you will be further robbing yourself, or sending back 6ᵈ in

stamps, or some such tiresomeness.—I have lent Bates'
Amazon, that you gave me, to Katharine. It is such a good
book—takes one into the sun & the waters.

au revoir

D. H. L.

[PS.]

Belt—*Naturalist in Nicaragua*	561
The Pilgrim Fathers	480
Autobiography of Edward Gibbon	511
Sheppard's *Charles Auchester*	505

Everyman's Library

---

1 Moore identifies the doctor as Dr. Feroze. See *I.H.*, p. 248. In a letter to
Katherine Mansfield, dated 27 December 1918, Lawrence describes a visit to the
home of Dr. Feroze. See *C.L.*, I, 571.

2 Lawrence did not leave for Hermitage until 2 May 1919, according to Moore
(*P.R.*, pp. 53–54); however, see note 1 to Letter No. 158.

3 Horne was part of the Lawrence-Koteliansky circle during 1914–15. See note 4
to Letter No. 1.

[MOUNTAIN COTTAGE]
Middleton-by-Wirksworth
Tuesday [?25 March 1919]

My dear Kot,

The books, the grapefruit and the tea came this morning, and
I was very glad. Please don't by [*sic*] Karavan tea—the very
name sounds beyond words costly, like camels and eastern
merchandise. I am ashamed at receiving so much from you.
If you were the banker of the portrait I wouldn't turn a hair:
but since you are the widow with the widow's mite, in *my*
excellent portrait of the future, it worries me.—I am sorry too
that those damned books have risen to 2/–. I rook you of
the postage now.

You read Anatole France[1] first, as I have got my books now.
They look *very* attractive. Often I would give you a book—
but I feel you would never read it, and it would only be an
encumbrance to you. Tell me if that is so. Tell me if you
would like me to send a book now and then—one that I
have read & found good. I should like to do it.

Tell Gertler I got his postcards & the book.[2] Tomorrow I will
start. I copied a *Teniers* in the meantime—very nice.—But
painting is not *my* art—only an amusement to me.

It is terribly cold here—deep snow still—and impossible for
me to set foot out of doors. But now I have books & paints I
shall be quite busy.

It is awfully nice to have China tea. Substitutes like the
ordinary tea and margarine & jam become just offensive when
one has been seedy. But I am really a lot *stronger*—if only I
could go out. Hope you & Gertler are both happy again by
now.

au revoir

D. H. L.

[PS.]
Horne didn't write again.

168

1 Pseudonym of François Anatole Thibault (1844–1924). The book is *Le Petit Pierre* (1918) as the subsequent letters make clear.

2 Lawrence's request to Gertler for some art books was made in a letter dated 20 March 1919. See *A.H.*, pp. 474–75.

[MOUNTAIN COTTAGE]
Middleton-by-Wirksworth
Derby
Monday [?31 March 1919]

My dear Kot,

Thank you for grapefruit, Karavan, & *Anatole France*.
Karavan I sip happily as I look out of the window at the
motionless valley: by the way I owe you half a dollar for it:
grapefruit I have eaten one & made a design for embroidery
with it: *Anatole* I have read four pages, and such a mess of
parturition, babies & puppies being spawned on the floor,
that I go outside and wipe my feet on the mat.

> No stir on the land, no stir on the sea
> The Murrys are silent as silent can be. [1]

That is, he's done me in over one of my essays, which now
becomes out of date, since he neglects to return it to me.—I
saw the notice of the *Athenaeum*: what a *rechauffé* of dead
men!

I have in preparation a very charming little present for you,
so you may as well know it beforehand, in case it never comes
off. Anyway it will be a week or two.

A letter from Margaret Radford;—how happy, dear Lawrence,
she is that she can be at Hermitage to receive us & stay ten
days with us. "Love rules the camp, the court, the grove." [2]

Another hair in Sonia's soup! Tell her to save it, she will have
enough to weave a rope to hang somebody with, soon.
Tell me about her & Amsterdam. [3] Say to Ghita I began the
tune of "Rule Britannia," because her father sings it so well.
Hope this is quite according to programme.

Heard from Arabella: Hilda's baby born last week: a girl:
"Gray behaving wretchedly, Richard very fine" (quotes.
Arabella). [4] *A*. herself seems in low water.—Hilda & baby
doing well.

Tell Ghita, for a second tune, we'll sing that inspiring hymn

> "We're marching to Zion
> Beautiful beautiful Zion
> We're marching homeward to Zion etc—"

I hope she'll join in. Don't say anything about Hilda—except to Sonia.

D. H. L.

[PS.]
My envelopes are awful, but they knock your long coupons into a cocked hat.

---

1 Cf. Robert Southey's lines:

> No stir in the air, no stir in the sea,
> The ship was still as she could be.
> > "The Inchcape Rock" (Stanza 1)

2 A quotation from Sir Walter Scott's "The Lay of the Last Minstrel":

> In peace, Love tunes the shepherd's reed;
> In war, he mounts the warrior's steed;
> In halls, in gay attire is seen;
> In hamlets, dances on the green.
> Love rules the court, the camp, the grove,
> And men below, and saints above;
> For love is heaven, and heaven is love.
> > (Canto III, Stanza 2)

3 Mrs. Farbman appears to have made a visit to Amsterdam at this time.

4 Hilda Aldington; Gray was the baby's name, and Richard was Richard Aldington, Hilda's husband. Arabella would be Dorothy Yorke.

MOUNTAIN COTTAGE
Middleton-by-Wirksworth
Derby
3 April 1919

My dear Kot,

I send you the *Scarlet Letter*—a very great book—no doubt
you know it already. But read it again. My next month's
English Review essay is about this.[1]—Keep the book if you
like it.

I heard from Murry, very editorial—he sort of "declines
with thanks" the things I did for him. He will publish one
essay next week—too late to ask for it back—and that is the
first and last word of mine that will ever appear in the
Athenaeum. Good-bye Jacky,[2] I knew thee beforehand.—But
don't say anything at 2 Portland Villas.[3]

I heard from Horne—foolish, I thought. He is living in
Acton—is still in the army—and "very busy" with
demobilisation—wants to get an "administrative" job—has
applied for a post in Palestine or Damascus or somewhere
else—thinks his barrister's qualification will help him to get an
appointment.[4] Let's hope they'll appoint him to the moon.—
Maisie[5] meanwhile is putting a "sketch" on the boards at
her own expense and starts her tour at Exeter next week.
"If it is not a success she will lose money by it—" (Horne).

Who is it that has been telling small petty mean lies, now, to
depress you?—instead of world-mighty Alexandrian lies.
Ach Kot, who cares about the little fleas, or the big fleas
either!

Don't bother about any book—in vulgar debt I owe you
2/- for postage for the others. And let me pay for Karavan,
please

I am very thrilled about Sonia. When she sees Grisha, she is
to be sure and give him my blessings. Let me know what
takes place.

It is true, one has to be in the mood to read books: no use
trying if one is out of the mood.

I have set to, revising my history.[6] It will take about three weeks—pray God not longer—and then I hope speedily to receive the £50. There is a sum for you!

Tell Ghita I received her bob-curtsey little letter, and wish to know if I am the little-boy blue of the illustration and exhortation: & if so, what tune shall I strike up.

Vale

D. H. L.

---

1 *English Review*, XXVIII (May 1919), pp. 404–17.

2 J. M. Murry

3 The Murry residence in London.

4 Horne's "barrister's qualifications" were called on at the Russian Law Bureau, where Koteliansky worked.

5 Probably a reference to Horne's wife.

6 *Movements in European History*.

MOUNTAIN COTTAGE
Middleton-by-Wirksworth
Derby
17 April 1919

My dear Kot,

We are still here—my sister with us, with her little boy—
she rather ill. She too had flu., and it left her with boils that
keep on coming. They make her weak & depressed—I do
wish they would stop.

We are coming to Hermitage next week—24th,[1] I think. I
shall let you know when we arrive. Perhaps you will come &
see us there. Margaret will be at the cottage till first week in
May, alas! I hate the bother of hauling out all my things &
shifting again.

Your present—evidently you did not deserve it, for it has
gone wrong in the post—envelope arrived torn across, little
box missing. I am filling up forms & hope still to recover it.
If not, I'll try & get another.—It is of no value, only it was
really nice, and not to be replaced—one could only get
something more or less the same.—It sounds cryptic, and even
shady, like a present posted by the Murrys. But it was a real
thing, & I have a faint hope it may turn up even yet.

I haven't heard from the M's—only received back the bit of
my MS. I hadn't asked for, containing also my own letter to
Jack—nasty bit of oversight; also last week's *Athenaeum*.
Of all the wet and be-snivelled rags, this *Athenaeum* is the
messiest: soulful, spiritual journalists moaning because they
can't, & probably never *will*, make pots of money, poor
darlings! The Athenaeumites are snivellers, *piagnoni* one &
all—even K's[2] sprightly wit has a wet-nosed sniff in it. Pah!

I see you are getting a little telegram-official fever. Keep
cool.—But it is irritating. Poor Sonia, hopping between the
frying-pan and the fire. I hope she'll get back all right. Are
you meanwhile all alone?

I read ½ *Anatole France*: but *Pierre* was so *Petite* [*sic*] that I
could hardly see him at all, and began to suffer from eye-

strain. But *Anatole* is a very graceful piffler, & so *easy* that to
me he becomes impossibly difficult. I feel like a parrot born
to crack nuts trying to feed itself on pap.—I'm glad you
like *The Scarlet Letter*. I shall send you another Hawthorne.
—Hope I don't sound conceited about *A.F.* & *P.P.*[3]

I have got only two more chapters of the history before me.
When these are done, I have nothing on hand at all, can
turn tramp or bolshevist or government official, any of those
occupations one takes up in one's leisure. It seems we are
to be kept dormant and apathetic and anaesthetised for ever.
I am afraid of becoming bored at last.

People are coming here for Easter. I nearly cut and run—
bolted to you. Seriously I thought of descending on you for
Easter. But I suppose I shall have to stick it out.

Thank you very much for the grapefruit. My sister shares
them with me. She likes them extremely, & I believe they're
good for her.—If I can get to Matlock I will send you an
Easter egg. But it rains: and I have never walked so far since
I was ill. I am better: can again chop wood & carry water and
potter in the garden. I mean no more questions are to be
asked about me, I am normal.

Poor Sonia: tell me how she gets on.[4]

au revoir

D. H. L.

---

1 See note 2 to Letter No. 152 and note 1 to Letter No. 158.

2 Katherine Mansfield.

3 Anatole France and *Le Petit Pierre*.

4 I have not been able to discover the source and the nature of Sonia's problems.

157

My dear Kot,

We are going away on Friday, leave here 8:00 o'clock—all the things packed up now. My sister with her boy leaves tomorrow evening. How many times have I packed our miserable boxes!—and when will they ever come to rest.—I feel as if we were setting off on a real new move now, as if we shouldn't be long in Hermitage, as if soon the bigger journey would begin, away from England. Perhaps they will make peace for the time being, & let us out.

If you won't come to Hermitage I will come to London & see you soon. The history is finished, I am a free man. The other day I got papers revoking the Cornwall order against us.—I think Sonia will come back soon. Meanwhile it makes you cross.

The Murrys do not write to me—which is what I prefer. K. writes to F.—foolish would-be-witty letters. They bore me merely.

I send you now your *Petit Pierre*—for which many thanks. I will send you more books from Hermitage. Margaret will be there. You remember the address: Chapel Farm Cottage, Hermitage nr Newbury *Berks*.

Let us have a meeting soon.

au revoir

D. H. L.

CHAPEL FARM COTTAGE
Hermitage
nr Newbury, Berks
Wednesday [30 April 1919] ¹

My dear Kot,

We came here last Friday—I am just recovering from the journey. The weather is not nice. Margaret Radford is here: under the circumstances I'd much rather be at Mountain Cottage.

What swine they are about Sonia.² They make my blood go a little darker—if that be possible. Tell me if your efforts have availed you anything.

Are we going to have peace?—Do you hear the Herald Angels Sing? Ah God!

I would come & see you at once, but have got a sort of obstinate sulky stupidity which prevents my doing anything. Partly it derives from the sweetly-loving Margaret. I wish one could exterminate all her sort under a heap of Keating's powder. I feel utterly "off" the soulful or clever or witty type of female—in fact, the self-important female of any sort.

I should like to come to London, if my disagreeableness would let me. I should like to talk for about half an hour: I should like to go with you to the opera, *en garçon*, in the cheapest seats: I should like to go to the National Gallery. But I don't want to see anybody at all—don't want to let anybody know I am there—save perhaps Cath. Carswell & Gertler. When I get over my fit I will come.

Tell me about Sonia. Tell me if you know of any charm to cure my fit of enduring hatefulness.

D. H. L.

---

1 In *C.L.*, I, 585, Moore gives the date of this letter as [?7 May 1919]. We know, however, that Letter No. 157 was written after 17 April 1919, the date of Letter No. 156. Since Lawrence planned to go to Hermitage on 24 April, the date for

Letter No. 157 would logically be 23 April, the Wednesday prior to the date set for his departure. If he came to Hermitage "last Friday," as Letter No. 158 states, then Letter No. 158 must be dated 30 April 1919. Moore's conclusion that the Lawrences must have moved in on Saturday 3 May 1919 is based on an unpublished letter from Lawrence to J. B. Pinker dated 5 May 1919 in which Lawrence thanks Pinker "for the cheque for fifty-five pounds which came so nicely on Saturday" (*P.R.*, p. 54). But for a man in Lawrence's financial circumstances, a cheque for £55 would still have "come so nicely on Saturday [3 May]" even if he had already been at Hermitage since Friday 25 April 1919.

2 Probably a reference to police authorities or government officials of some kind.

59 CHAPEL FARM COTTAGE
Hermitage
nr Newbury [Berks]
9 May 1919

My dear Kot,

So glad to hear of Sonia's safe arrival, & of your relapse into quiescence. From Sonia's letter I gather she has sent a bit of Dutch cake:[1] I shall write to her tomorrow, when it has arrived.

Now the weather is warm I am quite happy—*dolce far' niente*. The world is very lovely, full of flowers and scents. One can be out most of the day. Would you like to come down?

I haven't read Wm James *Religious Experiences*.[2] He is an interesting man. Lend it me if it is quite easy to do so. You really seem to be reading. I shall send you more books, in that case.

Katharine wrote to me, but somehow I couldn't answer her. When I can I will. Of him, nothing—and forever nothing.

I feel that soon we ought to be talking plans. I feel that soon we shall be scattering: God knows where to. We ought to have a meeting soon. Are you sure you wouldn't like to come down? I could get you rooms in the village, if you don't want to stay in the house here. Let me know.

D. H. L.

---

1 The reference would appear to imply that Sonia had gone to Amsterdam and suggests that she had some difficulty leaving Holland.

2 In Jessie Chambers' book about Lawrence, she tells us, however, that Lawrence "read also Herbert Spencer and John Stuart Mill and William James, whose *Pragmatism* especially appealed to him. He liked also *Some Varieties of Religious Experience* and recommended me to read it" (*D. H. Lawrence: A Personal Record* by E. T., second edition edited by J. D. Chambers [New York, 1965], p. 113).

160
Hermitage
nr Newbury [Berks]
Friday [? May 1919]

My dear Kot,

This is your present at last. The lost seal was chrysoprase—
bright green—lovely: this is jade. I drew a little man: a
thunder-evoker, from an African symbol—but they have no
proper engravers in Cornwall now, so I had to have your
initials. But I hope you'll like your seal, & keep it as a rather
bomb-like peace-sigil.

It is hot, & I had a little *colpa de sole*, so felt sick. Barbara is
here—chatters.—Cath. Carswell *et famille*, & Mme
Litvinov[1] *et fils* are coming to this village for Whitsun.—Not
to this house. If you hear of my disappearance don't wonder.

This isn't a letter—a barren note. Greet Sonia Issayevna &
Ghita Grishevna from me, tell them I am speechless, & am
rapidly becoming stone deaf, through the sound of voices.

D. H. L.

---

[1] Ivy Low. See note 2 to Letter No. 49.

---

161 [CHAPEL FARM COTTAGE]
Hermitage
nr Newbury, Berks
30 June 1919

My dear Kot,

I haven't been able to write to anybody lately—simply stiff-fed
with everything. However, the PEACE is signed—sweet
peace—Peace Perfect Peace—Pea-Pea-Pea-Pea-Peace: "the
very word is like a bell"—pah![1]

Murry suddenly descended on us on Saturday—a bolt from
the blue:— not very startling. Truly, he was quite nice. But

by now I am an old suspicious bird. He was looking for another house, *for Katharine*!!

Huebsch, the American publisher[2]—did you say to Murry that he was no good?—did Farbman suggest that?—but however, Huebsch is supposed to be coming to London "early in July": that is, within the next fortnight. There I am to meet him. Then we are to discuss my going to America: particularly a lecturing tour wherein I lecture on poetry. Pah! Pfui-i! But if it must be done it must. I put my faith in no man—and in no bundle of men.

What about you and Sophie Issayevna? You must have plans. I must get out of this country as soon as possible. But having no money, & all, it is hell. How on earth are you fixed? Curse, damn, & blast!

I want to come & see you very soon. I would come tomorrow, but feel I must wait a bit longer to hear from that Huebsch, who I am ready to call *Hässlich*.

Frieda of course wants to go to Germany as soon as possible. When do you think that will be possible? It is my plan to go straight to New York. Though I hate it, I shall do it. But if it is quite impossible, I shall go to Germany with Frieda, for a bit.

The Radfords, with stinking impudence, having let us this cottage, want us to clear out by July 25th, so then we shall have nowhere to go. However, I hope & trust that we can leave England by August, or during that month. But what about you? However, I must come soon—very soon—& talk. Perhaps I'll come this week[3]—shall I? Ask Sophie Issayevna.

Many mingled greetings.

D. H. L.

---

1 A reference to the Treaty of Versailles which was signed on the afternoon of 28 June 1919.

2 B. W. Huebsch published *The Rainbow* in 1917.

3 Moore records a visit to London on July 3. See *P.R.*, p. 54.

---

162 [CHAPEL FARM COTTAGE]
Hermitage
[nr. Newbury, Berks]
Saturday [12 July 1919]

Have written Goldring[1]—he is 7 St. James Terrace, Regents
Park, N.W.8.—& asked him to ring you up. I have agreed
to give him the play "Touch & Go"—for publication &
production both. He says he will see Fagan[2] about the Court
Theatre.—I'll enquire about Daniel.[3]

D. H. L.

---

1 See Douglas Goldring's account of his relations with Lawrence in *C.B.*, I,
490–96. Goldring was introduced to Lawrence by Koteliansky.

2 Probably a reference to J. B. Fagan, who was a well-known theatrical manager
and playwright. See *Oxford Companion to the Theatre* (London, 1967), p. 307.

3 C. W. Daniel, who published Lawrence's play *Touch and Go* (London, 1920).

---

63 [CHAPEL FARM COTTAGE]
Hermitage
[nr. Newbury, Berks]
Thursday [?17 July 1919]

My dear Kot,

What do you think of Huebsch. Somehow it puts me off
America: to lecture like a fool to fools.

I am glad you liked Douglas Goldring.

I think I shall come to town next week, for a week. Margaret
is coming here—& I can't be in the house along with her.—I
have written to Barbara, & shall stay in her rooms, probably.
She is going to Cambridge for a week or so. Her rooms are
in Guildford St. I shall be by myself and in peace. I won't
come so soon again to the Cave, lest I wear out my welcome.¹
But I'll be round to see Sophie Issayevna & all.

Huebsch makes me hang fire about America. If only one could
go as an independent man. Pah, these lectures, these innumerable *suffisant* swine.

I have a pleasant feeling about the Peoples Theatre—but take
nothing to heart these days.

D. H. L.

---

1 This suggests a previous visit, probably the one projected in Letter No. 161
and which Moore dated as taking place on 3 July 1919.

MYRTLE COTTAGE
Pangbourne
Saturday [?2 August 1919][1]

Dear Kot,

I have done a certain amount of the translation—*Apotheosis*.
I began "Russian Spirit," but either Shestov writes atro-
ciously—I believe he does—or you translate loosely. One
sentence has nothing to do with the next, so that it seems
like jargon. The *Apotheosis* is more intelligible. His attitude
amuses me—also his irony, which I think is difficult for
English readers. But he isn't anything wonderful, is he?
Apotheosis of Groundlessness will never do. What can one
find instead, for a title?[2]

Monstrous hot here.—My younger sister & family have
gone—my elder sister comes today. Beyond that no news.

Too hot to write & [*sic*] intelligent letter.

D. H. L.

---

1 Lawrence arrived in Pangbourne on 28 July 1919. See his letter to Catherine
Carswell dated ?15 August 1919 in *C.L.*, I, 590. The project of translating Shestov
into English seems to have resulted from Lawrence's visit to London alluded to
in Letter No. 163. Although there are a large number of letters in connection with
the Shestov translation, the letters are not dated by Lawrence except for the day
of the week on which they were written. I have tried to assign the dates on the
basis of internal evidence in order to present the letters in the right sequence. We
know that Lawrence arrived in Pangbourne on July 28th and that he planned to
leave on August 25th, as his letter to Catherine Carswell makes clear. The work
on Shestov continued at Grimsbury Farm and later at Chapel Farm Cottage.
See *P.R.*, p. 55.

2 The book was eventually published under the title *All Things Are Possible*,
translated by S. S. Koteliansky with a foreword by D. H. Lawrence (London,
1920). As this and the subsequent letters make clear, Lawrence's contribution to
the book was much more than the "Foreword" for which he received credit.

MYRTLE COTTAGE
Pangbourne
Friday [?8 August 1919]

My dear Kot,

I'm glad you went to the New Forest—it's a first step out,
anyhow.

I am sending in Frieda's application for a passport today.[1]

I have done 71 of the Shestov paragraphs[2]—more than half.
No, I don't hate doing it—rather like it—only he often
irritates me when he will keep on going on about philosophers,
and what they do or don't do. One gets sick of the name of
philosophers.—But sometimes he blossoms into a kind of
pathetic beauty.

I'll send you the MS when finished—shall you have to get it
typed? I might do a bit of typing at Hermitage. We go back
there on the 25th I expect.

I'll let you know as soon as I finish.

D. H. L.

---

1 Frieda needed a passport to visit her parents in Germany.

2 *All Things Are Possible* consists of a series of short paragraphs.

166

Dear Kot,

Could you get a little hand book of philosophics (or look at one in a public library) and find out the correct term for your "consequentialness," your "law of consequences," "law of sequence," "causality"—look at *Positivism*. I know nothing about Positivism. *Encyclopaedia Brittanica* [*sic*] will tell you —in any public library.

Also will you send me Shestov's "Introduction" if possible before—or with—Part II. Also will you send me a small "Introduction" of your own—the facts of Shestov's life & purpose.

Don't ask the Woolfs—we will make Heinemann or somebody such print the stuff.[1] Also why not print weekly in *The Nation* or *New Statesman?* We must do this.

Look up Moleschot and Vogt in a big biographical dictionary.

I hope "Part II" is not so long as "Part I." We shall have to cut down if it is. There is more chance of printing a smaller book.

I send you this part—let me have it back, & we'll make some selections to offer to *The Nation* or to *New Statesman.*

I don't want my name printed as a translator. It won't do for me to appear to dabble in too many things. If you don't want to appear alone—but why shouldn't you?—put me a *nom de plume* like Richard Haw or Thomas Ball. Also, when it comes to payment, in mere justice my part is one-third. Don't argue this with me. If you are a Shestovian, accept the facts.

We might try the *English Review.*

Please go through my version and alter anything you think fit.

D. H. L.

---

1 Martin Secker eventually published the book.

[MYRTLE COTTAGE]
Pangbourne
Tuesday [?12 August 1919]

My dear Kot,

I have done also "The Russian Spirit." Send it at once to
Austin Harrison [1]—tell him I recommended you to do so—
and tell him a few words about Shestov.

> The English Review
> 19 Garrick St.
> W.C.

Harrison is mean. *Manage* him about money. He might like
to print a series of Shestov-paragraphs. If so, go and see him
& have a definite arrangement with him.

D. H. L.

---

1 Editor of *The English Review*.

168

My dear Kot,

I have finished Shestov—have compressed him a bit, but left
nothing out—only "so to speak" and "as all know" and many
such phrases and volatile sentences—no *substance* at all.—
Sometimes I have added a word or two, for the sake of the
sense—as I did in "Russian Spirit." What I leave out I
leave out deliberately.[1] There is a many-wordedness often,
which becomes cloying, wearying.—I do get tired of his
tilting with "metaphysics," positivism, Kantian postulates,
and so on—but I *like* his "flying in the face of Reason,"
like a cross hen. I don't know what I have done with the
"Russian Spirit" which you returned to me. I have written to
Pangbourne to see if it's there. If not, I shall have to copy it
out from your MS.—let me have the "Preface" as soon as
possible: also everything you know about Shestov, and I'll
write a tiny "Introduction," & we'll approach the publishers.[2]

So you will be home Tuesday.—Greet Sophie Issayevna &
Ghita

D. H. L.

---

1 We have here Lawrence's own description of his role as an editor of Koteliansky's translations.

2 Lawrence made the initial approach to Martin Secker in a letter from Grimsbury
Farm dated 2 September 1919. See *A.H.*, pp. 481–82. This letter is not in *C.L.*

---

169 GRIMSBURY FARM
[Long Lane
nr Newbury, Berks]
Tuesday [?9 September 1919]

My dear Kot,

I got your letter this morning. I feel I can't come to London:
feel the town would be more than I could stand at this
minute: even the train journey would do for me. Here one
can chop bushes & milk the goats.

I had a letter from Secker—he said he would like to see the
Shestov, with a view to publishing it. Connie Garnett has the
Tchekhov letters[1] in print—is now correcting proofs for
Heinemann.—I hear that a book on Tchekhov, by Shestov,
is published in England—one of those black-covered transla-
tions. Could you find out about that, I wonder? Or shall I
write and borrow it?—We must find out enough about
Shestov.

Let me have the "Introduction" as soon as you can.

I'll write to Tidmarsh[2] about the Shestov "Tchekhov."

D. H. L.

---

1 Probably a reference to *Letters of Anton Tchekhov to his Family and Friends*,
translated by C. Garnett, with a Biographical Sketch (London, 1920).

2 The next letter (No. 170) implies that Lawrence was writing to Rosalind
Baynes, who might have been visiting "Lytton Strachey at Tidmarsh, near
Pangbourne, Berks." (*C.B.*, I, 514).

CHAPEL FARM COTTAGE
Hermitage
nr Newbury, Berks
Friday [?12 September 1919]

My dear Kot,

I got the Shestov book, & "Preface": also heard from
Rosalind Baynes[1] about the Shestov "Tchekhov." It was
your essay[2]—I thought she meant a whole vol. on Tchekhov.

I will send the Shestov[3] in to Secker on Monday. If only we
had a duplicate, we could send to America.

We came back here this evening[4]—wonderful autumn
weather.

When I hear from Secker, perhaps you will go and see him.

D. H. L.

---

1 "Rosalind Baynes, mother of three children, had been married since 1913 to
Godwin Baynes, a psychoanalyst of the school of Jung. Her father, Sir Hamo
Thornycroft, was the sculptor who set up the famous statue of Cromwell outside
the House of Commons" (*I.H.*, p. 253). Lawrence and Frieda were the guests of
Rosalind Baynes at Pangbourne.

2 Not identified.

3 The MS of *All Things Are Possible*, which has survived in Lawrence's handwriting. See *B.*, pp. 41–42, 323.

4 Lawrence was back at Hermitage by 15 September. See *P.R.*, p. 55.

[CHAPEL FARM COTTAGE]
Hermitage
[nr. Newbury, Berks]
Wednesday [?24 September 1919]

My dear Kot,

I have been a long time waiting to hear from Secker. He
always offers filthy terms. What do you say? Let me know, &
then I'll write & tell him you'll see him & make the agreement
direct.

What about an American publisher? Shall I write to one, direct,
or will you see an agent?

I am troubled about your finances. At present I've got to
see Frieda off to Germany—the policeman came Monday to
verify her passport application, & said the passport would
come all right—probably it will—so I must provide for
that trip, otherwise I could have given you something.—Have
you been to Harrison? Go to him, make him publish "Russian
Spirit," & even other sections. Try and get an advance out
of Secker—and really, out of common decency, do keep
whatever money can be made. I owe you heaven knows how
many pounds.—Soon I shall, I believe, begin to make money
in America. Then you can have some freely. At present
it's the same old hand to mouth.

I thought the Shestov "Preface" the worst part of the book—
don't think Secker will do badly if he omits it—I wrote a
4-page "Foreword."

Another thing—if you aren't busy, do you think you might
copy out for me three of the *American* essays?[1] Huebsch
worries me for them—an American came to see me last week.
If you would copy out three for me—I'll send my MS.—it
would save me weary work.—You would let me pay you, like
a type-writer [*sic*]. Your handwriting is so nice & plain.—
But be sure you don't do it if you don't want.

If Frieda gets her passport I shall be in London, & shall
see you.

Is Sonia home—yes surely. Remember me very nicely to her & Ghita.

D. H. L.

---

1 On the basis of the essays which had by this time appeared in *The English Review*, I would speculate that the three essays referred to here were those on Dana, Melville, and Whitman.

---

172 [CHAPEL FARM COTTAGE]
Hermitage
[nr. Newbury, Berks]
Friday [?26 September 1919]

My dear Kot,

I have written to Secker just what you said. I'll let you know as soon as he replies.—I have another publisher in America— Scott and Seltzer—I believe they'd be better than Huebsch.[1]

Will there be peace with Russia?

I send you the three essays. Will you please do them on smallish sheets like this—so that they can make one MS.— with the *English Review* pages. I wish I could have sent you a writing block—but none here—and it rains. I shall send you a few pears—for you and Sophie Issayevna—when it doesn't rain.

D. H. L.

---

1 Lawrence settled on Huebsch, as a letter to the American publisher dated 30 September 1919 indicates. See *C.L.*, I, 595–96. The Shestov book was at that time still called *Apotheosis of Groundlessness*.

73 [CHAPEL FARM COTTAGE]
Hermitage
[nr. Newbury, Berks]
Wednesday [?1 October 1919]

My dear Kot,

Yes, the paper is quite all right. I feel you'll hate doing it.

Secker says he has written to you, making offers.—He wants
a new title.[1]

Let us hope the insects will bite K. to death.[2]

Things will never be *lively*—they may be deadly. It is a
process of attrition, not violence.

Good for Grisha.

I *may*—just possible—go to Italy for the winter—but *not*
San Remo—which is really France still.

D. H. L.

[PS.]
Tell me what Secker says.

[PPS.]
Railway will compromise with Govt—*encore!*

---

1 The title eventually chosen was *All Things Are Possible*.

2 Katherine Mansfield, who had gone to the Italian Riviera.

---

174 [CHAPEL FARM COTTAGE]
Hermitage
[nr. Newbury, Berks]
Saturday [?4 October 1919]

My dear Kot,

The MS.[1] has come this morning—thank you very much indeed. Did it bore you very much to do it? I shall send it to America now.

I laughed at your fury with Secker. Didn't you know he was a scurvy little swine? They are all like it. Pah!—I wrote to him your terms—told him he could make the agreement with me— was quite plain to him: showed him what I thought of him.

Poor Fox:[2] after all, if he doesn't come back, he'll be *your* tragedy more than anybody's. But in my secret heart, *je voudrai qu'il soit perdu.*

I will send you whatever Secker writes.—I told him to send me Shestov back again, if he wasn't keen on him—& I'll try elsewhere.

D. H. L.

---

1 Although various MSS of the American essays have been discovered, the MSS in Koteliansky's handwriting have not yet turned up. For a full discussion of the various versions of the essays, see *The Symbolic Meaning: The Uncollected Versions of "Studies in Classic American Literature,"* edited by Armin Arnold, with a Preface by Harry T. Moore (New York, 1964). See especially "Introduction," pp. 1–4 and the headnotes to each essay.

2 The name of the dog referred to in note 3 to Letter No. 130.

---

75 [CHAPEL FARM COTTAGE]
Hermitage
[nr. Newbury, Berks]
Monday [?6 October 1919]

My dear Kot,

I send you Secker's letter & agreement. The world of business
is *never* decent—it lies & lies & lies again—by now I am
callous to it.—You will see the agreement is made with me—I
suppose you don't care.—I don't. Oh Lord, it is hard to
imagine the pitch to which I don't care. I'm always having to
kick myself into making an effort for my own rights.—I don't
care for Secker's "America" clause—why should he have
$\frac{1}{3}$ if we arrange rights?—and 10% of sheets sold won't
do—no. What do you think of this?—Anyhow, I so insisted
that Secker should return me the MS. if he wasn't keen on
publishing it, that he must go ahead now.

D. H. L.

176 CHAPEL FARM COTTAGE
Hermitage
nr. Newbury [Berks]
10 October 1919

My dear Kot,

I send you the agreement, & Secker's last letter.

Frieda has got her passport: waits for the Dutch visa—may set off next week. If so, we shall be in town & shall see you.

I really think I may go to Italy—if conditions are possible there.

I enclose 10/——to pay for paper and postage etc. of the MS.—for which I again thank you.

au revoir to all, including Fox.

D. H. L.

[PS.]
I offered Secker a set of possible titles. You keep the agreement—I am so careless.

177 [CHAPEL FARM COTTAGE]
Hermitage
[nr. Newbury, Berks]
Sunday [9 November 1919]

I shan't get away till Tuesday.¹ But I will come for certain on
Tuesday, arrive about 1:30. Shall bring all the luggage.

Hope this is all right for S[onia] & you.

D. H. L.

---

¹ Moore dates Lawrence's arrival in London *around* 10 November 1919. See *P.R.*,
p. 55, and Lawrence's letter to Catherine Carswell in *A.H.*, pp. 483–84.

---

178 [PENSIONE BALESTRI]
5 Piazza Mentana
Florence
Wednesday [26 November 1919]

I have your letter with enclosures this evening:¹ think I
shall see Secker in Rome, & will mention *Green Ring*:² but
he does not care for plays: doesn't *Constable* do a modern
play series?—and I'm sure Daniel would do it.—Let us
arrange English publishers first. I will be thinking, & will
write tomorrow. Turin, *les riches*, dried me up—& it was
Sunday, I arrived late Sat. evening.—Travelling is truly
horrible—it *feels* like accidents, the permanent way all
dilapidated. Have you any idea who sent the telegram about
the ship?

D. H. L.

[PS.]
My pen is stolen.

---

¹ Since Lawrence arrived in Florence on Tuesday 18 November 1919, the letter
to Koteliansky was likely written the following week.

² *The Green Ring*, a play by Zinaida Merezhkovskaya (née Hippius), was translated by S. S. Koteliansky and published by C. W. Daniel (London, 1920).

[PENSIONE BALESTRI]
5 Piazza Mentana
Florence
Saturday [29 November 1919]

My dear Kot,

I have your letter this evening, enclosing one from Herbert
Trench (Napoleon)[1] who is in London: a bus ran into his
taxi on Napoleon night & cracked his skull a little—he
invites me to go to Settingnano to stay with his *wife & daughter*
—*moi non!*

It is warm here, but a good deal of rain. Yes, it is *much*
better than England—not that pressure. One moves lightly—
and then there is wine. It is 3 francs a litre: but with the
exchange at 50, still possible.

Frieda comes on Dec. 2nd. We shall stay for 5 or 6 days:
then to Rome: and then nothing preventing, to that model
I told you of.[2] That will be: *presso il Signor Orazio Cervi,
Picinisco, Prov. di Caserta.* We shall be there, I think, by
Dec. 20. The Rome address I don't yet know. We leave
Florence, I think, on Dec. 9th or 10th. Letters apparently
take 5 days.—the moment the Huebsch parcel comes I shall
write to him about the *Green Ring*.[3] But alas, oh Lord, I
fear you may get no money out of him. Would you like to
see or write to Walter Peacock, 20 Green St., Leicester Square
W.C.2. He is a really decent dramatic agent, chiefly for
America. Tell him I said you would find him useful. I will
write to him also.—I am waiting to hear from Secker. If he
sees me in Rome, I will press the *Ring* on him. But he is a
slippery worm.—I have changed altogether £40 of my
money—and got Lira 2000 for it. They will take English
cheques here.—I wrote to Radford, perhaps she wants more
rent.—I can live here *well* for 100 francs a week—£2.
How are you to get money?

au revoir

D. H. L.

[PS.]
I have written to Peacock[4]—he is the man—go to him at once.

[PPS.]
I am being dentisted here.

---

1 See Ford Madox Ford's reference to "Herbert Trench, the poet" in *C.B.*, I, 106.

2 Lawrence's correspondence with Signor Orazio Cervi may be read in *C.B.*, II, 5–8. Orazio Cervi was an artist's model "who had worked for [Sir Hamo Thornycroft] and for other English artists . . . and who had retired on his savings to Italy and built himself a large house in his native village in the Abruzzi mountains" (*C.B.*, II, 5).

3 The letter to Huebsch was written on 3 December 1919. See *C.L.*, I, 599–600.

4 No letters from Lawrence to Walter Peacock have come to light.

---

180 [PENSIONE BALESTRI]
5 Piazza Mentana
Florence
Saturday [6 December 1919]

Have registered letter today—it enclosed £50. from Scott &
Seltzer, who will not send me back *Women in Love*, yet
can't see their way to publishing—fear!—I wrote to Huebsch
& everybody about the *Green Ring*. I sent Murry an essay
from here.[1]—I beg you, please *do not* send me ½ of the
"Russian Spirit" money:[2] if you have any regard for me,
don't bother me about this: please do keep it: I so much
wish you to make some money.—I am not Katherine [*sic*].—
I have a letter from the Altrincham Stage Society—they are
acting *The Widowing of Mrs. Holroyd* on March 10th to 13th
inclusive. I wish somebody saw it.—Frieda is here.[3] We leave
on Wed. for Rome. On the 17th we are at Picinisco: *presso
il Signore Orazio Cervi, Picinisco, Prov. di Caserta*. Write there.
The skunk Secker has not answered my letter to Capri: that
MS. must be printed by now. I'll write again.—The address of
the Altrincham Stage Society is Garrick Rooms, 8 Post Office
Hill, Kingsway, Altrincham, Cheshire.—The place is near
Manchester. Write to me at Picinisco—I don't know our
address in Rome.—I have been to a dentist here—everything
finished, 125 francs. Did Sophie Issayevna get my letters?
—Secker is c/o Compton Mackenzie, *Casa Solitaria, Isola
Capri*, Naples.—Or perhaps he is in London. Wring that
MS.[4] out of him.

D. H. L.

---

1 This despite Lawrence's protestation that Murry would get nothing more from
him. See Letter No. 155. The essay has not been identified.

2 The reference suggests that "The Russian Spirit" was published in some other
form aside from being part of *All Things Are Possible*, but I have not been able
to find the earlier publication.

3 The date of Frieda's arrival was 3 December 1919. See *C.B.*, II, 17.

4 The translation of Shestov's *All Things Are Possible*.

81 [PRESSO ORAZIO CERVI]
Picinisco [Prov. di Caserta]
17 December [1919]

My dear Kot,

I got your letters, both, today, when I struggled up the long
hour's goat-climb to Picinisco post-office.

About the "Foreword"—I will write to Secker, & tell him
you strongly wish it omitted—I will send him your letter.[1]
As far as I am concerned he can leave it clean out. But I mean
what I say in it: and as it would be my signed opinion, I
don't see that it matters: not a bit. Secker will no doubt
inform you.

When I get proofs I will go through them. But if he sends me
one set only, how can I post them to America. I have spoken
of them to Huebsch. But I will post them as soon as I have
them. Very many thanks for the notes of misprints.

This place is the devil of inaccessibility—I curse the post here.
I shall probably carry this, with Secker's letter, a long five
miles to Atina tomorrow.

Has Sophie Issayevna had any letters from me? My best
Christmas greetings to her & Ghita—wish distances weren't
so absolute.

I should be so glad if you would ignore that dividing of
Murry's miserable cheque.[2] Are you afraid of me? Don't I
owe you fifty times 35/- —*per Dio!*

D. H. L.

---

1 The letter to Secker was written on 17 December 1919. It is published in
A.H., p. 487.

2 This suggests that Murry published something which was a collaboration
between Lawrence and Koteliansky. I have not been able to identify the work.
From 4 April 1919 to 31 October 1919, *The Athenaeum*, which Murry edited,
published in serial form "Letters from Anton Tchekhov," translated by S.
Koteliansky and Katherine Mansfield. The issue of 4 April 1919 does not cite the
translators as do the succeeding issues.

PALAZZO FERRARO
Capri
(Naples)
4 January 1920

My dear Kot,

I have got all the letters today—no post for four days—sea too rough for the ship.

Now look here, I think all this about the "Preface" is perfect nonsense. What I say can't hurt Russian Literature—nor even Shestov: much more likely to *provoke interest*. You are being unnecessarily fussy. I haven't had a reply from Secker, so don't know what line he is taking. I am waiting for revised proofs, to send to America.

The letter from Huebsch contained an unexpected £25, so I feel I really can give you back £10 of the sums I owe you. It's the first time I've had a real *extra* £25, so it's very good. If Italy weren't so blasted expensive, I should feel momentarily rich. If any trifle accrues from Shestov, you will merely keep it till your ship comes home.

I found Mary Cannan here, large as life. But she's very nice, and brought us some butter.

I feel Capri isn't big enough to stay long in: and *so* cosmopolitan, in a small way. But I must get some work of some sort done, before I can move.

I have written to Pinker that I want to be rid of him.

Francis Brett Young—a Secker novelist, is here—with wife: humble waiters on Compton Mackenzie.

The weather is stormy, blowy, rainy—but not cold.

Don't be tiresome.

D. H. L.

[PS.]
The Green Ring will be published, anyway.

PALAZZO FERRARO
Capri
Prov. di Napoli
8 February 1920

My dear Kot,
Your letter today. The three weeks strike, & practically no
post all the time, made it seem useless to write. And now I've
had flu again—it is very bad in Italy—& am only just going
to get up.—Sonia's parcel has not come—parcels never come.
—I sent the Shestov to Huebsch—he asked for it—with
urgent instructions to pay a lump sum. We will await the
result—from him as from your Knopf—of whom I believe
I have heard, but know nothing. Post is very slow here, to
America. Secker of course is going on with Shestov—but
you know how *slow* Secker is—impossible. He will send you a
copy as soon as he has one ready.—He wanted to buy the
Rainbow out & out for £200. Of course I wouldn't, so we
broke off, & Duckworth is considering.—I have never heard
from Gilbert again—not since that letter you sent on.—Mary
is still here—but goes to Sicily soon—afraid of flu & death.
Very much afraid of death.—Gilbert is saying disgusting
things about "us writers" in American papers [1]—Mendelling. [2]
Mackenzie showed me cuttings. Curse Gilbert, if he's worth
it.—Douglas Goldring sent me his *Fight for Freedom*. A
nice thing for my play to be following on the heels of such a
shit: especially as, since I was purported to open the series,
I have got a little "Preface" on "A People's Theatre." [3]
O crotte mondaine!—I have broken with Pinker. [4] *Te deum
laudamus.*—It's fine & sunny here.—But I'm sick of this island:
a nice cats cradle of semi-literary & pleni-literary pussies.
Oh my dear English Countrymen, how I detest you wherever
I find you! Notwithstanding Mackenzie is nice.—But as soon
as I've got my legs I'm going over to the mainland to find a
cottage where, if possible, are none but Italians.—The
exchange, I hear, rose to 66: but they won't give it. Meanwhile prices soar up. I haven't heard anything from Daniel
about the play.
a rivederci e sia bene

D. H. L.

[PS.]
Katharine gone to Mentone—"L'Hermitage, Mentone"—as
I suppose you know. I wrote my final opinion of Jack to Jack.
Basta.

---

1 This may be a reference to Gilbert Cannan's essay "A Defence of D. H. Lawrence," *New York Tribune* (10 January 1920).

2 Coined after Gilbert Cannan's novel, *Mendel: A Story of Youth* (London,
1916), which was ostensibly based on the life of Mark Gertler, but in which the
characters and events are at great variance with reality. For further information
on *Mendel* and for its reception by Gertler and his friends, see the Appendix in
Mark Gertler: Selected Letters, edited by Noel Carrington (London, 1965),
pp. 253–56.

3 Lawrence's "Preface" on "A People's Theatre" has recently been reprinted in
Phoenix II (New York, 1968), pp. 289–93. Lawrence had written the essay as a
"Preface" to his play *Touch and Go.*

4 See Lawrence's letter to J. B. Pinker dated 10 January 1920 in *C.L.*, I, 611.

FONTANA VECCHIA
Taormina (Messina)
Sicily
9 March [1920]

I scooted round Sicily looking for a house—Capri was too
dry & small.—Now I have taken this, a nice, biggish place,
with great garden, for a year—2000 francs. The exchange will
need to stay at 62.—Mary is staying here, at the expensive
Timeo hotel.—Sicily is a queer place—a touch of Saracen &
the East in it—sort of explosive gunpowder quality. But I
like it. Wonder how I shall stand it for a year.

I watch the Russian news, as well as I can: and watch the
post. If only I can get a £10 I am expecting, I shall send it
you. But I had a blow—1000 Lire from America, which the
Credito Italiano wouldn't cash. I hope I shall get it back.
Oh these American cheques.

Women in Love has gone to print in America. Has Daniel sent
you *Touch & Go?*

I imagine you setting off for the Ukraina [*sic*].¹ God, what a
grand excitement, after so long! Do let me know. Tell me
about Sonia, what she will do. That parcel never came—.

I want to work—I mean I ought to. Perhaps I shall, here, it
is so still, & festooned with flowers, beautiful.

D. H. L.

---

1 Koteliansky was born in the Ukraine. Despite the suggestion here that he was
planning to visit his birthplace, Koteliansky never revisited his homeland.

FONTANA VECCHIA
Taormina (Messina)
Sicily
11 March 1920

My dear Kot,

I had your letter last night. I am waiting to hear from Huebsch. I sent him the Shestov, and asked him for a lump sum, some time ago. Let us see what he says.

I have been thinking about the other scheme. But I don't think I can come back to England. I don't much want to be associated with Mond[1] and Gilbert on a paper. What remaining belief I had in Socialism dies out of me more & more as the time goes by. I feel I don't care. I feel it wouldn't be worth while to give oneself to work on a rival show to little Murry. I am not interested in the public—it all seems so far off, here in Sicily—like another world. The windows look east over the Ionian sea: somehow I don't care what happens behind me, in the north west.—*Lasciami stare*. I am more or less busy on a new novel.[2] But if I can do anything from here, of course I will. Tell Sonia *please* not to bother about that parcel—I feel she will curse the day. Is Grisha happy in Russia?[3]—you will have had letters by now from him.

Has Gilbert come back to England?

Whatever I undertook with the public of today could merely fail. One has to be a Murry or a Squire or a Sassoon. Better stay still.

Best greetings to Sonia & Ghita.

D. H. L.

---

1 "Henry Mond (later the 2nd Lord Melchett) . . . became a cabinet minister under Lloyd George, and was raised to the peerage as Lord Melchett"(*C.B.*, I , 596). He was a close friend of Gilbert Cannan.

2 The novel referred to is *The Lost Girl* which Lawrence had begun writing in January 1913. "By April 5, 1913, he had abandoned *The Lost Girl* temporarily, after completing 200 pages. After the war this batch of manuscript was finally retrieved from Germany where it had been in the keeping of Frieda's family" (George Ford, *Double Measure: A Study of the Novels and Stories of D. H. Lawrence* [New York, 1965], p. 41).

3 Michael Farbman would, therefore, have been in Russia at this time.

FONTANA VECCHIA
Taormina
Sicily
Easter Monday [5 April 1920]

My dear Kot,

I wrote to you, & the letter got destroyed with old ones.—
Today is Easter Monday—sunny—and still a *festa*. All the
world goes to the sea today.—Today I have agreed with
Secker to publish *Women in Love* & *The Rainbow*, on a fair
royalty basis: beginning with *Women in Love*.[1] Good so far.
I trust to nothing these days.—I haven't heard from Gilbert
again, nor a single word of the 400 dollars etc:—only saw
the announcement of the marriage. Alas, the dollars. If my
name has been abused surely I should see the pence.—Here
is sunny and spring-like, and I like it. I have done half of
my new novel—quite amusing.[2] But I shan't say anything to
Secker yet, I shall probably sell it to the highest bidder when
it is finished. It is as proper as proper need be.—What are
your news in the world? I see Lloyd George is coming to
Italy—maybe he is Collyfogling something. The exchange is
over 80. In the village they offer 79.50, for cheques at sight.
I feel I ought to cash out my remainder—but don't know how
much I have: and there come such rumors of Italian financial
collaps [*sic*].—But it will not be yet.—Mary is still here—
seems to get old, but will never admit it: trips upstairs if
she dies of fatigue. Poor Mary—a burden also.—Shall we
offer Secker to sell Shestov for £20, or leave it on a royalty
basis as it is. I owe you money—you would get £20.—My
dollars from America are still absent—even those 100 which
the *Cambio Nazional* disputed. What do you think of Italian
affairs? I feel quite reckless.—What news of Grisha? I wish
this cursed Europe *did* explode.

Many greetings to you all.

D. H. L.

---

1 The letter of agreement is published in *C.L.*, I, 626.

2 *The Lost Girl*, published by Secker in November 1920.

187
Taormina
(Messina)
29 April 1920

We've been away in Syracuse for a few days—I find your
letter & this from Huebsch, on my return. I am cabling to
Secker to let Huebsch have Shestov if possible. Go to Secker
and explain about the *Freeman* also—if you don't hate to.

You see how long letters take to get here—sickening. It's
a great bore that one gets one's business so criss-cross. And
Secker is a little nuisance.

The draft Huebsch sends is 150 dollars that Gilbert collected
for me. But damn Huebsch, why does he translate it into Lire.
I get 2,700, whereas I myself here could easily make 3,400.
So I lose *at least* 700 Lire. And I *tell* them not to transfer.

I wish you could have this £50 from Huebsch. Compare even
£50 with Secker's dirty £10.

It is very lovely here. I feel I shall never come north again.
So hot at Syracuse.

What news of Grisha? I heard the Eders were arriving home
from Palestine.

Gilbert drops into oblivion.

Many greetings to Sonia & Ghita.

D. H. L.

88 [FONTANA VECCHIA
Taormina
Sicily]
4 May [1920]

Had your letter with cheque today—wish you hadn't sent me
the latter. Hope you have my letter & enclosed from Huebsch
about Shestov. Chivvy Secker.—Wonderful news that
Grisha has arrived [1]—tell me about him. I suppose Sophie
Issayevna hasn't time for a letter. Very hot here.

D. H. L.

---

[1] Presumably "arrived" in England from Russia, as the next letter (No. 189)
makes clear.

FONTANA VECCHIA
Taormina (Messina)
Sicily
7 May 1920

Your letter of 13th April, registered, came today. I had your letter with cheque for £5—, and news of Grisha in London, & the Caucasians, two days ago—and wrote you by return, as I always do when it is a matter of any moment.

Re—Shestov. I repeat what I have written before.

1. I had a letter from Huebsch a week ago, offering fifty pounds outright for Shestov. I telegraphed to Secker, and sent the letter to you. I thought if you were in need of ready money it would be a help to accept this £50. That is all.

2. Meanwhile—and I have written this long ago—I heard from Secker that the Robert MacBride Company had offered to set up a copyright American edition of Shestov on a 10% royalty basis, and that Secker had accepted this offer: on his own initiative, apparently. I don't know how final this is. See Secker and make it definite.

3. Huebsch makes no mention, as you will see, of separate payment for the articles from Shestov, in his paper *The Freeman*.[1] This paper I received—one copy—a few days ago. I send it you. It contains a batch of extracts from Shestov, not mentioning translator or anybody. If Secker has agreed with the Robert MacBride, write yourself to Huebsch & demand payment at once for the articles. I will write also.—*The Freeman* is the issue of April 7th.—Why it should arrive, & no letter from America is a mystery of the Italian post.

4. I only mentioned the £20 English rights from Secker because I thought you might want money. As apparently there is no pressing need, let him go forward on his damned royalty basis.

5. I *do* wish you would make my share in Shestov one-fourth. A half is too much.—And Secker is going to give me £100

down, advance of royalties for *Women in Love*, & another £100 for *The Lost Girl*—my new novel, which is finished —and another £100 3 months after publication of *Rainbow*, *if nothing has happened.* So behold, riches in anticipation.

Your letter, this letter, is perfectly dreadful—the flue [*sic*], and Annie, and all. Hope by now you are happier with Grisha & the Caucasians.—Nothing will happen to the world: Bloomsbury will go on enjoying itself in Paris & elsewhere, no bombs will fall, no plagues, Etna will not erupt and Taormina will not fall down in earthquakes. One may as well accept the dribbling inevitable of this pettifogging fate. I am planning next Spring to go to the ends of the earth. Sicily is not far enough.

I hope you've had all letters by now: even about that imbecile Gilbert, whom please bury.

Many greetings to Grisha.

D. H. L.

---

1 See *The Freeman* (7 April 1920), pp. 87–88.

FONTANA VECCHIA
Taormina
[Sicily]
29 June 1920

My dear Kot,

·Your letter, with Secker's £5 today. Bad luck about Shestov:
but he will start to sell later.—I have burnt your cheque:
consider you owe me £5, if you like, but refrain from paying
me till later on. I have sold a story for dollars 250: and have
plenty of money. I should like to lend you £10. now: would
you mind if I sent a cheque? You *must* be badly off. But you
are so beastly high-handed. Say if you will let me lend you
the £10. Don't be tiresome about money.

Ach Gilbert! Murry! all the wet little *schweinerei.* Can't be
bothered.

No news: it is extremely hot here: we lounge about half clad,
but feel limp. Sea-bathing seems to make one hotter afterwards.

Frieda wants to go to Germany in August or Sept.—We must
see if it can be managed—doesn't matter much anyhow. I have
a horror of trains this hot weather, particularly Italian ones.

Do tell me if you are hard up. You have too much respect for
money. What does it matter, so long as one gets along. I
can't take anything seriously any more.

D. H. L.

FONTANA VECCHIA
Taormina
Sicily
17 July 1920

My dear Kot,

I had your letter two days ago, with the renewed cheque for
£5. I am very glad you are a rich man, & sorry I gave you
the trouble of re-writing the cheque. I cashed it in the
village at 65.

I hope your Gorky book will have a success.[1] As for Shestov,
wait, he will start later. It is not all over.

Here it is hot, too hot to do anything, save at morning and
evening. Frieda has promised to go to Germany in August:
and I shall go north, to some friends near Rome, then on with
them perhaps to Venice—return here in October. All this is
yet indefinite. But I think we shall move in about a fortnight's
time. Summer is so long & dry, & already the leaves are
falling.—Though I am reluctant to move even so short a
step nearer to the "world."—I thought there *was* some sort
of peace with the Bolshevists. Think of a Garsington-tea-
party Bertie[2] pronouncing on Lenin! Pfui!—What *kind* of
realism is real nowadays—particularly on Gertler's part?—But
I am limp and misanthropic with a belly-ache today.

Vale

D. H. Lawrence

---

1 M. Gorky [A. M. Pieshkov], *Reminiscences of Leo Nicolayevitch Tolstoi,*
authorized translation by S. S. Koteliansky and Leonard Woolf (London, 1920).

2 Bertrand Russell.

FONTANA VECCHIA
Taormina
Sicily
3 December 1920

My dear Kot,

Your letter today. I feel I simply can't write letters—.

F. went to Germany—I was in Florence & Venice—we are back here for six weeks, & it has rained all the time. I will go to that "far country" when I can afford—as soon as I can afford.

All your news is entirely new to me. Poor Gertler, what a curse and a misery.[1] And what a pretty thought, of your mother. Hm!

I've got no news—merely wrestle with publishers. I'll send you *The Lost Girl*, don't buy it. I am not wildly interested in it.

I never received *Gorky's Reminiscences*.[2] Did you send it? When? By registered Book Post? Curse this Italian post. But let me know, & I'll enquire here, and warm their ears. Not that it has the slightest effect on the swine.

Mary is in Monte Carlo, wearing her glad-rags with gusto. Haven't heard more of Gilbert-Mond.

Suppose we shall sit here till March—might leave before. I promised to go to Germany for a while in spring, but am not sure.

Remember me to Grisha & Sonia.

D. H. L.

---

1 About this time, Gertler suffered his first collapse from tuberculosis and entered the sanatorium, Nordrach-on-Dee, Banchory, N.B. In a letter to Koteliansky, dated 19 November 1920, Gertler says: "... I don't feel well. I keep feeling so exhausted" (*Mark Gertler: Selected Letters*, edited by Noel Carrington [London, 1965], p. 186).

2 See note 1 to Letter No. 191 above.

---

93 [FONTANA VECCHIA
Taormina
Sicily]
24 December 1920

Gorki Reminiscences just came—what a charming little book!—
& just right, I think, *format* & matter. I shall enjoy reading
it. Hope Secker has sent you *Lost Girl* as requested. Christmas
here—a bit cold, today, but nice. All best greetings to you
all at the Cave.

D. H. L.

---

94 [FONTANA VECCHIA
Taormina
Sicily]
31 January [1921]

Have *The Green Ring*—and many thanks—read it again and
find something attractive in it as I did before.—Any more
news with you? Your mother?—And anything of Gertler?—
Ottoline was with Mary Cannan at Monte Carlo.—Lovely
summery weather here—all almond blossom. Where is
Grisha!

Greet everybody.

D. H. L.

FONTANA VECCHIA
Taormina
Sicilia
2 March 1921

My dear Kot,

Well your letter was a nice little kettle of old fish. How they
do but all stink! I hear the *Athenaeum* lost £5,000 a year
under our friend the mud-worm. But he is incorporated into
the *Nation.*—Nations foster such worms. I hear he is—or was
on the Riviera with K.[1]—who is doing the last gasp touch,
in order to impose on people—on Mary Cannan, that is. K.
pretending to be sick of Jack; another old dodge; in order to
pump the interlocutor to say things. K. also announcing that
the *Rowntrees*[2] couldn't bear *her* writing. Ah me, we have
become important. Two mud-worms, they are, playing into
each other's long mud-bellies.

I am tired to death of travellers. Taormina wriggles with them.
But there is a worse sort even than the british [*sic*]: *viz*, the
Scandinavian. There must be at least 600 Scandinavians in this
village at present: horrible greedy Pillars of Society escaping
their taxes. No wonder Ivy Low hates Stockholm, or wherever
she is.

I get bored with people altogether of any sort. But this house
is very nice, the world is green & flowery, the sun rises
bright over the sea, Etna with heavy snow is beautiful, and
there is a peculiar glamour—a sort of Greek morning world
glamour. Yet I itch to go away—and think once more of
America. But I have thought so often before. I have this
house till end of April: with option of another year. And it
costs only Lir. 2,500—and is beautiful, and alone, with much
land sloping in terraces. I love my *Fontana Vecchia: et
pretera nihil.*

I think Italy will not revolute or bolsh any more. The thing
will settle down to a permanent *socialisti v. fascisti* squibbling
—the old Italian faction, Guelph & Ghibellini—and so the
house will come to bits. It will have no one smash, like
Russia.

And what of Russia? And dear darling England?

Remember me warmly to Sonia, Grisha, and the long, two-plaited Ghita.

I hope you are better.

D. H. L.

---

1 Katherine Mansfield.

2 Not identified.

---

196 LUDWIG-WILHELMSTIFT
Baden-Baden
[Germany]
17 May [1921]

Here have I been for three weeks,[1] and never a word. We are in a little inn about 3 miles out of Baden—edge of Black Forest. The woods are very big and lovely—a sense of a big wide land and strong deep trees—so different from Italy. Germany very quiet and numb seeming—and all the old order completely gone. It feels queer and vacant. Baden-Baden hasn't really existed since 1914—and now a mere memory. Living for us very cheap, and plenty of food here—everybody quite nice—quite nice with me—the old show gone for ever—but a bit depressing, feels so life-empty. Don't quite know how long we shall stay—shall tell you when we move. Tell Sophie Issayevna I had her letter in Taormina: so sorry about the headaches. Any news of your people?—I asked Secker to send you *Women in Love*—but don't know when he is bringing it out.[2]

D. H. L.

---

1 Lawrence left Florence on 23 April 1921. See *P.R.*, p. 63.

2 The Secker edition of *Women in Love* was published in June 1921. See *B.*, pp. 45–46.

197
Baden-Baden
Germany
27 May 1921

My dear Kot,

Your letter and *Tchekhov's Note-Book* today.[1] They are
charming little books, in format & appearance, these.[2] I have
read only a bit, walking up here to Ebersteinburg through the
woods. It makes me want to sneeze, like pepper in the nose.
—But very many thanks for the book.—

Secker says now he will have *Women in Love* ready for
June 10th. He is not dependable. Tell me if you get the copy.
I have one: dirty paper.

So the Murrain[3] is renewing his bald youth like the vulture, is
he, and stuffing himself with Oxford garbage.[4]

And how is Gertler *personally?*

Well, your letters are really bad-to-worse bulletins. So there
is no end to anything.

As for me, thank God I have no news & know nobody. We
are in this peasant inn at Ebersteinburg, among geese & goats
& a pig—with the big *Schwarzwald* Woods near the door—
and the wild Rhine plain beyond. One eats quite well.—
Germany is queer & empty, & never a uniform save the
postman. There is really no authority at all—but everything
goes the same, in perfect order, because nobody wants to do
anything different. Only it seems so *quiet*. The Hotel Stephanie
in Baden was full of *Schieber* for Whitsun, & the manager said
they paid on an average 800 Mark a day: over £3. English.
We pay 35 M. a day each, & all we want we have. I cannot
but think that Europe is having a slight reactionary swing,
back to Conservatism. But underneath I feel that only some
sort of Bolshevism is inevitable, later.

The world at large makes me sick. I never want to think of it.
Hardly ever do think of it.—We have had hot good weather
—the deep woods—innumerable birds—& no people.
Alors—.

I have *nearly* finished my novel *Aarons Rod*, which I began long ago & could never bring to an end. I began it in the Mecklenburg Square days.⁵ Now suddenly I had a fit of work —sitting away in the woods. And save for the last chapter, it is done. But it won't be popular.

Tell Sophie Issayevna I am so sorry she was ill. There is not much fun for her in London, I am sure. I like to feel I can drift about.—And there is something very fine about this *Schwarzwald*—the big straight strong trees with all their power and their indifferent proud new leaves. One forgets people. Germany seems so *empty*. And nobody seems to care any more what happens politically.

Greet Sophie Issayevna and Ghita. It will soon be two years since I left Acacia Rd. & England. You were the last person I spoke to in England.

D. H. L.

[PS.]
Yes, Edgar Jaffe [*sic*] was my brother in law. But he had gone cracked after being Bolshevist Minister of Finance for Bavaria.

---

1 *The Note-Books of Anton Tchekhov Together with Reminiscences of Tchekhov by Maxim Gorky*, translated by S. S. Koteliansky and Leonard Woolf (London, 1921).

2 Koteliansky appears to have sent Lawrence several copies, or two books in a series.

3 J. M. Murry.

4 A reference probably to Murry's projected lectures at Oxford. See F. A. Lea, *The Life of John Middleton Murry* (London, 1959), p. 83.

5 Lawrence first began the novel *Aaron's Rod* in November 1917 when he was living at 44 Mecklenburgh Square, W.C.1 in a flat lent to him by Richard Aldington. In January 1918 Lawrence wrote to Lady Cynthia Asquith: "I have begun a novel now—done 150 pages, which is as blameless as Cranford" (*A.H.*, p. 427). There is no doubt that the novel referred to in the letter is *Aaron's Rod*. Discussing the critical confusion surrounding the composition of *The Lost Girl* and *Aaron's Rod*, George Ford, in what appears to be a typographical error, states that the initial 150 pages of *Aaron's Rod* were completed in January 1916. See *Double Measure: A Study of the Novels and Stories of D. H. Lawrence* (New York, 1965), p. 42. Since Lawrence was living in Cornwall in January 1916 and not at the Mecklenburgh Square address he refers to in his letter to Koteliansky, *Aaron's Rod* must have been begun in November 1917.

198

Lend me, or send me, a simple book on Einstein's *Relativity*
and I'll return it, or pay for it. Am sending you my
Psychoanalysis & Unconscious. But don't let anybody see it in
London yet. I want them to wait till it is published.[1] Barbara
etc. They shan't begin peeking at me beforehand. I shall
tell my friend Robert Mountsier to see you. He is my New
York agent, is in London and is coming here, presumably.

Greet Sonia.

D. H. L.

[PS.]
R. Mountsier. 36 Guilford [*sic*] St. W.C.1.

[PPS.]
Tell me how many words in the story, & which publisher
you think to offer it to.[2]

Alas that your gay desires can't take effect![3]

D. H. L.

---

1 The first edition of Lawrence's *Psychoanalysis and the Unconscious* was published
by Thomas Seltzer 10 May 1921. See *B.*, pp. 51–52. The English edition did not
appear until July 1923.

2 As the subsequent letters indicate, the story must have been Koteliansky's
translation of Bunin's "The Gentleman from San Francisco."

3 Reference is obscure.

HOTEL KRONE
Ebersteinburg
bei Baden-Baden
9 June 1921

My dear Kot,

Send the two stories along and I will have a shot at them now immediately.[1] I am doing nothing particular at the moment. Then you can offer them if you like to Woolf, & if that is no go, we will make Curtis Brown do something with them (if you like): & Mountsier in America. You know Curtis B. is now my agent: not very exciting, but more obedient than the impudent Pinker.—Mountsier I hear has gone to Ireland. See him when he comes back.

I couldn't send the *Psycho.* book: the damned Authorities sent it back and said I must get an *Erlaubnis* to send it out of the country. So I have written to Karlsruhe for the said *Erlaubnis*.

I am sure Sophie Issayevna's head will be better out of London. London is bad for one. Perhaps she will come to Baden. There is such a nice little house to let here for eight months.— And here in Ebersteinburg, 3 miles from Baden, higher, cooler, among the woods, one pays only 35 M. a day. Tell Sonia if she stays in Germany to come to Baden.

My mother-in-law is coming here next week so please write to this address.

And look, I have broken my pen. It is a *Swan* but the nib I got in Italy. Perhaps the nib too is no good. Ask them. The rest of the pen I have all right—only this section has the bit broken which goes up the back of the nib. Ask Mabie Todds, 79 High Holborn, if they will mend this, or if I need a new section or if I had just as well have a new pen entirely. I send only this section because they would make me get permissions for the rest.

As soon as *Einstein* comes I will send you a cheque for it & this pen. But read the *Einstein* first.

Will send *Psycho.* as soon as I get permit.

Many greetings to Sonia & Ghita.

I shall depart into the woods to write the stories when they come.[2]

D. H. L.

[PS.]
The nib is bent.
You may send what you like *into* Germany.

---

1 Koteliansky sent only one story; see Letter No. 201. He was, however, probably considering asking Lawrence to edit another story by Bunin as well.

2 Lawrence means, of course, "rewrite the stories."

200 [HOTEL KRONE
Ebersteinburg
bei Baden-Baden]
15 June 1921

Today came the *Einstein*—very many thanks. When you send
me the pen, I shall send cheque.—Today also I have posted to
you four copies of *Psychoan. & the Unconscious*. Will you
give Barbara two copies, one for herself, one for Eder. I
wrote Eder's name in one. Keep one for yourself.—I wrote your
name—and let the other one lie for a while, I may ask you
to send it to somebody else. I trouble you so far because of
the bother of getting permissions here.

Write to me Hôtel Krone, Ebersteinburg bie Baden-Baden.
I wait to hear about the stories.

D. H. L.

201　HOTEL KRONE
Ebersteinburg
bei Baden-Baden
16 June 1921

My dear Kot,

Yesterday the *Gent. from S. Francisco* & the pen: very many thanks. Have read the *Gent.*—& in spite of its lugubriousness, grin with joy. Was Bunin one of the Gorki-Capri crowd?—or only a visitor? But it is screamingly good of Naples & Capri: so comically like the reality: only just a trifle too earnest about it. I will soon get it written over: don't think your text needs much altering. I love a "little carved peeled-off dog"[1]—it is too good to alter.

For the pen many thanks. I write this with it.

I will send you *Einstein* when I leave Germany. Can't face another permission-form the size of a wall-poster just yet.

Haven't heard from Mountsier for two weeks. He was going to Ireland to journalise. Send him a p.c. to 36 Guilford St.— and to hell if he is fidgetty. But he's not fidgetty—you'll like him. And I really think *The Dial* might print the *Gent.* And if so, we get at least 100 dollars. Good for us!

Einstein isn't so metaphysically marvelous, but I like him for taking out the pin which fixed down our fluttering little physical universe.

Greet Sonia *vielmal*.

D. H. L.

[PS.]
Don't know what *Einstein* cost: but send 7/- —and don't cavil with me about it.—What was poor Ott [*sic*] nose out of joint for, I wonder: didn't the *Times* say that Hermione was a grand and sincere figure, among a nest of perverse puppies?

So the wet flea[2] has hopped to Switzerland—which Kurort? What is Campbell's address?

in *The Dial* (January 1922), where "The Gentleman from San Francisco"
was published. Later, when the story appeared in *The Gentleman from San
Francisco and Other Stories*, translated from the Russian by [D. H. Lawrence]
S. S. Koteliansky and Leonard Woolf (London, 1922), the animal had become
"a tiny, cringing, hairless little dog." For a full discussion of D. H. Lawrence's
role as a translator of Russian literature see my dissertation, "D. H. Lawrence's
Response to Russian Literature," *DA*, XXVI, 4678–79 (Seattle, 1965).

2 J. M. Murry.

202

VILLA ALPENSEE
Zell-am-See
Austria
25 August [1921]

I sent the *Gentleman* to Miss Monk [1]—she has typed it & is
posting one copy to Thayer [2] of the *Dial*, one to you. I wrote
to Thayer—he is in Paris—but have only his London address.

> c/o Brown Shipley & Co.
> 1 Pall Mall W.

Hope he will put the thing through.

We leave directly for Florence. Write there.

D. H. L.

[PS.]
Address: 32 Via dei Bardi
         Florence

1 Violet Monk, later Mrs. Violet Stevens, a friend of Lawrence during the Hermitage periods (1918–19). See "The Lawrence Circle," *C.B.*, I, 525; and "Who's Who in the Lawrence Letters," *C.L.*, I, liv.

2 Scofield Thayer, editor of *The Dial*.

203 32 VIA DEI BARDI
Florence
[26 August 1921]

Got here yesterday—found your letter—Miss Monk,
Grimsbury Farm, Long Lane near Newbury—is a Hermitage
friend, & ought to have sent you that MS by now. I have
written her about it. You can write also if you don't get it
soon. As for little JMM, he is too rotten to kick. I do hope
Thayer will take the *Gent.* You must find it dreary in No. 5.[1]

D. H. L.

---

1 No. 5 Acacia Road, St. John's Wood, London—Koteliansky's address.

---

204 [32 VIA DEI BARDI
Florence]
16 September [1921]

Your letter today. I heard from Miss Monk that she had sent
a copy of *Gentleman* to Thayer of the *Dial,* and a copy to
you. I wait to hear from Thayer. We leave next week—going
to Taormina. Write to Fontana Vecchia—I didn't want you
to pay *anything* for the typing—please cash the 15/–.—You
are not trying Squire.[1]—I want my new novel postponed till
spring.—Florence wildly festivating Dante—such a row.

Greet Sonia & Grisha & Ghita.

D. H. L.

---

1 "Sir John Collings Squire (1884—), early pseudonym Solomon Eagle, English
poet, journalist, and editor; founder and editor (1919–34) of *The London Mercury*"
(*C.B.*, III, 671). Although himself a contributor to *The London Mercury* (see
Lawrence's letter to J. C. Squire in *C.L.*, II, 645), Lawrence disliked Squire. See
Lawrence's letter to J. M. Murry dated 20 May 1929: "The animal that I am you
instinctively dislike—just as all the Lynds and Squires and Eliots and Goulds
instinctively dislike it" (*A.H.*, p. 801).

FONTANA VECCHIA
Taormina
[Sicily]
Friday [30 September 1921]

My dear Kot,

We got here last night.[1] I pick up the first bit of paper I find, in a medley of unpacking, to tell you that Thayer will publish *The Gentleman*, but that *page 5.* is missing from his manuscript. Can you see to that? His address is

Hotel Adlon, Unter der Linden
Berlin

I have no word from Thayer himself: my letter was from Robert Mountsier, 142 Marylebone Rd.

He will tell you anything you may want to know.

I am so glad to be back.—*So* tired of Europe—every new place one sees makes one more sick.

Greet everybody

D. H. L.

---

1 Compare *P.R.*, p. 64, where Moore suggests that Lawrence returned to Taormina on 27 or 28 September.

FONTANA VECCHIA
Taormina
Sicilia
10 November [1921]

My dear Kot,

I have meant day after day to write. But this summer my whole will-to-correspond has collapsed.

I had yours about Thayer. Did he ever properly acknowledge yours? And he ought to have paid you by now. I wonder if you are hard up. If you are, you won't hesitate to tell me, will you. My English money is at the last crumbs, but thank goodness I've got some dollars in America—when Mountsier will put me into touch with them. So just let me know if you are in need.

Mountsier I suppose has gone back to New York. He is one of those irritating people who have generalised detestations: his particular ones being Jews, Germans, and Bolshevists. So unoriginal. He got on my nerves badly in Germany.

What are you doing about the rest of the Bunin book?[1] Who is working over your translation? Perhaps Woolf. If it isn't very long, I'll do it if you wish me to.

I am getting my short stories into order, and settling up my MSS. I want to get all straight. I want to feel free to go away from Europe at any minute. I am so tired of it. It is a dead dog which begins to stink intolerably. Again I entertain the idea of going to America. A woman offered us a house, an adobe cottage in Taos, New Mexico, on a mountain with Indians near.[2] Really, I want to go. I will go to the States. Really, I think the hour has struck, to go. *Basta la mossa!* I hope we can go in January. I hope we can get a merchant ship from Palermo or Naples to New Orleans or to Galveston in Texas. You will say it is just my winter influenza which makes me think of America. But finally I shall go. But don't tell anybody.

I feel very sick with England. It is a dead dog that died of a love disease like syphilis.

Here nothing happens. It has been very warm and *scirocco*, and one's head feeling as if it were going to float away. Now suddenly it is very cold, and snow on Calabria. The devil's in the world. We see a few people here. But nobody who means anything at all to me.

Secker wrote in a great funk because Heseltine is threatening a law suit against *Women in Love*, for libel. He says Halliday is himself & the Pussum is his wife. Well, they are both such abject shits it is a pity they can't be flushed down a sewer. But they may try to extort money from Secker.

I ought to have written to Barbara, but I simply hadn't it in me. Why should I? I see Murry and the long-dying blossom Katharine have put forth new literary buds. Let 'em. I did a second volume to *Psychoanalysis & the Unconscious*,[3] and sent it to America. Nowadays I depend almost entirely on America for my living. I think Seltzer has just published at five dollars the slight travel book *Sea and Sardinia*. If he sends me copies I will send you one.

Tell me if there is any news. I know there isn't, except the old startler that All is Bloody.

Greet Sonia, Grisha, & the long-plaited Ghita.

And be greeted.

D. H. Lawrence

---

1 *The Gentleman from San Francisco and Other Stories* (London, 1922).

2 Mabel Sterne, better known now as Mabel Dodge Luhan, whose memoir of Lawrence, *Lorenzo in Taos*, was published in 1932.

3 *Fantasia of the Unconscious* (New York, 1922).

---

207 [FONTANA VECCHIA
Taormina
Sicily]
20 December [1921]

I sent you and Sonia a book for Christmas—though I feel very unChristmas-like. We really do think of going to *New* Mexico—which is still U.S.A. A compromise. No, I can't come back to England—can't. Don't believe in your "good simple people"—all Murrys etc.

Has that miserable *Dial* paid you? I wish we could sail in Jan.

D. H. L.

FONTANA VECCHIA
Taormina
Sicilia
26 December 1921

Dear Kot,

I got the cheque for £12-odd. I *wish* you would let it be 1/4
for me.—I am not justified in taking half.—The *Dial* should
have paid you *more*, also.

I had a return touch of influenza—and Christmas in bed. But
I don't care. It saved me going out to a horrible Xmas
dinner.

We really think of going to New Mexico. I am toiling to
find a ship. A woman¹ offers us a house in Taos, near Santa
Fe: mountains—6000 ft. high—aboriginal indians [*sic*]—sun
worship—fine bright climate. I want to find a ship to New
Orleans or Galveston or Los Angeles. Will sail in Jan. or
Feb. if possible. It is U.S.A., so not off the map. I am afraid
there is a colony of New York artists in Taos. Evil everywhere.
But I want to go—to try.

We only saw the Carswells in Florence in September—
voilà tout.

Be kind enough to send me a packet of primus stove *needles,*
will you—they only cost a few pence—as *sample*, registered
is the best way to post. Don't do it except when it is absolutely
no trouble.—I sent you *Contes Drolatiques*—hope you got
it.

Cold here.

Saluti

D. H. L.

---

1 Mabel Dodge Luhan. Some of Lawrence's misgivings about accepting Mrs.
Luhan's invitation are clearly expressed in his letter to her dated 5 November
1921. See *C.L.*, II, 671–72.

FONTANA VECCHIA
Taormina
Sicily
14 Jan 1922

My dear Kot,

I had the *Dial* by the same post as your letter. They are impudent people, I had told them not to put my name.[1] Of course they did it themselves. But I don't really care. Why bother.

I had the empty envelope of the primus needles: just ripped a bit at the side, & the packet extracted. Inevitably. But that also doesn't matter, because Smythe brought me three packets from England, two days ago.

I keep chasing ships to get to New Orleans, so as to avoid New York. But every ship seems either to go somewhere else, or to decide not to go at all at the last minute. I may get a *Cie Transatlantique* boat from Bordeaux next month—or I may go White Star, Naples to New York, next month. We will see. I feel like you, that I am messing about on the edge of everything. But I feel also I *can't* come back into Europe.— Taos I hear has a colony of New York artists there. Oh God! Yet I feel it is my destiny at least to *try* the States, if only to know I hate them. *Dunque*—!—And here, everybody is pleasant and has tea-parties and at least £500 a year. And it feels so empty. What isn't empty—as far as the world of man goes.

I too think of the Bucks Cottage fairly often, and still sometimes lull myself with:

> "Ranane Sadihkim
> Sadihkim Badanoi."[2]

If only there were some of the dark old spirit of that, left in the world! Meanwhile one is eight years older, and a thousand years more disconnected with everything, and more frustrated. *Quoi faire! Che fare?*

I am glad you liked the *Gent* when he was done. Of course you do exactly as you like about the Wolff [*sic*] book:[3] that has

nothing to do with me. Only send me a copy when it comes.—
Apparently Secker is going to buy sheets of *Sea and Sardinia*
from Seltzer. I will send you a copy of that when it appears:
which, if I know Secker, will be in about ten month's time.

Well, at least it is sunny and there is a bit of spring in the
air, the sun is warm & the almonds are in bud. Why should
one get depressed. But I have had flu—not badly—for three
weeks.

If we go to Taos, and if we get on there, perhaps you will
come too: if there could be something doing: and if you
would like to back me up. *Vediamo!*

*a rivederci, e sta bene, e molti saluti a Sonia anche a Ghita e
Grisha.*

D. H. L.

---

1 *The Dial* (January 1922), pp. 47–68, had published Ivan Bunin's "The Gentleman from San Francisco," translated from the Russian by D. H. Lawrence and
S. S. Koteliansky.

2 This song appears to have been the origin of Lawrence's *Rananim*, the name he
chose for his ideal community. For some further notes on the meaning of the
word, see K. W. Gransden, "*Rananim*: D. H. Lawrence's Letters to S. S. Koteliansky," *Twentieth Century*, CLIX (January 1956), pp. 23–24.

3 Ivan Bunin, *The Gentleman from San Francisco and Other Stories*, translated by
S. S. Koteliansky and Leonard Woolf (London, 1922). See note 1 to
219.

FONTANA VECCHIA
Taormina
Sicily
20 Jan 1922

My dear Kot,

Will you post me a copy of the *Occult Review*: & if possible
a catalogue of books on Occult Science: there is a publisher
whose name I forget. Any time when you are near Charing
Cross Road will do. You said you wanted to send me
something.—*The Occult Review*—or *The Occultist Review*:
that also I forget. I should just like to see this month's issue.

Well, I said I was going to America. But the moment I feel
the ship is there to take me, I fight shy. I *can't* go to America.
Not yet. It is too raw for me, & I too tender for it. We must
wait a bit. I have got a friend in Kandy, Ceylon, who asks me
to go there & stay with him.[1] I think I shall do that: quite
soon. I feel I can fortify myself in the east, against the west.
You will say I am foolish: but it is my destiny. I do intend
later to go to America. But I must first have something else
inside me.

I believe Secker is going to bring out *Sea & Sardinia*.[2] It is
just a light sketch book: but personal: so it would amuse you.
I will send you a copy when it is ready.

You will be glad to have Sonia back.[3] I shudder to think of
that cave, the flood of newspapers rising silently in a fog of
cigarette smoke, and you swimming slowly and hopelessly,
in the heavy ocean of printed slush, gasping to sink.

Greet Sonia, and I hope she is happy to be back in the
cavern, and I hope she'll order the cart for the newspapers at
once.

D. H. L.

PS. The brilliant idea strikes me that you might ring up
Thomas Cook's, Ludgate Circus, and ask them what boats
there are from *Malta* or *Naples* to *Colombo*, Ceylon, and
what is the price of a cabin for two, first class: or berths for

two, first class. I have written to Malta & to Naples, but you never know those people, plus the Italian post.—Any ship from S. Italy or Malta to Colombo.

D. H. L.

---

1 Earl Brewster. See "The Lawrence Circle," *C.B.*, II, 430.

2 Published by Secker in April 1923.

3 Sonia, i.e. Mrs. Farbman, must have, therefore, continued to live at No. 5 Acacia Road, St. John's Wood, London.

FONTANA VECCHIA
Taormina
Sicily
2 February 1922

My dear Kot,

Thank you for your letter, for the *Occult Review*, and for the Cook's letter, all safely come.

The fares are awful! But I want to go. Probably we'll go second class from Malta, & bust my dollars. I want to go to the east: I believe one will find a bit of peace there. After all I am not so clever but that my life consists in a relation between me myself, that I am, and the world around me, that I am in contact with, & which may or may not be illusory. But anyhow I need now another illusion: palm-trees & elephants and old old religions and yellow-dark people.[1] Vado pure! anche questo mese. Ci ho lì un amico americano, Brewster lui vuol studiare il buddismo. Ha una casa grande e vecchia vicina a Kandy—non è mica ricco—sposato, con una bambina. Andiamo aggiungerci a lui. Sai che sono stanco qui, a sbraitare con tutta questa gente. Sai che bisogna andarmene, via, via: sì, sì, non posso più qui. Sai che ci sono sempre gli angeli e gli arcangeli, troni, poteri, cherubini, serafini—tutto il coro costà. Ma qui sempre queste bestie battisate chi fanno udirsi, questo e nient altro. Io me ne vo. Camminando si arriva: neppure nel sepolcro: ma un po' fuori di questo mondo troppo troppo umano. Tante cose che ci sono nascoste: devo attaccarmici, a quellè.

Perchè scrivo italiano, sbagliato anche? Perchè son'sciocco, ma stanco a modo, e vorrei cambiarmi la pelle, come la biscia. Ogni modo me ne vo. C'era una volta il paradiso laggiù, in Ceilan. Tu non credi? Io sì. Cerco anche un po questo paradiso. Abitava proprio li, Adamo, quell' antenato.

Cosa vuoi, dunque? Cosa me ne vuoi? Ch'io me chiudo in una grotta Numero 5, come tu? Dio liberi!—in una tana pieno zeppo di giornali? Mai, amico mio, mai. Foglie di cannella, non di giornali.

Un poco triste anche, come quella biscia quando deve cambiarsi la pelle. Ma senza guai non ci sono guadagni. Ti!— tu mi dispiaci: rannichiarsi là in fondo di una tana No. 5, senza arrischiarti nemmeno un pelo della barba:—cosa devo pensare di te?—anche il rospo va alla caccia: ma tu, accoccolato in un cantuccio della tana, non fai niente che gracchiare. No no! La vita è da spendere, non da conservarvi.

Benedicite

D. H. L.

[PS.]

Comando a Seltzer di mandarti questi *Tartaruge*. Non ti piaceranno pure.

---

1 Following is an English translation of Lawrence's Italian: I am going, too, this month. I've got an American friend over there, Brewster, who wants to study Buddhism. He has a big, old house near Kandy—he is by no means rich—married, with a daughter. We are going to join him. You know that I am tired here, gabbing with all these people. You know that I must go away—away, away: yes, yes, I cannot stand it here any longer. You know that there are always the angels and the archangels, thrones, powers, cherubs, seraphs—that whole hierarchy. But here are only the baptized beasts who make themselves heard—this and nothing else. I am going away. Travelling you arrive: not to the grave—but somewhere outside this much too human world. So many things are hidden from us: I must attach myself to those.

Do you wonder why I write Italian? Because I am dull and weary, and I should like to shed my skin as the snake does. I am going definitely. Paradise was there once, in Ceylon. Don't you believe it? I do! I am tentatively searching for that paradise. That is where he lived, Adam, that forefather of ours.

What are you after, then? What must I do? Shut myself up in the Cave at No. 5 as you do? God forbid!—in a den plumbful of newspapers? Never, my friend, never! Leaves of cinnamon for me, not of newspapers.

I am sad, too, like the snake which must shed its skin. But one does not gain anything without suffering. You!—you irk me: hiding yourself at the bottom of that Cave at No. 5, without even risking one hair of your beard. What must I make of you? Even a toad goes out hunting: but you, crouching in the shelter of the cave don't do anything but croak. No, no! Life is ours to be spent, not to be saved.

Benedicite

D. H. L.

[PS.] I asked Seltzer to send you *Tortoises*. You won't like it.

---

212 FONTANA VECCHIA
Taormina
Sicily
Friday [17 February 1922] [1]

We leave Taormina on Monday for Palermo—throes of
packing—we sail from Naples on the 26th—by *S.S.
Osterley*, Orient Line for Colombo—about 14 days. Address:

> "Ardnaree"
> Lake View Estate
> Kandy, Ceylon

Write me a line at once. I ordered you *Sea & Sardinia* from
Secker—tell me if he sends it. Feel so queer, actually to be
going. But am glad—so glad.—Palm trees & elephants &
dark people: *incantevole!*

D. H. L.

---

1 See *P.R.*, p. 65, for the date of Lawrence's departure from Taormina.

---

213 NAPLES
Saturday [25 February 1922]

We sail tomorrow on the *Osterley*—write to Ceylon.

D. H. L.

R.M.S. "OSTERLEY"
Tuesday 7 March [1922]

My dear Kot

I got your cable to the ship—so nice of you to think of us.
Here we are ten days at sea. I like it so much: everybody
pleasant and no showing off, and plenty of room. The ship
isn't half full, except the third class. We have come second,
and it is perfectly comfortable and is good as anyone could
wish. I enjoy it very much.

We are now in the Arabian Sea steering straight for Colombo,
where we arrive on Sunday night or Monday morning. The
sea is lovely, with white "lambs" everywhere, but the
boat is as steady as a street.

We had a few hours in Port Said, and it is still just like
Arabian Nights, with water-sellers & scribes in the street, &
Koran readers and a yelling crowd. And I loved coming through
the Suez Canal—It takes 18 hours—and you see the Arabs
and their camels and the rosy-yellow desert with its low
palm-trees and its hills of sharp sand. Almost one seems to
walk through it. It gave me rather a nostalgia for the
desert. Then Mount Sinai like a vengeful dagger that was
dipped in blood many ages ago, so sharp and defined and
old pink-red in colour.—I spend the day talking small-talk
with Australians on board—rather nice people—and
translating *Mastro-don Gesualdo*[1] and having meals—and
time passes like a sleep—the curious sense that nothing is
real except just this ship—nothing exists except just this ship. I
do wonder how we shall feel when we get off and are in
Ceylon. At the moment it seems as if we should just go on for
ever on this boat. But it is so nice too.—You have the address:
"Ardnaree," Lake View Estate, *Kandy*, Ceylon. Greet
Sonia.

D. H. L.

---

1 By Giovanni Verga, published by Thomas Seltzer (New York, 1923). For a
discussion of Lawrence as a translator of Verga, see Giovanni Cecchetti, "Verga
and D. H. Lawrence's Translations," *Comparative Literature*, IX (1959), pp.
333–44.

215 KANDY,
[Ceylon]
3rd April [1922]

So hot here—and I don't like Ceylon—shall probably go on
in about three weeks time to Australia—one may as well
move on, once one has started. I feel I don't care what becomes
of me.

D. H. L.

---

216 ARDNAREE
[Lake View Estate]
Kandy, Ceylon
17 April 1922

My dear Kot

I had your letter. You are right, Ceylon is too hot. One
sweats & sweats, & gets thinner and thinner. I am not staying.
We are sailing next Monday, 24th, for West Australia—the
address c/o Mrs. Jenkins,[1] Strawberry Hill, *Perth*, West
Australia.

It has been lovely to *see* Ceylon. But I feel the East is not
for me. It seems to me the life drains away from one here.
The old people here say just the same: they say it is the
natives that drain the life out of one, and that's how it seems
to me. One could quite easily sink into a kind of apathy,
like a lotus on a muddy pond, indifferent to anything. And
that apparently is the lure of the east: this peculiar stagnant
apathy where one doesn't bother about a thing, but drifts
on from minute to minute. I am not at all sure that we shall
like Australia either. But it seems to me *en route*. We shall
stay with Mrs. Jenkins for a time: if we don't care for that,
go on to Sydney. I am taking a ticket to Sydney, as it only
costs £6 more. And then after trying Sydney & New South
Wales, if I don't like that we shall go across the Pacific to

San Francisco, and then I shall have to sit down and earn some money to take the next stride, for I shall be blued. But I don't care. Now I have started, I will go on and on till I am more or less sure. And if I like none of the places I shall come back to Europe with my mind made up, and settle down permanently in England or Italy. So there's the programme.

Of course one doesn't work here at all—never would.

I send you a little Kandy brass tray *via* my sister. I hope it won't take long for you to get it: if the post doesn't swallow it. The lion is supposed to be a Buddha symbol, but it might just as well be the lion of Judah.—By the way I detest Buddha, upon a slight contact: affects me like a mud pool that has no bottom to it.—One learns to value what one actually knows & possesses, and to have a wholesome indifference to strange gods. Anyhow these little rathole Buddhist temples turn my stomach.

Well, next from Australia.

Yrs.

D. H. Lawrence

---

1 "Mrs. A. L. Jenkins, an Australian friend, who met the Lawrences aboard the *Osterley* from Naples to Ceylon in Feb.–Mar., 1922, and helped entertain them during their visit in W.A. in May 1922" ("The Lawrence Circle," *C.B.*, II, 434). Mrs. Jenkins' meeting with the Lawrences is described by H. E. L. Priday in *C.B.*, II, 131–33, 150–52.

217 P & O. S. N. Co.
S. S.
20 May 1922

Dear Kot

Here we are in the Gt. Australian Bight, rolling on again. We
stayed two weeks in Western Australia: weird land, marvellous blue sky, clear air, pure & untouched. Then the endless
hoary grey "bush"—which is gum trees, rather thinly
scattered, like a thin wood, with a heathy sort of undergrowth,
like a moor with trees. People very friendly, but slow and
as if unwilling to take the next step: as if everything was a
bit too much for them. We are going now to Sydney—
calling at Adelaide & Melbourne. We get to Sydney on May
28. I don't know how we shall like it—but Frieda wants to
have a little house & stay a few months anyhow. She is tired
of moving on. But I like it. I like the feeling of rolling on.
I shall have to cable to Seltzer to give me money & he'll
have to give it me. I don't care.—I think from Sydney we
shall visit the South Sea Islands—think of our "*Rananim*"—
on the way across to San Francisco. If you were here you
would understand Katharine so much better. She is *very*
Australian—or New Zealand. Wonder how she is.—I got a
mail in Perth just as I left—nothing from you. Things
follow after me in time. I haven't got an address—perhaps
c/o Thomas Seltzer, 5 West 50th. St. N. York—or else wait
till I can tell you. It's a long time now to England—boat
takes six weeks—fortnightly mail.—I'm not working—don't
want to.

How are you all?

D. H. L.

218 [WYEWURK]
Thirroul, N.S.W.
[Australia]
5 June [1922]

We have come down here about 40 miles south of Sydney—
taken such a nice little bungalow on the edge of the Pacific—
can bathe all to ourselves. It is queer—a big, free land, rather
fascinating. But I feel awfully foreign with the people,
although they are all English by origin. It is rather like the
Midlands of England, the life, very familiar and rough—and
I just shrink away from it. If I can write we shall stay a few
months. Then I really think we shall cross to San Francisco.

Write me a line c/o Robert Mountsier, 417 West 118 Street,
New York. So long since I had any mail.

D. H. L.

[PS.]
Pardon the p.c.—I can't bring myself to write letters here.

219
Thirroul, N.S.W.
[Australia]
9 July 1922

My dear Kot,

I had your letter, and the Bunin book next day.[1] But not the
Mrs. Tolstoi reminiscences.[2]

What a pretty cover Bunin has! But the tales are not very
good: *Gentleman* is much the best. Some of Wolf's [*sic*]
sentences take a bit of reading. Look at the last sentence on
p. 71.[3]

You should have had *Sea and Sardinia* and *Aaron's Rod* by
now: unless Martin Secker is playing me dodges and not
sending out the presentation copies as I asked.—I shall be
able to read this famous *Ulysses*[4] when I go to America. I
doubt he's a trickster.

We still propose sailing on August 10th by the *Tahiti*, to
San Francisco: arrive Sept. 4th. Send me a line and tell me all
the happenings. I heard from a friend in Paris that the Bunin
book was noticed in the *Times*. What was the notice like?
I had Cath. Carswell's *Camomile* here: slight, but good, I
thought. What are the notices of that?—By the way, don't
you think Secker ought to try that *Shestov* again now?
You press him about it, & I'll write him too. It would certainly
sell some now.

I have nearly finished my novel[5] here—but such a novel! Even
the Ulysseans will spit at it.

There is a great fascination in Australia. But for the remains
of a fighting Conscience, I would stay. One can be so
absolutely indifferent to the world one has been previously
condemned to. It is rather like falling out of a picture and
finding oneself on the floor, with all the gods and men
left behind in the picture. If I stayed here six months I should
have to stay for ever—there is something so remote & far
off and utterly indifferent to our European world, in the very
air. I should go a bit further away from Sydney, and go

"bush."—We don't know one single soul—not a soul comes
to the house. And I can't tell you how I like it. I could live
like that forever: and drop writing even a letter: sort of come
undone from everything. But my conscience tells me not yet.
So we go to the States—to stay as long as we feel like it.
But to England I do not want to return.—Though no, I
don't think you flatter me. I do think I've got more in me
than all those fluttering people, good & bad, in London.
But they are *antipatico*. They are distasteful to me.

Write me a line, c/o Mountsier—or else just to *Taos*, New
Mexico, U.S.A.

Greet Grisha & Sonya [*sic*] the tall Ghita, and starve Fox for
one day, for my sake.

Yrs.

D. H. L.

---

1 *The Gentleman from San Francisco and Other Stories*, translated from the
Russian by S. S. Koteliansky and Leonard Woolf (London, 1922). In the first
edition, an erratum slip was enclosed as follows: "'The Gentleman from San
Francisco' is translated by D. H. Lawrence and S. S. Koteliansky. Owing to a
mistake Mr. Lawrence's name was omitted from the title-page. The three other
stories are translated by Mr. Koteliansky and Mr. Woolf."

2 This would be *The Autobiography of Countess Sophie Tolstoi*, translated by S. S.
Koteliansky and Leonard Woolf (Richmond, 1922).

3 The sentence reads as follows: "Perhaps, too, there was in her soul a drop
of purely feminine pleasure that here was a man to whom she could give her
small commands, with whom she could talk, half seriously and half jokingly as
a mentor, with that freedom which their difference in age so naturally allowed—
a man who was so devoted to her whole household, in which, however, the first
person—this, of course, very soon became clear—was for him, nevertheless,
she herself."

4 James Joyce's *Ulysses* was published in America in 1922.

5 *Kangaroo*, published in September 1923. See *B.*, pp. 65–66.

220

"Countess Tolstoi" came two days ago— have read her
rather sad, & bit ridiculous: very interesting. Had your letter
too. Hope Secker sent you *Aaron* as bidden. We are packed
up, and go to Sydney tomorrow—sail on Friday. The sea
is lovely & calm—I look forward to the voyage—hope it will
be pleasant.—America will seem much nearer to England—
probably we shall be in London next spring. How do you
like the look of Thirroul?[1] The houses are all wood & tin
—but it is nice here, so easy & sunny.

Greet the Cave-dwellers.

D. H. L.

---

[1] A reference to the picture of Thirroul on the postcard.

221 [PALACE HOTEL
San Francisco]
8 September [1922]

Been here a day or two—sunny, hot, noisy, but not unpleasant. Leave tonight for Santa Fe—will write properly
from Taos, where I expect my mail.

Greet everybody.

D. H. L.

---

222 TAOS
New Mexico
U.S.A.
18 September 1922

My dear Kot.

I have your letter. We arrived in Taos from San Francisco on
the 11th—but Mabel Sterne immediately sent me motoring
off to an Apache gathering 120 miles away across desert &
through cañons. Weird to see these Red Indians. The Apaches
are not very *sympatisch*, but their camp, tents, horses, lake
very picturesque. This is high tableland desert country,
6000 ft. up: & then mountains near. Mabel Sterne, who is a
rich American woman, lends us this new & very charming
adobe house which she built for us: because she wants me to
write this country up. God knows if I shall. America is more or
less as I expected: shove or be shoved. But still it has a
bigness, a sense of space, & a certain sense of rough freedom,
which I like.—I dread the pettyfogging narrowness of
England. Still, I think to come on in the spring. It is still hot,
sunny here, like summer.

I am so sorry you are ill & forlorn in the Cave. I wish you
could come out.

If Secker hasn't sent you a copy of *Aaron*, it is because he is a nasty little fellow.—I think the book sells pretty well here. Seltzer had a "suppression" trial—*Women in Love*, & *Schnitzler* & *Young Girls Diary*—and he won with triumph.[1] So he telegraphs. I believe I have got £500. in the bank, so if you want any, I hope you'll say. Say if you are hard up. I have taken money from you & not felt in any way constrained, so surely you can do the same with me.—I am paying back at last the little bit that Eddie Marsh and Ottoline once gave me: so long ago.—If you are short of money, just say "Yes, I am hard up."

I will write again very soon. Letters should not take more than a fortnight now. This is not so far away: but 30 miles from the railway, over the desert.

Hang on, & don't let them get you under.

D. H. L.

---

[1] For a full account of Lawrence's struggle against the "suppression" of his works, see "D. H. Lawrence and the Censor Morons" by Harry T. Moore in *D. H. Lawrence: Sex, Literature and Censorship* (New York, 1953), pp. 9–32.

DEL MONTE RANCH
Questa
New Mexico
4 December 1922

My dear Kot

I have been waiting for an answer from you to my last letter. I asked you too to send to Mountsier a copy of each of the *Signatures*[1] if you still had any. Why this non-answering. I hope you're not downright ill at last. That Cave! You ought to be out of it.

You see we've moved. Too much Mabel Sterne at Taos. This is only 17 miles away—but another world. The last foothills of the Rocky Mts.—forest & snow mountains behind—and below, the desert, with other mountains very far off, west. It is fine. We have an old 5-room log cabin—and chop down our trees & have big fires. It is rough, but very agreeable. Then we ride horseback when we have time. I feel very different.

America makes one feel hard—would make one feel bitter, if one were not too old for bitterness.

I asked Seltzer to send you a copy of *England my England*, short stories. I won't send you *Fantasia of the Unconscious*, that would bore you. And you must be sick of books, anyhow.

I'll send a word to Katharine, *via* you. Perhaps. Anyway greet her from me.

I intend to stay here till March or April: if I don't move before. Seltzer is coming at Christmas to see me. Oh God!—I am repeatedly invited to go East & lecture. I might be a rich man. But shoulder to shoulder with Gilly[2] and Hughie Walpole, no. I won't go.

I still think to come to England in the spring. What is happening in the world? We never see a newspaper, save the *Denver Post*, which is all Headlines & Murder. I know nothing. What is going to happen? Anything? I dreamed that Albert Stopford[3] came to see me and told me that something big, very big, was imminent: like another war. Dreams! I don't care anyhow.

Do you remember the Christmas in Bucks? 4—a cycle seems to have revolved since then, and come back somewhat to the same place. I feel a *bit* like I felt in Bucks. *Rananim!*

Well, be well. God knows what a state you're in. Are you fat, fox-like?

Many greetings to Sonia & Ghita & Grisha.

D. H. L.

---

1 Lawrence probably wanted these in connection with "The Crown" which was published in *Reflections on the Death of a Porcupine and Other Essays* (Philadelphia, 1925).

2 Gilly is probably Gilbert Cannan, but see *C.L.*, II, 729, where Moore suggests Gilly might refer to Chesterton.

3 According to E. W. Tedlock, Jr., Frieda remembered Albert Stopford "as an English friend, an aristocrat" (*The Frieda Lawrence Collection of D. H. Lawrence Manuscripts: A Descriptive Bibliography* [Albuquerque, N.M., 1948], p. 319). Writing to Mary Cannan on [?12 February 1922], Lawrence reported: "Albert Stopford is here—the man who made some sort of scandal, I don't know what. He's really very nice: but getting oldish" (*C.L.*, II, 692). No further information appears to be available.

4 1914.

DEL MONTE RANCH
Questa
New Mexico
12 February 1923

My dear Kot

Your letter just come with Murry's enclosed.—Yes, I feel with
you about that institution—there is no easy way out—no way
of ecstasy and uplifting—it's just a bitter fight through thorns
—and one must fight, or die, like Katharine.[1]—It is terrible
to live and see life after life collapse, and more & more
ruin pile up.—I feel bitter in America: it makes one suffer,
this continent, a nasty, too much suffering.

I did write to Murry at once. And from New Zealand I sent
K. a post card care of Ottoline.

I ordered you *Fantasia*.

I hope you are well.

D. H. L.

---

1 Katherine Mansfield died 9 January 1923. For an account of her death and
burial, see Antony Alpers, *Katherine Mansfield: A Biography* (New York, 1953),
pp. 359–60.

225

DEL MONTE RANCH
Questa
New Mexico
25 February 1923

My dear Kot,

I had your registered letter only last night: & then brought out from Questa by a man coming here.

I have such a deep mistrust of England. When I want to come, I can't, I feel my endless mistrust won't let me. And I have fixed up everything to go to Mexico City. We leave here in two weeks time, and I expect to be in the City of Mexico on March 20th. I will let you know the address there. And then I will tell you again how I feel about coming to England. Maybe suddenly I shall decide to come? *Quién Sabe?*

I am writing this to Murry too.—I ordered you various books from Secker & Seltzer.

D. H. L.

[PS.]
I have not much faith in literary ventures, either! *vieux jeu!*

226

[TAOS
New Mexico]
March 16 [1923]

We leave tomorrow for Mexico City—expect to get there 23rd. I will send you an address as soon as I have one. Many thanks for *Signature* MS. Did Mountsier ask for it? He is no longer my agent.

D. H. L.

HOTEL MONTE CARLO
Av. Uruguay 64
Mexico City
11 April 1923

Dear Kot—

We have been here about three weeks—in this noisy, ram-
shackle town. But it is anyhow very free and easy. We are
going tomorrow to Puebla—then Tehuacan & Orizaba. It is
just possible I shall take a house here for the summer—if I
don't come to England.

I find it is hard, when it comes to the point, to make up my
mind for England—I don't know why.—Do you remember,
during the war I always wanted to come to Mexico. I like
it here, too: so few pretenses of any sort.—The young man
is a young Californian [1]—in the picture—& the others the
two Mexican chauffeurs. Has Secker sent you all the books I
ordered for you?

Grüsse

D. H. L.

---

[1] Probably Willard Johnson. For his connection with Lawrence, see *C.B.*, II,
492–94.

Jalisco
10 June 1923

Dear Kot,

Your letter today—hope the magazine[1] does well.

Don't think of the money—you don't owe me anything. Truly I don't want it, at the present have enough. I intend to leave here at the end of this month if I can finish the novel on which I am working.[2] We go to New York, and ought to be in England by August. It only depends, now, on my finishing the first draft of this novel here.

So—auf wiedersehen

D. H. L.

---

1 The magazine was *The Adelphi*. For an account of Murry's and Koteliansky's roles in the publication of *The Adelphi*, see F. A. Lea, *The Life of John Middleton Murry* (London, 1959), pp. 105–19. Koteliansky was the business manager and also contributed translations of Russian writers to the magazine. Lawrence's and Koteliansky's contributions to *The Adelphi* are given in Appendix II.

2 *The Plumed Serpent.*

ZARAGOZA #4
Chapala, Jalisco
Mexico
22 June 1923

My dear Kot

The Dostoevsky & Tolstoi books have come: & many thanks.[1]
What a dismal time Dostoevsky brought upon himself.

The *Adelphi* also came, & oh dear, I was badly disappointed.
It seemed to me so weak, apologetic, knock-kneed, with
really nothing to justify its existence. A sort of beggar's
whine through it all. Mr. Wells' parsnips floating in warm
butter. Mr. Joiner screamingly ridiculous.

No really! Is this the best possible in England?

We are going to New York in July—care Thomas Seltzer.
God knows if I shall be able to bring myself across the
Atlantic. Probably I shall come back to Mexico. But I will
let you know.

One's got to *hit*, nowadays, not apologise.

How can I write to Murry?

What do you think yourself?

Write to New York.

D. H. L.

---

1 The Dostoevsky book would have been *Dostoevsky: Letters and Reminiscences*,
translated from the Russian by S. S. Koteliansky and J. Middleton Murry (London,
1923); the Tolstoi book would have been *Tolstoi's Love Letters* (to Valerya
Arseneva), translated by S. S. Koteliansky and Virginia Woolf (London, 1923).

230 [SAN ANTONIO
Texas
U.S.A.]
Friday [?13 July 1923]

Here in U.S. again going to New Orleans—then to New York—shall find letters there.[1] This already feels much nearer England.

D. H. L.

---

1 Lawrence arrived in New Orleans 15 July 1923. See *P.R.*, p. 72.

---

231 c/o THOMAS SELTZER
5 W. 50th St.
New York
7 August [1923]

My dear Kot

Have your second letter. I will write the *Dial* & ask them to let me have the MS.,[1] in case they accept it.—Isn't Thayer still in Europe?

I feel I can't come yet to England—though I came here on purpose. But it's no good, I shall have to put it off.

Thank you so much for inviting us to the Cave.

Frieda intends to come. I think she will sail on the 18th to Southampton. I asked Mary Cannan to let you know if her flat is still available, in Queens Gardens No 49. Mary herself is in Worcestershire. I think Frieda would stay a week or two in the flat, then go to Germany. For my part, I shall go to Southern California, to the mountains—and perhaps stay the winter, in which case F. will join me. We will see.

Seltzer is publishing my translation of *Mastro-don Gesualdo*— Verga's novel—in September.

It's a pity one can't go ahead with the old thread of life. But I can't take it up again this moment.

I'll see about that MS.

D. H. L.

---

1 The MS referred to here was Koteliansky's translation of Gorky's *Reminiscences of Andreyev*. For a discussion of Lawrence's part in the translation of this work see my "Introduction," pp. xxix–xxx to this volume of letters.

---

c/o THOMAS SELTZER
5 West Fiftieth Street
New York
13 August [1923]

Dear Kot

I'm not coming—not yet. *Pazienza!*

Frieda sails on the *Orbita*—Royal Mail Steam Packet Line, to
Southampton, on Saturday.—She is due in Southampton on
the following Sat. night: 25th—or on Sunday 26th. I asked
Murry to look after her all he could—and I ask you the
same.[1] Meet her at Waterloo if you can, will you. I'll ask
her to wire.

I got your MS from the *Dial* today. They accept it, & I am
going through it at once.

I think I shall go to California—perhaps sail the Pacific
Ocean.

But one day I'll come back.

D. H. L.

---

1 Murry seems to have interpreted Lawrence's request rather liberally, for when
Lawrence arrived in London in November 1923, he noticed the "chumminess"
between Murry and Frieda. It has since been revealed that during this time in
1923, Frieda "proposed to Murry that they become lovers," but "Murry turned
away from her although he was sorely tempted. They became lovers for a while
after Lawrence's death." See *C.L.*, I, xii–xiii, and *I.H.*, p. 322. The correspondence
between Murry and Frieda after Lawrence's death is revealing; see *Frieda Lawrence: The Memoirs and Correspondence*, edited by E. W. Tedlock, Jr. (New
York, 1964), pp. 352–54 *et passim*.

---

219 WEST 100th STREET
New York
17 August 1923

My dear Kot

We were on board the *Orbita* this morning. They say she will
probably not get in till Tuesday morning—the 28th. Which
is very slow. So I expect Frieda will leave Southampton the
Tuesday afternoon—be in London by evening.

I went through your Gorky MS. & returned it to *Dial* [*sic*].
I made the English correct—& a little more flexible—but
didn't change the style, since it was yours & Katharine's.
But the first ten pages were a bit crude.

I do *not* like New York. An empty place. I am going to
California on Monday:

care Knud Merrild[1]
    628 W. Twenty-Seventh St.
    Los Angeles
    Cal.

Then I'll see how I feel.

Trust all goes well.

D. H. L.

[PS.]
Perhaps you will phone Cooks or the Royal Mail Steam
Packet Co. & ask when the *Orbita* gets in.

---

1 Knud Merrild's memoir of Lawrence has been reissued as *With D. H. Lawrence
in New Mexico* (London, 1964).

LOS ANGELES
17 September 1923

My dear Kot

Your letter came on here. Thank you so much for promising to look after Frieda. I hope she landed comfortably & is having a nice time.

I sent your word to Seltzer, about the *Adelphi*. But he's not very good at doing extraneous jobs like that.

Here I've been in California eighteen days.[1] The time slips by quickly.—It is a loose, easy, rather foolish world here. But also, a great deal of falseness is also left out.—It's not so bad, in some ways.—But I think I shall go down to Mexico about this day week. I shall look once more for a little ranch. We might all meet there one day. Who knows. And it's not far from the Pacific, whoever wants to sail that sea.

I am sending F. two books: one is merely a copy of *Studies in Classic American Literature*, the other a novel by Will Comfort, a man here.[2] If Frieda is away, don't bother to send them on. If Seltzer didn't send you a copy of *Studies*, & if F. doesn't want this copy, take it. I ordered a copy sent to you.

It seems hard to me to imagine England. It's not very real to me. But I shall come back one day—if only for a time. When I am more decided about this side of the world: & this Pacific seaboard.

Am waiting for news from you all.

Grüsse

D. H. L.

---

1 Lawrence arrived in Los Angeles on 30 August 1923; he left for Mexico 25 September 1923. See *P.R.*, pp. 73–74.

2 Will Levington Comfort, who died in 1932, was an American novelist, journalist, and short story writer. His best-known novel, *Routledge Rides Alone* (1910), emerged from his experiences as a war correspondent in the Russo-Japanese War of 1904. The novel was recommended by Edwin Markham for a Nobel Prize. H. L. Mencken said of Will Comfort: "He has done, indeed, some capital melodramas. What Comfort preaches is a sort of mellowed mariolatry, a humorless exaltation of woman. Arm in arm with all this exaltation of woman, of course, goes a great suspicion of mere woman." The year 1923 marked the publication of Comfort's novel *The Public Square*, which may have been the book which Lawrence sent Koteliansky.

35 HOTEL GARCIA
Guadalajara
Jalisco
22 October 1923

My dear Kot

There, now I've tried Mexico again. I was at Chapala for a
day yesterday. The lake lovelier than before—very lovely:
but somehow gone alien to me. And a sense of suspense, of
waiting for something to happen—which something I want to
avoid.

I really think I shall come back to England now: in about a
fortnight's time, when I have arranged money & ships. I feel
it is time I saw you all again: time to talk with you & Murry
again, even if one only talks & goes away again. And I
think I would stay in England—not go to Sicily for the
winter.

It's some time since I got a letter from Frieda—my travelling.
But wherever she is, let her know, will you—or I'll write
her a note.

D. H. L.

MEXICO D. F.
20 November [1923]

My dear Kot

I sent a wire to Seltzer yesterday to tell him I was sailing
on the 22nd—two days hence—on the Hamburg-Amerika
boat *Toledo* to Plymouth. She is due in Plymouth on the 11th
or 12th. of December—but she may be later. I sail from
Vera Cruz, and touch at Havana, and at Vigo, Spain.

I am not very keen to come, but this time it is settled, I have
bought my ticket & leave in the morning for Vera Cruz.
Going out to dinner with English people here makes me
already a bit weary with Europe. It is not, as you say, that I
fight with shadows: but that I feel I don't belong. As for
being angry, I am not angry unless someone annoys me. I've
lost my faith in the old world. Murry says so confidently—
"The New will happen over here, certainly not in Mexico."—
Quién sabe! I'll tell you better in six weeks time.

Pero vengo. And I may be as glad to be back as Frieda appears
to be. Anyhow I am glad to see you & pick up again the
old connections.

Pues, hasta luego

D. H. L.

[PS.]
I hope you don't get very tired of having F's letters & my
letters forwarded to you.[1]

---

1 One of these letters, dated 10 November 1923, is now preserved in the *Kotelian-sky Papers* among the letters from Lawrence to Koteliansky. This letter to Frieda
was first published in *Encounter*, I, No. 3 (December 1953), p. 33 as if it were
addressed to Koteliansky, but parts of the letter were omitted. The inclusion of
Frieda's letter among those published in *Encounter* is puzzling, since it must have
been Koteliansky himself who made the selection. The letter, correctly printed,
is now published in *C.L.*, II, 762.

237 [110 HEATH ST.
Hampstead
London, N.W.3]
Christmas 1923[1]

Kot

Let the old warrior put his hat on and make ready.[2]

D. H. L.

---

1 Lawrence wrote a letter from this address to Mabel Dodge Luhan dated 27 December 1923. See *C.L.*, II, 765. I assume he was at the same address on Christmas of that year.

2 Probably a reference to an invitation from Koteliansky to celebrate Christmas. Lawrence was in London by 7 December 1923. See *P.R.*, p. 76.

---

238 HOTEL DE VERSAILLES
60 Bvd. Montparnasse
[Paris
25 January 1924]

Had a good journey.—Paris quite lovely, much nicer than London—and cold, but sunny.

D. H. L.

HOTEL DE VERSAILLES
60 Bvd. Montparnasse
Paris
Thursday [31 January 1924]

My dear Kot

I send back the proofs.[1]

I haven't heard from you or Murry, only a letter from Brett to say there is great gloom. Why be gloomy! Did the man[2] not offer the money for the publishing scheme? You've still got Schiff.

I read his book—quite good in a rather awful way.[3] Gives one a sense of depravity not faced out, back of it all.

Paris is rather nice—the French aren't at all villains, as far as I see them. I must say I like them. They are *simpatico*. I feel much better since I am here and away from London. I can't tell you how I loathe London and those six weeks.

Don't worry about things. All there is to do is to go ahead as far as you can with what you want to do, and not trouble further.

We think of going to Baden-Baden next Wednesday—the 6th —stay about two weeks.—Then I'm not sure. If I can get out of going to New York so soon, I think we shall go to Arles & Avignon for a few weeks, come to London about 25 March, & sail at end of month. But I'm not sure of anything.

I was trying to write a couple of stories, keep myself going.

Paris quite cold, but better than London: cleaner, not quite so dark—

Thank you so much for sending that history book to my niece.

I'll pay when I come back.

Do you want the Schiff book again?

I still have no word from Seltzer. Have you?

Greet Sonia & Grisha.

D. H. L.

---

1 The proofs could have been those of Lawrence's essay "On Being Religious," which was published in *The Adelphi*, I (February 1924), 791–99.

2 Not identified, but the reference might be to Vivian Locke-Ellis, as Letter No. 241 suggests, "who had put up £400 to start *The Adelphi* [and] was involved with Koteliansky, Murry, and Schiff in their publishing scheme" (*C.L.*, II, 774).

3 "Sydney Schiff wrote novels under the name of Stephen Hudson; Lawrence may be referring here to *Tony* (1924)" (*C.L.*, II, 774).

---

240 [HOTEL DE VERSAILLES
60 Boulevard Montparnasse]
Paris
5 February [1924]

Leave in the morning for Strasburg—address c/o Frau
Baronin von Richthofen
    Ludwig-Wilhelmstift
    Baden-Baden

Am quite ready to be on the move again.—

Greet Sonia.

D. H. L.

241

[HOTEL DE VERSAILLES
60 Boulevard Montparnasse]
Paris
Tuesday night [5 February 1924]

Dear Kot

We go in the morning.

We met Lock [*sic*] Ellis tonight. I don't like him. I think he doesn't like you. I said two words to him only about the publishing scheme—then felt a certain contempt for him. Don't *ask* him again. Better Schiff. But think of something else.

A postcard from Cath Carswell that there is a registered parcel for me from Seltzer. It may be *Memoir of Maurice Magnus*.[1] I asked her to open it & see, and if it is, to ring you up & you or Murry would call for it. You won't mind, will you.

That Lock [*sic*] Ellis is one of those birds I don't like.

D. H. L.

---

1 Lawrence's "Introduction" to *Memoirs of the Foreign Legion* by M. M. (Maurice Magnus) was published by Secker in 1924. See *B.*, pp. 206–07, for a note on Lawrence's involvement with Magnus.

LUDWIG WILHELMSTIFT
Baden-Baden
[Germany]
9 February [1924]

Dear Kot

I had a letter from Murry. He says he is putting £500 & you
£200 to the publishing scheme. As soon as I can get to
America & can see what I've got I will let you have the other
£300. Meanwhile nothing from Seltzer, & the latest I learned
in Paris was that income tax must be paid by March 15th.

Murry seems to have got another man up his sleeve. It means
he'll fasten on to somebody else, & not come to Taos.
Thank God for that. I don't want him, flatly. You keep him
in London & do businesses [*sic*] with him.

Germany is queer—seems to be turning—as if she would make
a great change, and become manly again, and a bit dangerous
in a manly way. I hope so. Though everything is poorer,
terrible poverty, even no tram-cars running, because they
can't afford the fares, & the town dark at night, still there is a
certain healthiness, more than in France, far more than in
England, the old fierceness coming back.

We think of going to Munich for a few days.

If Murry talks to you about America at all, dissuade him from
going, at least with me.

Greet Sonia & Grisha & Ghita.

D. H. L.

[PS. in Frieda's hand]
Lawrence quite cheerful here with my mother and sister! Good
wishes for your happiness!! Frieda.

LUDWIG WILHELMSTIFT
Baden-Baden
[Germany]
12 February 1924

My dear Kot

I have your letter. Very good, go ahead with the publishing scheme. I'll be in London before long; and we can settle it all up. We are due to leave here on the 20th—stay a few days in Paris—and be in London by about 26th. I have no word at all from that dog of a Seltzer, so it looks as if I shall have to go quickly to New York. God knows what he may be up to.—I haven't much money in England, but there should be plenty in New York to make up all you want: unless Seltzer has gone all wrong.

Don't think about doing that *Magnus* MS. till we have talked it over. I didn't want my memoir to be published apart from Magnus' own *Foreign Legion* book. There doesn't seem any point in it.

If we are only going to stay in London a week or so, we shall not go up to Hampstead, but shall stay in some hotel down town. You might tell me if you know a decent quiet place.

This Europe still wearies me. I shall be glad to leave it.

wiedersehen

D. H. L.

244 [LUDWIG WILHELMSTIFT]
Baden-Baden
[Germany]
Monday [18 February 1924]

Thanks for sending letters. Haven't you had mine? I wrote
by return—agreeing heartily. We leave Wednesday for
Paris—expect to be in London by 26th at latest.

Pardon post card. I am incorrigible.

D. H. L.

---

245 HOTEL DE VERSAILLES
60 Bvd Montparnasse
Paris 6
Thursday [21 February 1924]

Got back here this morning—stay probably till Tuesday,
but will write. Had your letter: nothing from Seltzer.

D. H. L.

246 [HOTEL DE VERSAILLES
60 Boulevard Montparnasse]
Paris
Saturday [23 February 1924]

Dear Kot

We arrive Victoria from Dover at 5:10 on Tuesday afternoon.
I asked Brett to get us a room at Garlands Hotel in Suffolk
St.,—near National Gallery. Adelphi too close to Martin
Secker. I asked Brett & Murry to meet us if they felt like
it—you too if you feel like it. Anyhow let us all dine together,
Garlands or elsewhere, Tuesday evening, and discuss every-
thing.[1]

wiedersehen

D. H. L.

---

1 The dinner took place at the Café Royal instead and ended rather ignominiously
for Lawrence, who had drunk too much wine. Catherine Carswell's account of
the dinner, first published in *The Savage Pilgrimage* (New York, 1932), is now
reprinted in *C.B.*, II, 295–302. According to her, Koteliansky was infuriated when
Donald Carswell began to speak Spanish with Lawrence. Then Koteliansky made
a speech "in praise and love of Lawrence, the speech being punctuated by his
deliberate smashing of a wine-glass at the close of each period. As—'Lawrence is
a great man.' (Bang! down came Kot's strong fist enclosing the stem of a glass,
so that its bottom came in shivering contact with the table.) 'Nobody here realizes
how great he is.' (Crash! another good wine-glass gone.) 'Especially no woman
here or anywhere can possibly realize the greatness of Lawrence.' (Smash and
tinkle!) 'Frieda does not count. Frieda is different. I understand and don't include
her. But no other woman here or anywhere can understand anything about
Lawrence or what kind of being he is'" (*C.B.*, II, 298). Part of Murry's recollection
is also reprinted in *C.B.*, II, 302–03, as is the Hon. Dorothy Brett's account in
C.B., II, 303–05.

47   [Garland's Hotel
Suffolk Street, Pall Mall
London]
3 March [1924]

Dear Kot

Will you please give the MS of *Memoirs of Maurice Magnus*
to Secker's man. Secker wants to read it because he knew the
people.

Yrs.

D. H. L.

248

My dear Kot.

We landed here in a gale, & snow, cold & horrible.[1] But today there is brilliant sunshine. New York looks as ever: stiff, machine-made, and against nature. Still it is more stimulating than Europe. It is so mechanical, there is not the sense of death. And another destiny. Brett so far is very nice: self contained and detached, which is the best.[2] Seltzer & Mrs. Seltzer are not so nice. She is the bad influence. He says he lost $7,000 last year. And simply no money in the bank, for me. I don't like the look of their business at all.—But Curtis Brown's man here seems very decent & reliable: a north of England man. He'll attend to the thing for me.

We shall leave next week for Taos, as soon as this is a bit straightened out. My dear Kot, it's no good thinking of business unless you will go at it like a lion, a serpent, and a condor. You're well out of publishing. The world is a very vast machine, that grinds the bones of the good man gladly, if he's fool enough to let it.

D. H. L.

---

1 Lawrence sailed from England 5 March 1924. See *P.R.*, p. 78.

2 The Hon. Dorothy Brett accompanied the Lawrences to New Mexico. For her memoir of Lawrence, see *Lawrence and Brett: A Friendship* (Philadelphia, 1933). Portions of the memoir are reprinted in various parts of the three volumes of *C.B.*

VILLA BERNARDA
Spotorno
Prov di Genova
6 December 1925[1]

My dear Kot

Curtis Browns sent me the letters—unless these are copies—
they are, I see—& the £5. for the Bunin book. Seltzer is
hopeless, he ought to go bankrupt & have done with it.
But his creditors won't *make* him bankrupt hoping to squeeze
him bit by bit.—I wish he'd never existed, poor devil.

We've got this villa here till end of March—then what, I
don't know: either back to America, to the ranch, or I think
I'd like to go to Russia. Should I, do you think? and could I?
I have a feeling inside me, I should like to go to Russia.

It's cold here, but sunny. Frieda's daughter Barbara is in
Alassio, coming over tomorrow: the other daughter coming
after Christmas. The Riviera doesn't interest me, & I'm a bit
bored: but the sun shines on the Mediterranean, I like that.
Brett is down in Capri.—I'm trying to clear off bits of work
I've promised.

How is Sonia & Ghita, & Grisha? Is 5 Acacia still cavernous?
—with Fox for the prehistoric animal? *Bisogna sapere!*—And
newspapers?

I wrote Barbara but haven't heard from her. The world needs
a move-on.

Send us news, if there is any.—You are still Frieda's pet
enemy, which is almost straining constancy.[2]

stia bene

D. H. L.

---

1 There is a large gap in the correspondence from March 1924 to December 1925.
By December 1925, Lawrence had returned to Europe from New Mexico and was
living in Italy. I have not been able to account for the hiatus in the correspondence,
unless it is that Lawrence's letters from this period are among those which Koteliansky has designated as not to be made available to the public.

Letter No. 249, however, gives no hint of a break in the friendship between the
two men.

2 The enmity between Frieda and Koteliansky was of long standing. Frieda
herself acknowledges that Kot did not like her. See my "Introduction," p. xvii
and p. xxv.

250 VILLA BERNARDA
Spotorno
Prov. di Genova
18 December 1925

My dear Kot.

I had your letter. Oh, but don't let's bother any more about people & lies. I am so weary of human complications. I expect I know you well enough, of myself, no matter what anybody says—though they *don't* say anything. In the end one's very heart gets tired. But somewhere, inside myself, I don't change: and I don't think you do. We are both much simpler than a man like Murry, whom I don't really understand. —I remember very well the famous walk in the Lake district, how you suffered having to sleep in the same bed— & how we got water-lilies—and came down to Lewis' unattractive home, & it was war, & you departed in a cloud. It's part of one's life & we don't live twice. Neither will Slatkovsky [*sic*] ever peep in again on our sour, sour herrings, in the Russian Law Bureau: nor shall we ever see Maisie sit on Campbell's knee. Oh *basta!* We won't grow old yet— *Son' tempi passati!*—but there are other days. Next time we're in London we'll see if we really can't cheer up and rouse the neighbourhood: like Fox.—Does Ghita still call him *Foxie?*—The war, somehow, gave us a bad kick in the wind, all of us: and we felt the damage most, in the after years. Now we've *got* to begin to rouse up a bit, or we shall all be old before we know where we are.

As for Russia: I still think I should like to go, in spite of all the "rulers." Don't I remember Litvinov[1] in a steam of washing and boiled cabbage? And isn't he, too, in the seats of the mighty? But there must be something there, besides & beyond.

So Sonya [*sic*] will never cook us another goose, only marmite pie and nut-cutlet.[2] I tried that Shearns[3] place, & thought it horrid—a real blow-out. What is the Cave coming to, with the Cave-lady herbivorous![4]

274

But perhaps it is good for the headaches.

Make a bow for me, to your *sacra famiglia*: except Ghita isn't
a *bambino*!

Tutte le buone cose!

D. H. L.

---

1 Maxim Litvinoff, Russian foreign commissar (1930–39), and ambassador to the
U.S. (1941–43). See "The Lawrence Circle," *C.B.*, I, 521.

2 Vegetarian dishes.

3 Probably a restaurant.

4 Mrs. Farbman appears to have become a vegetarian.

VILLA BERNARDA
Spotorno
Prov di Genova
4 January 1926

My dear Kot

I had Farbman's book,[1] & actually read it all, with much
interest. It was really interesting. Many thanks for sending it.

I do hope the domestic tragedy[2] in the Cave was only a
mishap. I simply feel I can't stand tragedies anywhere any
more. Why can't things smooth out a bit?—But send a line,
& say it was nothing serious.

It was very sunny & nice here today, feels like spring coming.
We had a warm sunny Christmas. It is extraordinary, the
change, when one crosses the Alps. I think on the whole I
like the Mediterranean Countries best to live in. The ranch
still doesn't attract me, though sometimes in my sleep I hear
the Indians drumming and singing. I still wish my old wish,
that I had a little ship to sail this sea, & visit the Isles of
Greece, and pass through the Bosphorus. That *Rananim* of
ours, it has sunk out of sight.

If you will send me a grammar book, I'll begin to learn
Russian. Just an ordinary grammar book. Even if I never do
go to Russia, it'll do me no harm. And when I come to
England you can give me a few lessons. I am forty years old
now, but the world is still an unopened oyster, probably will
always remain so. Nevertheless, one can go on trying to
prise it open.

I wonder if Russia has had all her troubles & her revolutions,
just to bring about a state of complete materialism and cheap-
ness. That would be sad. But I suppose it's on the cards.

What are those people like, on the *Calendar*?[3] Do you know
them?

I think Frieda has forsaken you, as a pet enemy. I won't
tell you who the later one is, perhaps you've guessed. For
my part, I wonder if we don't lose the faculty for making

new connections, & if the old ones are all broken we're a
bit lost. I feel suddenly rather grown up, feel I'd better be a
bit wary how I let fly.

Say nice things to Sonia from me, & to Ghita & Grisha.

D. H. L.

[PS.]
I should be very pleased if you'd buy Ghita a small thing with
the change, & give it her for a Valentine.

---

1 Probably Michael Farbman's *After Lenin: The New Phase in Russia* (London,
1924). Farbman also wrote *Russia and the Struggle for Peace* and *Bolshevism in
Retreat.*

2 Reference is obscure.

3 *The Calendar of Modern Letters*, which published Lawrence's novelette "The
Princess" (March, April, May 1925). See *B.*, p. 269.

VILLA BERNARDA
Spotorno
(Genova)
11 January 1926

My dear Kot

I have your letter—no doubt the Russian Grammar will soon come. Many thanks for sending it.

I have been thinking lately, the time has come to read Dostoevsky again: not as fiction, but as life. I am so weary of the English way of reading nothing but fiction in everything. I will order *Karamazov* at once.

Our little friend[1] also wrote to me, asking would I write the *Adelphi* with him—just us two—as a sort of latter-day *Signature*. I told him, to drop it altogether, as the public wanted neither the one-man show of him alone, nor the Punch & Judy show of him and me. To which he replied with more spite & impudence than I have yet had from him, & which makes me imagine he must be nearing the end of his tether. "The time was long, yet the time ran—"[2] *Fra poco sarà finito, quella commedia sacra e buffa degli Adelphi. Per me, non sono adelphos di nessuno.*

Barbara has also written to Ivy Lowe [*sic*], concerning my coming to Russia. *Ha fatto bene?*

I am ordering you a copy of *Reflections on the Death of a Porcupine*, from Philadelphia, because it contains *The Crown*: in memory of *Signature* days. And I will order my new novel for Grisha, not expecting him to care for it. Many thanks to him for *Lenin.*[3]

Yes, get a passport. It is time you moved out of England a bit. You could come & see us here, then: it is so sunny & nice. But wait a bit for me, & we'll go to Russia together: when the green leaves are coming, there.

Hope Ghita likes her purse: may it never be empty.

I had no idea our little friend had gone hawking the *Adelphi* around town. I believe he's in one of his money-panics, *benedetto lui!*

Greet Sonia, *tutta la sacra famiglia*.

If our little friend had stuck to me or my way a bit, he wouldn't be where he is.

D. H. L.

[PS.]
Smerdyakov [4] always suggested the French *merde* to me. The beshitten! Damn all magazines—except for the bit of money they pay.

[PS. in Frieda's hand]
Halloh [*sic*]—Kot! My greetings to you in the New Year and let's be friends.

Frieda

---

1 J. M. Murry.

2 The line is taken from Dante Gabriel Rossetti's poem "Sister Helen":

> "Why do you melt your waxen man,
>   Sister Helen?
> Today is the third since you began."
> "Time was long, yet the time ran,
>   Little brother."
>
>   (Stanza 1)

3 See note 1 to Letter No. 251.

4 One of the characters in Dostoevsky's novel *The Brothers Karamazov*. In Russian, Smerdyakov has the connotation of "stinking" or one who causes things to stink owing to his own befouled nature.

VILLA BERNARDA
Spotorno
(Genova)
15 January 1926

My dear Kot

I have the FOUR grammar books, & feel like the man who asked for a piece of bread, & was given a field of corn. Why four, all at once? The extra three only frighten me.

But I have bravely started, and am in the midst of those fearful *лц* and *ть бц ьб э* and *ч* things. I hope the bolsheviks [*sic*], with the end of the Romanovs, ended a few letters of the alphabet. Did they?

And where is Ghita's purse coming from, if all the money went on books? I enclose another ten bob, hope it'll reach. I thought you'd just buy *one* 5/– book.

It has actually *snowed* here, and been vilely cold. Today it is slackening off, hinting at mildness. The beastly Italian louts are out *alla caccia, hunting*—O *cacciatori!*—the hedgesparrows, robins, larks and finches. The tiny birds are driven down by the snow, and I don't exaggerate when I say one hears five or six shots a minute, all day long. You hear a huge man say: *sono cacciatore apassionato!*—which means he's just shot a robin.[1] Oh world of men!

My sister is coming out here for the second half of February, and is very thrilled. Martin Secker returns to London on Monday. He's quite nice, really, & perfectly unassuming—shy.

Nothing further from our little friend.[2]

tanti saluti!
D. H. L.

---

[1] For Lawrence's views on bird hunting, see his essay "Man the Hunter," published for the first time in *Phoenix* (New York, 1936). Edward McDonald comments on this essay in his "Introduction" to *Phoenix*, pp. xii–xiii; however, the date of Lawrence's letter to Mabel Luhan should be 16 January 1926, and not "March 18, 1926" as McDonald states. See *Lorenzo in Taos* (New York, 1932) p. 289.

[2] J. M. Murry.

I am here a few days with my sister—she leaves for England
tomorrow: lovely hot weather, & romantic scenery, but the
place rather come-down in style: weary, weary people walking
about. I'm going tomorrow to Nice, & perhaps alone to
Spain. F. has her two daughters & another girl at the Villa
Bernarda.

I am glad you liked those parts of the *Plumed Serpent*.[1]

D. H. L.

---

[1] Koteliansky particularly liked the Quetzalcoatl hymns in *The Plumed Serpent*.
See Frieda's letter to Koteliansky in *Frieda Lawrence: The Memoirs and Corre-*
spondence, edited by E. W. Tedlock, Jr. (New York, 1964), p. 225.

255

Came on here from Capri—weather wildly cold, snowed yesterday—the sun hot again! How are you?—send me a line to Spotorno, expect to be back there soon.

Tante Cose!

D. H. L.

RAVELLO
[Amalfi]
17 March [1926]

My dear Kot

Will you tell me what you think of this letter.[1] Frieda sent it
on. I don't know whether she *lost* the address mentioned in it.
Is that a good address on the letter-head?

I shall probably go back to Spotorno next week: write me
there, & send me the letter back, please.

It's rather horrid weather down here—feels earthquaky.

If you think I should write to these people, transcribe the
address for me, will you? Since I had influenza I abandoned
my Russian Grammar in despair.

I think in April we shall go to Germany. From there to
Moscow would not be so wildly far.

But send me a line.

tante cose

D. H. L.

---

1 The reference is obscure, but see note 1 to Letter no. 257.

VILLA BERNARDA
Spotorno
Italy
10th April, 1926

My dear Kot,

I came back here a couple of days ago, after wandering about
and getting myself better after 'flu. Italy is still very nice, and
I feel more at home here than in America.

I don't want to go to Russia now: I hear such dreary tales
about it from people in Florence. As for those Nazcompros [*sic*]¹ people, damn them! I could never stir Frieda to
write to them, and as for myself, I am beyond it.

Swine that they wouldn't give you a naturalization paper.²
Wasn't there anybody you could take by the nose? I suppose
you will stay in the Cave until you are a real grizzly. Sorry
Farbman has 'flu. Everybody in Italy has it, and mine keeps
flicking me in the eye with its tail.

Murry writes to me with sneaking impudence. I have not seen
the letter, as Frieda destroyed it without sending it on. I
shouldn't have answered it anyhow. Let the green mildew
grow on him.

Brett says she is going back to America to look after the
ranch. Myself, I don't quite know what I shall do, but I
may go to Umbria, Perugia, and collect material for a book
more or less about the Etruscans. We leave here on the 20th
and are going to Florence.

I have never met Gertrude Stein, but if you remember the
deaf fellow in *Aaron's Rod*, that is her brother. I really will
write oftener once we are settled a little into quiet ways again.

Remember me to Sonia, Farbman and Ghita,

D. H. L.

[PS.]
I actually dictated this letter to Frieda's daughter Elsa—to
see if I could do it. Hope you don't mind. F's daughters are

really very funny: they sit on their mother with ferocity,
simply won't stand her cheek, and fly at her very much in her
own style. It leaves her a bit flabbergasted, & is very good for
her, as you'll guess.

D. H. L.

---

1 Nazcompros people might be "these people" in Letter No. 256.

2 Koteliansky's application for naturalization in 1926 was refused; however, he
became a "British subject/by Naturalization of Russian origin—Imperial Certi-
cate/London No. 17752/dated 27 November 1929."

---

258 VILLA MIRENDA
San Polo Mosciano
Scandicci
Florence
17 May [1926]

My dear Kot

We've made another little move¹—taken the top half of this
old villa about seven miles out of Florence, for a year. It's
very cheap, only £25 the year, so we can leave it or lend it
when we like.—Brett has gone back to America, to look after
the ranch. I feel I don't want to go.

The weather is atrocious—a few fine days, then thunder &
rain. Never was such a wet May. How is it in England?

We're right in the country, very pretty, & 1½ miles from the
tram-terminus. The tram takes us into Piazza in half an hour:
very convenient.

I'm supposed to be preparing material for a book on the old
Etruscans, but don't know if I shall do it.—The postcard is
one of their things—called the Chimaera—Vth Century B.C.

I hear from Murry—I suppose his second baby is born by
now.² He writes with the same impertinence, but I feel he is
a defeated man.

The strike³ is over, apparently—I'm very glad. Myself, I'm
scared of a class war in England. It would be the beginning
of the end of all things. What do you think of it?—And
why did the *Lira* fall so suddenly?

We may come to England in the later summer, then I shall
see you. For the moment I am not deciding anything.—I
only wish the weather would be dry, this wet is bad for one's
bronchials.

Remember me to Sonia, & Grisha, & Ghita: also they will be
glad the strike is over. What is Grisha doing?—My desire to
go to Russia has disappeared again. I feel the Bolshevists

are loutish and common.—I don't believe in them, except as disruptive and nihilistic agents. Boring!

What are you yourself doing?

tante cose!

D. H. L.

---

1 For material regarding Lawrence's move to Scandicci, see *P.R.*, p. 87. It was at the Villa Mirenda that Lawrence wrote *Lady Chatterley's Lover.*

2 Murry married his second wife, Violet le Maistre, on 24 April 1924. She died on 30 March 1931.

3 The General Strike by the trade unions of Great Britain in May 1926, undertaken in support of the Miners' Federation in their dispute with the coalowners. It ended inconclusively on 13 May 1926.

259
VILLA MIRENDA
Scandicci
Florence
28 June 1926

My dear Kot

Your letter today—also a long screed from Barbara to Frieda.

We are sitting very unobtrusively here: but think to leave
this day fortnight, July 12th, for Baden-Baden, & stay there a
fortnight: then probably to England for August. Of course
the thought of England, as it draws near, depresses me with
infinite depression. But perhaps we may manage a month.
Perhaps we may shirk it after all. But I'll tell you.—It is
awfully nice here, now the summer is hot & more or less
steady, and the days pass by so quickly and without notice, it
seems a pity to stir oneself up again.

I feel the same about Secker: absolute mistrust, which grows
deeper instead of lighter. Why hadn't he sent you that
£2.16.—long ago, if he owed it? I think he is in low water.
He keeps asking me to write another novel. But I don't want
to. He can whistle. Why should I write books for any of 'em!
I've had enough—And if the New Agers smell no better than
the Old Agers, they too can whistle, & keep their £1. per
1000.—They hadn't written me.—Don't send me any of that
miserable Shestov fragment. And if ever you want any
money, tell me, & I'll send it along. Don't have a silly Jewish
money complex. We've lived too long.

I haven't done any of the Etruscan book yet: & shan't do it,
unless the mood changes. Why write books for the swine,
unless one absolutely must.

I like it here. One can stay out & be quite remote. Or go into
Florence in an hour, & see a few people who aren't exciting,
but all the better. I don't ask excitement. I was very busy
typing out F's translation of the *David* play—and working it
up a bit. Thank heaven it's done, & just sent off. A real
German play now! What next?

288

The parents of the Sitwells have a castle about 14 miles away. We went to see them: queer couple. Thursday I am lunching with the world's champion fencer. How's that?

If we come to England, I expect we shall take a little flat Chelsea way for a month—then I shall go to my sisters for a week, probably to the seaside.—We shall see you—& we must make a little trip somewhere, like the memorable trip to the Lakes. *Aspettiamo!* Shall we go down to Murry's Dorset together?—and see his second baby, son & heir, another John Middleton, ye Gods!

It seems I don't know anybody in London any more.

Remember me to Sonia & Ghita & Grisha.

tante Cose!

D. H. L.

[PS.] Note the address can be shortened

260 BADEN-BADEN
[22 July 1926]

Germany rather nice & peaceful—but a bit rainy again, after the heat.—We expect to arrive in London on the 30th, & go to a little flat: 25 Rossetti Garden Mansions, Flood St.—Chelsea S.W.3—So shall see you soon.

D. H. L.

---

261 25 ROSSETTI GARDEN MANSIONS
Flood St. Chelsea S.W.3
Friday [?30 July 1926]

Dear Kot

Got in this evening [1]—very tired—found your note.

We shall expect you to tea tomorrow about 4:00: It's the very top floor, Mrs. Stanley Fay's flat. Hope you'll find it.

wiedersehen

D. H. L.

---

1 Moore dates Lawrence's arrival 31 July 1926. See *P.R.*, p. 88.

25 ROSSETTI GARDEN MANSIONS
Chelsea S.W.3
Sunday [8 August 1926]

My dear Kot

We have got back here today.[1] The Aldingtons were very
nice.—I am leaving for Scotland tomorrow morning, Monday,
at 9:50: so in the evening I should be in Edinburgh.

I forgot to tell you to take the *Early Greek Philosophies*. If
you would care for it, then tell Frieda, & come and fetch it.

My address is c/o Miss M. Beveridge
  "Bailabhadan"
  Newtownmore
  (Inverness) N.B.

I hope Sonia came home safely, & is feeling well; and that I
can see her when I come back.

I will write from Scotland.

au revoir

D. H. L.

---

1 The date is obviously 8 August 1926; but see *P.R.*, p. 88.

---

263 ["BAILABHADAN"
Newtownmore, Inverness-shire]
12 August [1926]

Scotland is very nice, rather cold, & showers—but the
shadows & lights on the low hills are queer & northern &
alive. Of course there are motor-cars everywhere—which is a
nuisance—& they are building new roads through the
quiet valleys.—

I hope Sonia is home, & feeling better.

au revoir.

D. H. L.

I had your letter—so sorry Sonia has such a poor time. Frieda wrote she had seen you.—We had a trip to the west coast, & the Isle of Skye—very wet, but one lovely day: and I was very much impressed. It seemed so remote and uninhabited, so northern, and like the far-off old world, out there. One day I shall go again.—I hope to be in London at the end of next week, but will let you know. The address is "Ravenstone," George St., Mablethorpe, Lincolnshire.

Remember me to all.

D. H. L.

265 "DUNEVILLE"
Trusthorpe Rd.
Sutton-on-Sea, Lincs.
28 August [1926]

My dear Kot

Frieda arrived last evening. I've taken this bungalow for two weeks—& for a month if we like it. The weather is lovely, & the sea very nice. I like this flat coast, it's where I first knew the sea.—We're just moving now from Mablethorpe—Sutton is only two miles away—my sister departed yesterday. I'll write again.

D. H. L.

P.S.—Do ask Gertler about a doctor to examine our friend Gertie,[1] & about the sanatorium—how much it costs etc.

I am so bored by the thought of all things literary—why not sell cigarettes!

D. H. L.

---

1 Gertrude Cooper, who during Lawrence's youth was a member of the band of young Eastwood people who called themselves "the Pagans". In later years she made her home with Mr. and Mrs. Clarke (Ada Lawrence) at Ripley, Derby. Gertrude Cooper was tuberculous, like Lawrence" (*C.L.*, I, xxxiv).

"DUNEVILLE"
Trusthorpe Rd.
Sutton-on-Sea, Lincs.
2 September [1926]

My dear Kot

Many thanks for the booklet & letter. I am sending both on to my sister[1]—I want to get Gertie away as soon as possible to some cure, she's delayed too long. I suppose I shall have to go over next week to see to the business—& probably take her to London—or direct to Mundesley.[2]

Frieda has asked her two daughters down here—whether they'll come or not, I don't know—I rather hope they won't.

I like being here. We've had now two dull days, with some rain, but I'm hoping it will brighten up today. I really rather like being back in my native Midlands. This is the first place— or Mablethorpe is—where we ever came for a holiday, to stay. It's all just flat sands—but very fresh & bracing. And the people are common, but alive. For the first time for years, I am rather glad to be at home in England. Though if the grey weather continues, I shall have to move off after the sun.

I haven't heard a word from the Whitworth people about the play.[3] When I do I'll let you know: when I come to town. I must find some cheaper hotel to stay at, Garlands is too dear. But I'll let you know.

How is Gertler, by the way? I should like to see him when I come to London.

Frieda sends her *Grüsse*

D. H. L.

[PS.]
I wish you would address the letter to Mrs. Whitworth— I hope I've spelled her right. [Crossed out]

(I'm an ass—you don't know the address—she's the woman who is producing the play.)

---

1 Mrs. Clarke, Lawrence's sister Ada.

2 A sanatorium in Norfolk.

3 Lawrence's play *David*.

"DUNEVILLE"
Trusthorpe Rd.
Sutton-on-Sea, Lincs.
Monday [6 September 1926]

My dear Kot

Dull weather, rain & a low grey sky—not much fun here. I
think we'll leave in a week's time. I wish you'd ask Gertler
if he knows any place in Hampstead where we could have a
couple of rooms, & eat in or eat out, doesn't matter which. I
don't want to be down in town: & Frieda hated Chelsea. Or
even your St. John's Wood?—We'd then stay at least a week,
& longer if it were necessary for the play—of which, so far,
I've heard nothing.—It's being produced by the Stage Society
& 300 combined—a Mrs. Geoffrey Whitworth bossing the
show, & Robert Aiken,[1] who produced Shakespeare at the Old
Vic, producing it. But how long do they think I'm going to
wait in England for them!—I like it here all right, when it's
fine—but in the rain & mist it's no good, & gives me another
cold.

Apparently F's daughters aren't coming—that is, they've not
written. Before I come to London I must go to Ripley. My
sister thinks we might get Gertie examined *first* at Nottingham, & x-rayed there—& then proceed to other doctors if
necessary. I think maybe she's right. I'll have to go at the
week-end & talk it all over.

I am writing also to Miss Morrison—who is at 1. Elm Row,
Hampstead—to ask her if her people—in her house—know
of rooms for a week or fortnight for us.[2] I'll ask her to drop
Gertler a line to Penn Studio, Rudall Crescent—is that right?
—if she has wind of anything.

So I trust we shall see you next week. You will be no more a
solitary.

au revoir

D. H. L.

[PS.]
Frieda suddenly says that Miss Morrison will probably be
away, & her house shut. If so, then let it be so!

---

1 Lawrence here means Robert Atkins who was associated with the Old Vic
both as an actor and as a director. The production of Lawrence's play *David* was
eventually staged on 22 and 23 May 1927. See Letters Nos. 279 and 281. Who
Mrs. Geoffrey Whitworth was or what her responsibility for the production was I
have been unable to discover. Lawrence's letter to Robert Atkins may be read
in *C.L.*, II, 941–42.

2 See Lawrence's letter to Miss Morrison in *C.L.*, II, 935.

---

268 ["DUNEVILLE"
Trusthorpe Rd.
Sutton-on-Sea, Lincs.]
Wednesday [8 September 1926]

Got your letter this evening in town—no time to go home.
Frieda at least will arrive Monday, & we shall be very glad
of the rooms. You didn't give the address. But say we will
take the rooms from Monday.

Send me the address. I shall go to Ripley for two days.

Many thanks for all your trouble.

D. H. L.

69

"DUNEVILLE"
Trusthorpe Rd.
Sutton-on-Sea, Lincs.
Thursday [9 September 1926]

My dear Kot

I hope you weren't shocked at the post card.[1] But I got your letter only at evening, on the beach, & had to scribble the nearest thing possible.

Very many thanks for finding us a place. It sounds very good, and I think we shall be all right there. But send me the address, won't you?

We leave here on Monday. I shall go to Ripley from here, but Frieda will come straight up to London, and take a taxi to the lodgings—arriving somewhere about tea-time. I'll let the landlady know, if I have her address.

So we shall see you soon. I do hope Sonia is feeling better.— I expect I shall be in town by Wednesday evening, or Thursday at latest.

auf wiedersehen

D. H. L.

---

1 Lawrence's postcard (Letter No. 268) depicts a frolicsome female in a bathing suit. The caption "This is how I feel" would not have matched Lawrence's mood at the time; hence the explanation in this letter to Koteliansky.

TORESTIN
Gee St.
Ripley nr Derby
15 September 1926

My dear Kot,

Of course it's grey & a bit rainy here: these Midlands!

Gertie doesn't seem so very bad. She was examined in Derby
—the x-ray shows a hole at the top of the left lung, but
new. I have written to Dr. Lucas, to ask when they can take
her in to Mundesley. The doctor said she couldn't do better
than go there. So as soon as we hear there is room, my sister
will take her over. She ought to be cured by Christmas.

I shall be coming to London tomorrow—don't know the
time yet: probably in the evening.

This strike has done a lot of damage—& there is a lot of
misery—families living on bread & margarine & potatoes—
nothing more. The women have turned into fierce communists
—you would hardly believe your eyes. It feels a different
place: not pleasant at all.[1]

I hope Sonia is better. You'll come up to Willoughby Rd.

weidersehen

D. H. L.

---

1 See Lawrence's fuller description of the miners' strike reprinted in *C.B.*, III,
90–92. The description is taken from his "Autobiographical Fragment" in
Phoenix (New York, 1936), pp. 822–24; but it recalls this visit to the Midlands
in September 1926. See also "[Return to Bestwood]" published for the first time
in *Phoenix II* (New York, 1968), pp. 257–66.

30 WILLOUGHBY RD.
Hampstead
N.W.3
Thursday [23 September 1926]

My dear Kot

Such a lot of people we see!—Tomorrow we are in after lunch—but that weary Enid Hopkin[1] with husband threatens to come for tea—Margaret Radford threatens between 6:00 & 7:00—and Frieda's son Monty is coming to dinner, & I expect we shall stay in the evening. If you feel like facing any of these people, come any time.—Saturday also we shall be here till evening—though Frieda's daughter comes to lunch, & maybe others to tea. But come when you like, notwithstanding.

We're fixed to leave on Tuesday.[2]

Perhaps I'll be able to pop in at 5 Acacia on Monday.

D. H. L.

---

1 Enid C. Hopkin was the daughter of William Edward Hopkin, whom Lawrence knew well in Eastwood. She married Laurence Hilton. In the late 1920's she visited the Lawrences in Italy, and later when Lawrence's *Lady Chatterley's Lover* was published, Enid Hilton helped to distribute it in London. After Lawrence's death she helped Aldous Huxley to collect letters for his edition of Lawrence's correspondence. See *C.B.*, III, 637.

2 Lawrence left London 28 September 1926. See *P.R.*, p. 89.

PARIS
Thursday [30 September 1926]

Very pleasant here, sunny & nice—we go on tomorrow as far as Lausanne—shall be at the Mirenda by Monday.

D. H. L.

VILLA MIRENDA
Scandicci
(Florence)
Sunday 17 October 1926

My dear Kot

It's a fortnight tomorrow since we got back—we stayed a
couple of days in Lausanne, Frieda having caught the gastric
flu. Which everybody had in Paris. But she's better.—And
it is nice to be here in the big quiet rooms again, no traffic &
no bothers. It is still very warm, at midday hot: but heavy
mists in the morning. Lovely weather, though. The peasants
finished the *vendemmia* two days after we got here—but the
wine is still to be made.—I haven't told anybody in Florence
that we are back, yet. It's so nice to be still.

I heard from Gertie,[1] she has gained two pounds and a half in
weight—but they are still keeping her in bed.

I sent off the music to *David* the other day. Wonder if you'll
recognise the prophets singing *Ranané Sadikim* [*sic*]. But it
won't sound the same.—Wonder if they'll make anything of
the play, anyhow. I don't feel very sanguine.

Will you send me the Dobrées'[2] number in Well Walk, when
you write, so I have their address. I liked them—him too.

And don't forget, if you want to borrow some money, you
can borrow from me as from the Lord, who doesn't mention
payment till the Judgment Day, when all is over.

How is Sonia by now? quite well I hope. And Ghita, at
Oxford, getting more superior every day, I'll bet.

There is an enormous fusillade going on in the *boschi*—
shooting little birds as they go south—*vivi pericolosamente!*
must have been intended for the *uccellini!* *à la* St. Francis.

Saluti!

D. H. L.

---

1 Gertrude Cooper. See note 1 to Letter No. 265.

2 The well known English literary scholar, Professor Bonamy Dobrée, and his
wife, Valentine Dobrée.

VILLA MIRENDA
Scandicci
Florence
14 December 1926

My dear Kot

Here's Christmas near, & I've not written you for ages! But the life goes by so quietly & quickly. We are nice & comfortable here in the Mirenda, with a cosy room & a warm stove, & F. has hired a piano. I practically never go in to Florence, & really see nobody: which pleases me better. I've lost interest in people, & find I can amuse myself very well.

Lately I've been painting—quite a big picture, my last, about 1 1/2 yards by 1 yard—of Boccaccio's story of the nuns & the gardener.[1] I'm sure it would amuse you—it does me. Think I'll turn into a painter, it costs one less, & probably would pay better than writing. Though for that matter I'm patiently doing a novel[2]—scene in the Midlands.

How are you all? Have you found some way to make a living without emerging from the cave? Is Sonia better?—Is Gertler coming to Florence in the New Year? Tell him we shall be pleased to see him—wonder how *The Widowing of Mrs. Holroyd* went off, on Sunday.[3] Suppose I shall hear. But London seems remote.

I send you two quid for Christmas festivities. If I sent you more, you'd probably have a complex. If you want to feel you've earned them, sing *Good King Wenceslas* for me, for a carol. Anyhow have a good time, & buy a bottle of something cheerful.

Many greetings to all—write me a word?

D. H. L.

[PS. in Frieda's hand]
Dear Kot! A merry Xmas, we often wish you and Gertler would come in for an evening! Glad we are no longer enemies! Greetings to Sonia. F.

1 It was this painting that was apparently damaged by the police when Lawrence's pictures were seized at a London exhibition in 1929. For details, see *C.B.*, III, 351–52.

2 *Lady Chatterley's Lover.*

3 For details of this production of Lawrence's play on 12, 13, and 19 December 1926, see Edward Nehls's note 143 in *C.B.*, III, 673–74.

VILLA MIRENDA
Scandicci
Florence
20 January 1927

Dear Kot

I had just heard from Secker, & told him to pay the money to you.—I'd sort of forgotten the Shestov.[1] But annoying those things are!—I'll ask Secker why he didn't pay the money when he got it. It's an awful bore, that pettiness.

If I haven't written, it's because I'm finding it harder & harder to write letters. The will-to-write seems to be departing from me: though I do write my new novel in sudden intense whacks. And I paint away at my pictures, to amuse myself.

It's been bad weather—gave me a cold—but today the sun shines & one can sit still in the sun—which is all one asks, at the moment. It's not a winter to boast about, even here. Yet the time goes by quickly.

I had a letter from Dobrée, telling me we could stay in their house: very nice of him indeed. But now I think *David* is being put back until April, so that I should not need to come to England before end of March. The later the better, for me, in the hopes of spring.

There is no news at this end of the world. Frieda expects her children out in March.

Where is Gertler? Every day I mean to write to him, & thank him for the little book of pictures,[2] & I never do it. What's happened to me?

How is poor old Sonia? She does seem to be having hard luck lately. I'm awfully sorry.

Well, I'll really catch myself in a nice moment, & write a proper letter.

I'll tell Secker to deal with you for Shestov. In fact I'll send him your letter, as it contains nothing personal or libellous, & I'll add what I say to him.[3]

Yrs

D. H. Lawrence

[PS.]
When you get the money from Secker, keep it.

D. H. L.

---

1 *All Things Are Possible*, which was published by Secker in 1920.

2 "The small book on Mark Gertler published by the Fleuron in 1925" (*Mark Gertler: Selected Letters*, edited by Noel Carrington [London, 1965], p. 224).

3 Lawrence's letter to Secker follows.

VILLA MIRENDA
20 January 1927

"—dear Secker

I enclose letter from Koteliansky about the Shestov affair. Will you in future deal with him entirely in the matter of the Shestov translation, as the work was really his. And it seems to me a pity you didn't pay in that small sum of American dues, at the time. However, I suppose by now it is all settled.

Yrs

D. H. L."

276 VILLA MIRENDA
Scandicci
(Florence)
24 January 1927

Dear Kot

Thanks for the cheque. I am putting it in the fire, so you can say no more about it.—And I hope your letter will have some small effect on Secker.

But the world's a bad egg.

Yrs.

D. H. L.

---

277 VILLA MIRENDA
Scandicci
(Firenze)
13 April 1927

My dear Kot

I got back yesterday and found your book[1]—had no idea that you were sending it, or even had written it. But it looks quite thrilling, & I shall read it as soon as I feel I'm here.—I was away at Ravello, above Amalfi, with friends, then walking & driving in Maremma, looking at Etruscan tombs in Cerveteri & Tarquinia & Vulci & those places. I was away about a month—liked it very much. Frieda went to Baden for a week or two, & got back a week before me. Now yesterday has arrived her younger daughter Barbara, so somehow it feels a bit of an upset. However, I suppose I shall soon settle down. At present I feel a bit abroad, somehow.

How have you been all this time? Is Sonia better, and Ghita getting on well at Oxford? It is spring, and very lovely here, with all the trees in blossom and the birds singing, and the sun good and strong. I don't think I could live in a sunless country any more.

I heard from Mrs. Whitworth that *David* is now due in May. The man Monck, the producer, also shirked it: so I don't know whom they'll get, & don't care much. It feels forever so uncertain, I don't think I shall come over.

Is there any news? I have none. Brett is still in Taos, flourishing as a cow-boy figure, and urging us to come out. But not this year, I think.

If you see Barbara, tell her I'll write—I'll really have to start in and do some letters. What's happened to us?—I feel a stranger to myself. Is it a "change of life"? Do you feel that way?

Write and tell me how things are.

D. H. L.

---

1 I have identified the book as V. V. Rozanov's *Solitaria*, translated by S. S. Koteliansky (London, 1927). For the importance of this work in Lawrence's creation of *The Man Who Died*, see my article "The Phallic Vision: D. H. Lawrence and V. V. Rozanov," *Comparative Literature Studies*, IV, No. 3 (1967), pp. 283–97.

VILLA MIRENDA
Scandicci
Firenze
27 April 1927

My dear Kot

I read Rozanov as soon as he came: and wrote a criticism as
soon as I'd read him: and send you the criticism[1] so you will
know what I think. Do you agree at all?

As for my crit., will you send it on to Curtis Brown—
Magazine Dept. They may get someone to print it, though
it's an off-chance. But they usually place anything I send. The
Calendar would print it, but since it's their own publication,
I'd rather it went somewhere else. If you know anybody,
give it them. If not, no matter.

I was very pleased to have Rozanov—I'm really rather tired
of Tchekov & Dostoevsky people: they're so Murryish.
By the way, any news of Our mutual friend?

It is full summer here—quite hot. I'm taking this house for
another year, because nothing else occurs to me to do. I think
we shall stay here later, this summer: til [*sic*] end of July: but
I'm not sure. My old instinct, not to come to England, is still
strong. And it is an instinct rather than anything else. Italy I
like, when I'm in the country and there's nothing but peasants.
But the towns are most irritable and tiresome, & Rome very
antipatica nowadays. I've half a feeling I shall go to Spain
before very long. Or Egypt! How do the Dobrées like it?
If you'll send me their address, I'll write to them. I never
read her book,[2] because children-literature bores me, especially
Proustia. But I must get it, & actually try. Anyhow I'm
glad it was a success.

I did a novel,[3] too: English Midlands scene. The public
would call it pornographic again, though it's the reverse: so
I'm holding the MS. and shan't even have it typed, yet awhile.
Secker wants it this year, but won't get it. Now I really want
to do a series of *Travel Sketches of Etruscan Places*. I liked
my trip to Cerveteri & Tarquinia and Vulci so much, I'd

like to jot them down while they are fresh. Then later go to
Cortona & Chuisi & Orvieto etc. It's such good weather now,
hot without exhausting. And so make a little book of
Etruscan places. But I'm nearly like Rozanov, anything I
say I'll do, I seem never to do: but something else. But there
are so many little jobs on hand, that I've neglected & have
piled up.

I'm sorry about Sonya [*sic*] not being well. I get to dread the
thought of sickness. Gertie has been a horrible business—in a
hospital in London these last two months—left lung removed,
six ribs removed, glands in neck—too horrible—better die.
Yet she's managed just to live through it. Good Lord, what
next! Why aren't we better at dying, straight dying! What is
left, after all those operations? Why not chloroform & the long
sleep! How monstrous our humanity is! Why save life in this
ghastly way?

They say the govt. is mobilising soldiers here. Lord knows
what for. The exchange is down to 88, and everything dearer
than England—no fun.

Frieda's daughter Barbara has been here the last two weeks—
leaves next Tuesday. She's a bit hard to please. What ails
the young, that they get nothing out of life? For certain,
life doesn't get much out of them.

How is Gertler? Did he go away? Does he keep pretty well?
As for me, I've not done any painting lately. Feel I'd like to
paint something red—

I still haven't written to Barbara. *Ay di* me! So many words
exist already!

I'll read the Tchekov book[4] next. But Tchekov, being particularly a pet of Murry & Katharine, is rather potted shrimps
to me.

D. H. L.

---

1 The criticism was a review of Rozanov's *Solitaria*. It was published in *The
Calendar of Modern Letters*, IV (July 1927), 157–61. The review is readily available
in *Phoenix* (New York, 1936), pp. 367–71, or in *D. H. Lawrence: Selected
Literary Criticism* (New York, 1956), pp. 245–49.

2 Valentine Dobrée, the wife of Bonamy Dobrée, published several works of fiction. Lawrence refers here to her book *Your Cuckoo Sings by Kind*, which appeared in 1927.

3 *Lady Chatterley's Lover*, which Lawrence was yet to rewrite twice.

4 Anton Tchekhov's *Literary and Theatrical Reminiscences*, translated and edited by S. S. Koteliansky (London, 1927). This book was published in March 1927.

---

279   VILLA MIRENDA
Scandicci
Firenze
30 April 1927

My dear Kot

I hear *David* is on May 22 & 23—and they urge me to come. I suppose they'll make a mess of it without me. So I shall pretty well have to come. Therefore I shall be in London by end of next week, I suppose—Friday or Saturday. I'll let you know precisely. I'm not sure where I shall stay—perhaps in Rossetti Garden Mansions for a time, in Miss Beveridge's flat, while she is away. I'll see. The Dobrées are still away.

I had the *Adelphi*—the penultimate: next to the last gasp. What are the "domestic circumstances"? More little Murrys arriving?

Well *au revoir*

D. H. L.

[VILLA MIRENDA
Scandicci
Florence]
5 May [1927]

Have got a cold in my chest, as usual—shan't risk travelling till it feels better—so heaven knows when I'll be in London. I'll write again,

D. H. L.

VILLA MIRENDA
Scandicci
Florence
27 May 1927

My dear Kot

Your letter today—I was very glad to hear about *David*[1] from
you. It seems to me just as well I wasn't there.—You can't
make a silk purse out of a sow's ear. But if ever the thing is
regularly produced, I'll come & see what I can do: though I
doubt if it would be much. Actors haven't enough *inside* them.
Anyhow I have a fairly good idea from what you say, of what
it was like.

I too am sick of these bronchial colds, mixed with malaria.
I've never been right since I was ill in Mexico two years
ago—beastly bronchial trouble, & the germs get it in an
instant. But *really*, I am stronger. I think this climate here is a
bit sudden and trying, too. In July we'll go to Bavaria, and
see what a bit of an altitude will do. I loved Bavaria, before the
war.

Osbert & Edith Sitwell came to tea the other day.[2] They were
really very nice, not a bit affected or bouncing: only absorbed
in themselves & their parents. I never in my life saw such a
strong, strange *family* complex: as if they were marooned on
a desert island, & nobody in the world but their lost selves.
Queer! They've gone back to England now.

It is summer, so I'm not doing much—finishing a *Resurrection*
picture & doing bits of things. Oh, I wish you'd ask Edgell
Rickword[3] to ask Dobrée to do a "Scrutiny" of Bernard
Shaw. I've done Galsworthy already—I don't really want to
do Shaw: slaying my elders only interests me in spasms. Do
ring up Rickword, & say I suggest *Dobrée* for the "Scrutiny"
on Bernard Shaw.

You say they—the Dobrées—will be back in London in June.
I'll write to them then. I have lost their Egyptian address.

I there any further news of Jesus' biographer & better?[4]

I ordered you, & Gertler, a copy of *Mornings in Mexico*—a little book Secker is just bringing out. I am holding back the novel till next year, anyhow.

How is Sonia?

Remember me to everybody.

D. H. L.

---

1 *David* was produced at the Regent Theatre, London, 22 May 1927. A reviewer for the *Times* called the production "neither drama nor poetry" and added that it "grows wearisome long before the last of the sixteen scenes" (*The Times*, 24 May 1927, p. 14). Writing in the *Spectator*, Richard Jennings asked: "What is it that persuades a writer of such intense conviction and so little sense of humour as Mr. D. H. Lawrence into an adventure like that of *David*...?" Jennings called the play "not necessarily anything dramatic at all" (*The Spectator*, No. 5161 [28 May 1927], p. 939). Koteliansky's account of the production is preserved among the *Koteliansky Papers* in the British Museum.

2 For Sir Osbert Sitwell's account of this meeting with D. H. Lawrence, see *C.B.*, III, 142–43. See also "A Visit with D. H. L." in the *New York Herald Tribune* (20 December 1960).

3 Edgell Rickword was the editor of *The Calendar of Modern Letters*. Lawrence's critical essay "John Galsworthy" originally was published in *Scrutinies*, by various writers, collected by Edgell Rickword (London, 1928), pp. 51–72. See *B.*, p. 213.

4 A reference to the fact that J. M. Murry had published *The Life of Jesus* (London, 1926).

VILLA MIRENDA
Scandicci
Florence
13 June 1927

My dear Kot

Your letter today! No luck with Rozanov! I'm sorry!
But not surprised. What dirty rag of a paper would dare
print the review! The world goes from bad to worse. But
cheer up, we're not dead yet!

Maria Huxley came yesterday, with the Franchettis. He is a
Jew, Barone Luigi—and as rich as Croesus. He plays the
piano very well, & is quite nice—but I agree entirely—I have
absolutely no basic sympathy with people of "assured
incomes." All words become a lie, in their mouth [*sic*], in their
ears also. I *loathe* rich people.

We are going on Wed. for a couple of days with Maria to
Forte dei Marmi—north of Pisa, not very far from here.
Aldous did not come in to Florence with Maria, as he is
working very hard, to finish a book by July. God help him.—
Sullivan[1] arrives there—at the Huxleys—on Monday—20th
—but we shall be back here by then. Two days is enough.—
Perhaps Maria will bring him over—Sullivan—to see us. I
should like to see him, because of associations, but I no
longer expect to care about people, one way or another.

I am working at my Etruscan book—a piece of hopeless un-
popularity, as far as I can see.[2] But the pictures may help it.
We shall probably do a bit of a tour to Etruscan places when
we get back from the Huxleys.—I think we shall be here
till end of July—though the weather is queer & uncertain.

I feel a bit like you: nothing nice ever happens, or ever will
happen. I dreamed I was made head of a school somewhere,
I think, in Canada. I felt so queer about it: such a vivid
dream—that I half wonder if it is *my* destiny! A job!—But I
manage to make a living still.

I feel sometimes tempted to go back to America. Europe is
like a dying pig uttering a long, infinitely-conceited squeak.—
At least America isn't so depressing. I feel tempted to go, in
the autumn.

I wish you would go & see Milly Beveridge—she too was at *David* & the discussion—and she had a little house here this spring. The address is 20 Rossetti Garden Mansions, S.W.3.— You remember—we had 25 last summer. She is nice & intelligent—not young—has an assured income but not a very big one—paints—and I like her, and I think you would. Ring her up one morning about 10:00, and go to tea with her. I told her I'd tell you.

Suddenly pouring with rain. It'll be no fun motoring to Forte if it continues. I'll let you know what the visit was like.

Poor Ottoline! I really begin to sympathise with her. I shall write a book from *her* point of view—all the little artists coming—etc—etc. That Turner is small beer:[3] may even be successful small beer, as he has a cadging sort of nature.

Brett flourishes in Taos—has a fine motor-car of her own, which she drives herself—two horses, which she rides—& fell off lately—and exhibits pictures in the "hotel" which cause a "furore." She is furious because we don't go out there—but really, these wonderful women begin to scare my soul.

I'll tell you any news if any crops up. Meanwhile it's a desert.

Greet everybody from me.

D. H. L.

[PS.]
Where did Murry get the *Adelphi* money, do you know? And is he yet come to Italy? The *Calendar* is in all probability dying next month.

---

1 J. W. N. Sullivan, a friend of Koteliansky, was an "English writer on scientific subjects, had served in the Censorship Department under John Middleton Murry during World War I, and by 1917 was contributing to the *Athenaeum*, *Nature*, and *TLS*, and, later, to Murry's *Adelphi*. He was also the author of *An Attempt at Life* (1917), *Aspects of Science* (1923), *Three Men Discuss Relativity* (1926), *Beethoven* (1927), *But for the Grace of God* (1932)" (*C.B.*, II, 512–13).

2 The book was called *Etruscan Places*; it was published in 1932 by Secker, after Lawrence's death.

3 W. J. Turner. See *C.L.*, II, 985. Lawrence also mentions W. J. Turner in Letter No. 300.

283 VILLA MIRENDA
Scandicci
Florence
12 July 1927

My dear Kot

Poor me! I'm in bed again with bronchials & bronchial
hemorrhage—for the last week—so sick of it. I have the
best doctor from Florence—but he can only give coagulin—
says not to bother—but I really get depressed. The doctor
says best go to the mountains, about 2000 feet, to pine woods.
If I'm well enough, I think we shall go to Austria, to the
Worthersee, near Villach, in a fortnight. I hope I can go, I
am sick of this business.—Frieda's sister & husband from
Berlin will be there, at the Worthersee—for August. There
isn't any other news, except that I am sick.

How are you all? Don't be black-moodish, think, you might
have bronchial hemorrhage and many other ills.

D. H. L.

HOTEL FISCHER
Villach
Kärnten, Austria
10 August 1927

My dear Kot

We got here on Friday—had a bed on the train all the way,
so stood the journey all right. I am feeling much better, here
in the cool. That heat & dryness of Tuscany was just too
much for me, when I wasn't well. It seems still heavenly to
go to bed in a cool bed, & not to have to sweat all the time.
My chest is still a bit sore—I have to go carefully—but I can
go [sic] little walks, & go in the motor to the lake—so feel
myself in the land of the living once more.

Frieda's sister is staying on the lake—about six miles away.
F. has gone swimming. We remained in this *gasthaus* in town
—amusing, with all the Tyroler people coming through—no
English nor American.

Austria is the same as ever—the land itself poor, very poor—
the people healthy and easy-going—they don't really bother
themselves—never try to get a grip on anything, not even
the cash. They aren't very honest, swindle you when they can,
but even then in a vague, happy-go-lucky way, very different
from the Italian intensity. There seems to be no government
at all—the whole show just drifts on—to another collapse,
everybody says. I hope not. I can't help sympathising with
them for not caring—why should one care!

I suppose we shall be here another fortnight, then move
towards Bavaria, where we are to spend September. I hope
my chest stays good: it is an affliction.—How are you
feeling. Better, I hope. If only you went out more!

Remember me to everybody.

D. H. L.

285 [HOTEL FISCHER
Villach
Kärnten, Austria]
24 August [1927]

I had your letter—cross as ever. As for Frieda, it is mere
heedlessness, nothing worse.—Still quite sunny & hot here,
but not too much. We leave next Monday, 29th—for Salzburg
—and on 1st Sept. are at

c/o Frau Dr. Jaffe-Richthofen
Irschenhausen
Post Ebenhausen
nr Munich

Are you alone in the Cave? like that hot summer when we
came too? It's a pity you can't go really away somewhere
for a while—I'll write a letter properly, just now.

D. H. L.

---

286 IRSCHENHAUSEN
Post Ebenhausen
bei München
9 September [1927]

It is so quiet here, one forgets how the days go by. Bavaria
is just the same, at least the Isartal—and one looks for one's
old self.—I am a good deal better—but the cough still a
nuisance—still, *really* better. We'll be here till end of month,
then Baden. Are you alone still!—Barby Weekley[1] comes next
week!

Grüsse

D. H. L.

---

[1] Frieda's daughter Barbara

IRSCHENHAUSEN
Post Ebenhausen
bei München
26 September 1927

My dear Kot

I had your last little *De Profundis*: the worst of you is, there's never any *oro te* follows. Now what's the matter? anything new, or just the continual accumulation of the same old badness? It seems to be a fight between you & time: whether Time will wear out your inertia, or your inertia will wear Time out. *Caro*, there's nothing to be said to you: one has long realised the futility. But if I can do anything for you, let me know. And meanwhile, *omnium desperandum*.

We are still here: shall be here I suppose another week. The weather alternates between marvellous black steady days of rain, & marvellous warm bright days of sun. I likewise alternate between feeling much better, & almost sprinting along the road in my old self, & then feeling still a bit of a wreck. The Lord knows what's in it. I feel a bit like Noah's dove who has lost the ark & doesn't see any signs of an olive bough—& is getting a bit weary on the wing. An olive tree is a low little tree, & doesn't grow on mountain tops. How is it that dove didn't come home with a sprig of fir or birch or beech? I think I'll take a pine-needle in my beak, not wait for olives.

There's no news—except the govt. now takes 20% of the royalties of persons living abroad. I begrudge it. I don't feel very keen on going back to Italy—don't know why. But the climate will drive us back. We're due to stay in Baden-Baden a fortnight, anyhow. I like it here, the stillness & the forest & the still-unbroken quality of the silence. The deer go rushing past in front of one.—Let me know when I can be of any avail.

D. H. L.

HOTEL EDEN
Baden-Baden
[Germany]
Thursday [6 October 1927]

My dear Kot

Had your letter & MS[1] in Irschenhausen. I'll try & work the stories up, when I have an inspired moment, & let you see what I can make of them. As they stand they wouldn't sell, of course, though the kernel is interesting.

We are very grand in an hotel here, with rooms & bathroom & all very fine for 10/– a day each. It would cost full double in Italy. But I suppose we are living off past splendours. Germany is very much revived & more prosperous, yet curiously for me has gone suddenly dead. It is as if the angel of death again were waving his wings over the middle of Europe. I don't know where I get the feeling from. My mother-in-law at seventy-six is younger than ever. Perhaps now only she has reached her real spontaneous youth: probably her teens were self-conscious and old, so her seventies are spontaneous & young, & she doesn't care a fig about anything.

The Dobrées ask us to Egypt. Shall we go, if we can scrape together the money? I doubt if I can manage it financially— but I might—the passage is so dear. It's the English govt. takes 20% tax on royalties of persons abroad—& Curtis Brown 10%—on every small penny of royalty.

I wish you had a job, I do really. I even wish we started a non-yellow magazine—I'd make mine pink. But the way is long the wind is cold etc.[2] We *never* get round a certain corner.

I suppose we'll be here till Monday week.

Grüsse

D. H. L.

1 Probably "Two Jewish Stories," recorded by Beila Koteliansky (b. 1852; d. 1929), translated with Notes by S. S. Koteliansky, *The London Mercury* (February 1937), pp. 362–70. For further details, see my Introduction, p. xxviii.

2 Lawrence recalls here the beginning of Sir Walter Scott's "The Lay of the Last Minstrel":

> The way was long, the wind was cold,
> The Minstrel was infirm and old.

HOTEL EDEN
Baden-Baden
[Germany]
8 October 1927

My dear Kot

Your letter about your scheme¹ came on today. I am a useless
person to consult commercially. You know Secker asked me if
*Jud Süss*² was worth publishing in translation—and I said
no! Luckily he did it, & saved his life & almost made his
fortune. So there am I, as a business adviser!

Do you think you could sell such little books as 8000 words
at 15/– each? I doubt it: unless you had something very
special, & a bit risky, inside. But where will you get anything
very special and risky? It's as good as impossible. Unless you
think of something clever. You see no man today will risk
himself in print, at least under his own name. Everybody
turns out the expected stuff. Unless you could persuade a few
people to do you an *anonymous* declaration: a *confessio* or an
apologia in which he really said all he wanted to say—really
let go. If you could get Wells to do a black prophesy &
somebody else to reveal other intimate things that can't get
into print—that Mayo woman say [*sic*] the *worst* about
India³—that kind of thing—all say the worst they all feel—
you might get something even worth 15/–.—But they'd
have to be anonymous. And you'd have to have at least half
a dozen MS [*sic*] before you made any announcement.—Otherwise, I doubt if you'll possibly get anything worth printing.
You won't be able to pay enough.—What you might do, you
might write to a few people who have strong feelings, & ask
them if they have anything that no paper would print, which
they would like to have printed—anonymously or otherwise.
Then see. Otherwise nobody will give you anything really
worth having. And you can't offer the world tripe at 15/–.
for 10,000 words.—Then if you want to do Nonsuch [*sic*]
Press Stuff, you must leave out Kuprin & me. That Nonsuch
[*sic*] sort of stuff is for the pretty-pretty public. If you can
really catch the pretty-pretty public, all right—but not with
corn like mine. My dear Kot, *do* do something. But it must

be feasible. Publish books at 15/– for 10,000 words if you like. But first find the things to publish, worth publishing. I should be a bit ashamed to see a story like *The Man Who Loved Islands* 4 done up at 15/–, when the *London Mercury* will print it in the ordinary course. What is your point? very exquisite production? Then do the classics, that people feel safe about.

I believe you could do something. But you've got to hit a special line. I'll try & think of something. But I of course incline to something cheap—a tiny little magazine at 6^d that honestly says something.

But I'll try to think of something.—Did Leonard Wolff's [*sic*] stuff5—his little books—sell?—But they didn't cost 15/–. Why 15/–? What justification?

D. H. L.

---

1 The "scheme" is the subject of several letters. Koteliansky planned to become a publisher and sought Lawrence's assistance. As Letters Nos. 289–94 make clear, Lawrence was willing to help, but he remained frank and forthright in voicing his opinions as to the nature of the project and its chances for success.

2 The book Lawrence means is *Jew Süss* by Lion Feuchtwanger, translated by Willa and Edwin Muir (London, 1926).

3 Moore identifies the Mayo woman as "Katherine Mayo" (*C.L.*, II, 1006). An American journalist (1868–1940), Miss Mayo went abroad during the First World War to study the workings of the Y.M.C.A. Her name is chiefly associated with her book *Mother India*, which she published in 1927. Regarded by some as a sensational study of child-marriage in India, the book was burned by indignant students in Calcutta.

4 "The Man Who Loved Islands" by Lawrence was published in *The Dial*, LXXXIII (July 1927), pp. 1–25, and in *The London Mercury*, XVI (August 1927), pp.370–88.

5 Leonard Woolf's "stuff," as Lawrence calls it, did sell. The Hogarth Press, which was operated by Leonard and Virginia Woolf at Hogarth House, Richmond, was begun in 1917. By 1924 it had published thirty-two books, among them seven translations from the Russian by Koteliansky. For further details on the Hogarth Press and on Koteliansky's part in it, see Leonard Woolf, *Autobiography: Downhill All the Way* (London, 1967) pp. 64–74.

KURHAUS EDEN
Baden-Baden
[Germany]
Monday [?10 October 1927]

My dear Kot

I can more or less see the possibility of your "intimate
series," if you can get hold of any MSS. that are in any way
really intimate. But as far as I know authors, it's next door to
impossible. Myself, I find it terribly difficult to write intimately
—one feels colder & colder about unbosoming oneself.
And you'd need at least six genuine good MSS. before you
start. I shall see Douglas[1] & Huxley in Florence—& I'll put
the matter to them, privately. Then there's E. M. Forster—
perhaps A. E. Coppard—Osbert Sitwell—Edith Sitwell—
Gerhardi[2]—Dos Passos—Sherwood Anderson—Gertrude
Stein—Robert Graves—all *might* do an interesting thing,
if they will. And one could think of others. But I doubt so
terribly if anybody will write & *sign* anything truly intimate
or particularly worth having. And there must be some point
to the series: you don't want just to start out cadging 15/– or
21/– for limited edition stuff which is only like all other stuff.
Myself, I'll give you anything I can give: but what in God's
name am I to write *intimately*? If there were some clue—some
point upon which we're to be intimate, so that the things
hung together a bit: if even only a suggestion from everybody
of what they think the most important thing in life—something of that sort.—But you *must* have a point.

And I'm a bit doubtful of the sixpenny stories. Better perhaps
a little fortnightly or monthly of ten or twelve thousand
words: a little magazine something like that *Laughing Horse*
from Sante Fe—did you see the number Spud Johnson did
on me?—it wasn't good, but a little private sort of magazine
like that can be made to pay, just to pay, especially if you
canvass personally for material, and appeal only to a decently
educated public—not like the *Adelphi*, which wanted all the
chapel & church imbeciles, & fell through the holes in its own
socks. The point is, you've got to offer something genuine:

there's plenty of hotch-potch already. You'll never make much money with genuine stuff, but you'll be sound.

There goes the dinner bell.—But you've got to get down to some bed rock somewhere—there have been too many piffling little "enterprises."

D. H. L.

---

1 Norman Douglas, the author of *South Wind* (London, 1917). "He knew Lawrence in London before World War I, and renewed the acquaintance in Italy in 1919 and afterwards" (*C.L.*, I, xxxvi).

2 "William (Alexander) Gerhardi (1895–   ), English novelist, was born in St. Petersburg (Leningrad) of English parents. His career as a 'polyglot' began as a child, when he could already speak fluent English, Russian, French, and German .... His works include *Futility* (1922), *Anton Chekhov* (1925), *The Polyglots* (1925) ... [etc.]" (*C.B.*, III, 657).

KURHAUS EDEN
Baden-Baden
[Germany]
Sunday [16 October 1927]

My dear Kot

All right! though personally I don't like expensive limited
editions, if it's a good way to start, then let it be so. I'll
try & write something suitable when I get back to the
Mirenda, & I'll tackle Huxley & Douglas—though it's hard
to get anything out of Douglas, he's so irritable & nervy &
can't work much. You'll have to keep E. M.[1] up to the
scratch—he's not dependable either.

Personally I think nothing of Gertrude Stein, & not much of
Gerhardi. But they have the sort of limited edition public,
I believe.

As for the *Jimmy* story,[2] you'd be perfectly welcome to it,
only Secker is bringing out a volume of short stories, my
stories, in January probably, & including that, of course.
We'll have to think of something else.

We leave on Tuesday morning early, and should be at the
Mirenda by Wednesday evening.

Do you know anything of Murry, & his wife?—how is she?

And do you know Campbell's address? Perhaps I'll write to
him.

I'm still doubtful of the 6ᵈ story series—so hard to get 'em
going.

Will write from Italy.

D. H. L.

[PS.]
We might get something decent from Compton Mackenzie,
or Francis Brett Young.[3]

---

1 E. M. Forster.

2 Lawrence's "Jimmy and the Desperate Woman."

3 An English novelist, author of *The Red Knight* (London 1921). See *C.L.*, I, lvi.

VILLA MIRENDA
Scandicci
Florence
31 October 1927

My dear Kot

Huxley said he was writing to you to say he's tied up to
Chatto & Windus, & can't give you anything. And I enclose
Douglas' letter [1]—don't mind that he calls you a little Jew,
it's merely Douglas.—That's how people are! They're like
fish that will only nibble at a fly that looks like a lot of
diamonds. They do so love to say No!—because that gives
them a sense of power. Myself I began a thing for you—but
the thick morning fogs gave me a bit of cold again, & I've
left off trying to work. But still, if you can get anybody else,
I can have my MS ready for Christmas for you.—Perhaps
you might try A. E. Coppard—I know they "collect" him.
But I'm afraid you'll find most writers too cautious, too
anxious for their own selves & pockets. If I said you were a
millionaire just starting publishing, they'd rise at once.

Altogether the world is depressing—and I feel rather depressed.
My bronchials are such a nuisance, and I don't feel myself
at all. I'm not very happy here, & don't know where else to
go, & have not much money to go anywhere with—I feel I
don't want to work—don't want to do a thing—all the life
gone out of me. Yet how can I sit in this empty place & see
nobody & do nothing! It's a limit! I'll have to make a change
somehow or other—but don't know how.

I'm sorry about Douglas & Huxley—but rather expected it.
People are very small and mingy nowadays. Tell me if there's
anything else I can do. Anyhow if you want my MS by
Christmas I'll get it done—though it may be a bit *long*.[2]

Ever!

D. H. L.

---

1 Douglas' letter is preserved among the *Koteliansky Papers* in the British Museum.
2 There is no hint as to which MS Lawrence was working on at this time.

VILLA MIRENDA
Scandicci
Firenze
22 November 1927

My dear Kot

Well how are things with you now? I was disheartened,
because I had a cold and didn't feel myself, and nothing seemed
worth while. But I'm bucking up again now. And now
Frieda is in bed these two days with a cold. But I expect she'll
be up tomorrow: she's much better. It's this unnatural autumn
—now hot like an orchid-house, hot and damp.

Have you done any more about your scheme? Judging from
the notice of Forster's last book,[1] he must be rather a piffler
just now. And I read the *Celestial Omnibus* again—and found
it rather rubbish. Those things don't wear. But if you can
get anything out of him, do. The devil will be to get
manuscripts: and it's entirely useless your beginning till
you've got *four*: a series must at least begin to be a series.

I'm thinking I shall publish my novel *Lady Chatterley's Lover*
here in Florence, myself, privately—as Douglas does—700
copies at 2 guineas. It is so "improper," it could never appear
in the ordinary way—& I won't cut it about. So I want to do
it myself—& perhaps make £600 or £700. Production is
cheap here. And the book must come out some day.—But
don't mention it, will you, among people.

Michael Arlen[2] came to see us Saturday—ill poor devil—
tubercular trouble. He's much thinner—not much changed—
the Florence snobs cut him dead—he's absolutely *persona
ingrata* now, after they made so much fuss of him. He turned
all his money in America into a trust, can't touch it till he's
35—now he's 31.—But then he'll have a large income,
perhaps £10,000 a year. But what's the good! he's a sad dog.

But tell me about the scheme, & what's to be done. Huxley's
"Proper Studies" is a bore!

D. H. L.

1 In 1927 E. M. Forster was made an honorary fellow of King's College, Cambridge, where he delivered the Clarke Lectures in literature which were published as *Aspects of the Novel* (London, 1927). It is probable that Lawrence refers to this book. The *Celestial Omnibus* appeared in 1911.

2 Dikran Kouyoumdjian (1895–1956) was a novelist and dramatist who wrote under the name Michael Arlen. He visited the Lawrences in Cornwall in 1916. See *C.B.*, I, 520.

VILLA MIRENDA
Scandicci
Florence
8 December [1927]

My dear Kot

I was very much distressed to hear about Ghita, but thankful
there'll be no ill consequences. I hope by now you've got her
safely at the Cave, and she's about well, & all serene. Damn
all motor cars:[1] and I hope they've got to pay good substantial damages.

I suppose the Cave is not being abandoned, after all?

About the printing—dear Kot, what *is* the good of beginning
with just one? My novel[2] I'm writing all over again, so that's
in abeyance. But *how* can you begin the little books with
just me? You'd begin and you'd end there. You've just got to
wring a few MSS out of people, if you're going to start.
The worst of it is, what people? They've all got commercial
contracts.

Have you seen the German magazine *Querschnitt*? It's a very
good modern—popular sort of magazine. I believe, if one
were going to do anything new & popular today, one would
have to be quite bold, jump in with two feet, be unconven-
tional, improper at times, print good nude pictures, & give the
thing a *kick*. There's absolutely no public for merely "good"
stuff: there really isn't. The public wants pictures & bits
of text. But *live* pictures. I'll send you a copy of *Querschnitt*.
The good Jehovah has got to be a bit of a devil—if he's
going to do anything today. You'd far more easily find
artists & draftsmen for a magazine, than writers. Then the
text becomes subsidiary—all the better—& you can put in
snappy things of all sorts.

If we don't go to the ranch in the spring, I think we really
shall go to Ireland.

Can you get from Gertler any explanation of Dobrées
curious behaviour? He wrote very warmly in Sept. asking us
to go to Egypt. I replied we'd like to, if we could. And since

then, not a word from him—only a note from her, saying she hadn't been able to think of journeys—& evidently not badly wanting us. She's a perfect right not to want us— but then in mere politeness he should answer my letter, & say, do we mind putting the thing off.—I'm surprised at his lack of manners. But I suppose there was some mischief made somewhere. However, I was polite, & so can they be.

I expect we'll be here for Christmas—weather dull, most other things too.

D. H. L.

---

1 Ghita Farbman was involved in an automobile accident. See also Letter No. 295.

2 *Lady Chatterley's Lover*, the third version. For further details of Lawrence's writing of this novel, see *B.*, pp. 97–101.

---

295 VILLA MIRENDA
Scandicci
Firenze
23 December 1927

My dear Kot

Well here is Christmas once more—and such beastly weather you never saw—first bitter cold, now clammy wet warm mist. Talk about the sunny south!—and never any rain, the wells dry: only *damp*. At the ranch it is sun every day, and frosty nights!!!

I'm glad it's not so bad with Ghita, but my goodness, bad enough. Makes me furious, damned automobiles.

My dear Kot, I do think this is the low-water mark of existence. I never felt so near the brink of the abyss. But in 1928 something is *bound* to begin new: must. We're trampled almost to extinction—we *must* have a turn soon.

As for my novel, it's half done, but so improper, you wouldn't dare to touch it. It's the most improper novel ever written: and as Jehovah you would probably find it sheer pornography. But it isn't. It's a declaration of the phallic reality.[1] I doubt if it will ever be published. But certainly no English printer would print it. When one is in despair, one can only go one worse. I am driven so *le plus plus pis aller*.

O dear, why are you so Jehovahish! I could wish you a little Satanic. I am certainly going that way. *Satanasso!* It's a nice word. I'm weary of Jehovah, he's always so right.

So your scheme will have to wait a bit. But I think others besides ourselves are being driven to extremity. And when it reaches the limit, then surely something will begin. I'd come to England if there were anything to come for. I'd work in England if there were anyone to work with. But I don't want to found either a beshitten *Adelphi* or a noble magazine.

It's a low-water mark, it really is. As for Christmas, damn it. We're having in the peasants to the tree, Saturday night, & spending Sunday in Florence with people the Huxleys are staying with. Nothing more!

De profundis oremus omnes

D. H. L.

---

1 For a discussion of "phallic reality," see my article "The Phallic Vision: D. H. Lawrence and V. V. Rozanov," *Comparative Literature Studies*, IV, No. 3 (1967), pp. 283–97.

CHALET BEAU SITE
Les Diablerets
Vaud, Suisse
22 January 1928

My dear Kot

We got here Friday night—a rather lovely journey over the Simplon, sun & snow: but a bit long. Came tinkling from the station in a sledge. There are about a hundred tourists in the place, winter-sporting; but I'm not starting in yet. We've got a little flat in this chalet, cosy and warm. Outside there is good snow, dry—and it isn't cold, because there's no wind. I really like it, for a change, and I really think it will do me good. One needs a tonic, after Italy.—I suppose we shall stay a month at least—see how it suits me.

What about you? have you got a job yet? and are you flattening out your employer?

I am getting my novel typed out, & think I shall make a private edition in Florence, & an expurgated edition for Secker & Knopf. Meanwhile I'm collecting poems together for my *Collected Poems*. I'll sort of feel I've got everything behind me, when they are done,—& the novel. Then what next? Some sort of a new start? If we don't go to the ranch, I shall come to London at least for a time. But I am terribly sceptical of being able to do anything. The swine, as you call them, are too many: & vulgar finance & Beaverbrook are laying their hands on the last remaining remnants of freedom. Well, let them! Perhaps when nothing independent remains at all, a few people will stir up. Meanwhile I see no signs.

I hope anyhow this place will be good for my health—that's all I'm here for. I'd like really to feel well again.

How are Ghita & Sonia?

[D. H. L.]

VILLA MIRENDA
Scandicci
Florence
15 March 1928

My dear Kot

So long since I've written!—but I was sort of hoping that
something would turn up, some publication hope, to write
about. But nothing! Only in Diablerets Aldous & I talked,
that it would be good if a few authors joined together to
publish their own books—the "Authors Publishing Company."
And they, the authors, provide the capital, & get a good man
to run the show, on shares. Would that interest you? It's
feasible, anyhow: & a good idea.—Aldous should be in
London now, though I've not heard, & have only the
Athenaeum Club, Pall Mall for his address.

Meanwhile my novel is with the printer here, being set up. I
feel very bold. But I must do it. And I doubt if you could
have got a printer to tackle it in England. English printers
refuse to print words like "arse" or "shit"—just refuse.
Which is nonsense. My novel, the second half, is phallic, &
intentionally so. I believe in it. It can't be done publicly,
so I do it privately. It will be on nice hand-made paper, &
I hope will be handsome.—The printer's shop is an oldfashioned little place—nobody understands a word of
English—nobody can be shocked. What a mercy! I hope to
have the book ready by May 15th. I shall send you a few of
the order-forms,[1] & perhaps you would give them to one or
two of your friends, like Schiff. Then we'll see how it goes.
It's a beginning anyhow.

We've been back a week. Diablerets did me really a lot of
good. But *this* is a rotten climate. It's rained every day
since we're back, & my chest is sorer. I can't stay here long:
I suppose we'll have to summer somewhere up in Switzerland,
to see if I can't make a cure of myself. Oh if only one were
tough! But I'm so much better.

If we go to Switzerland in May, we shall most likely come to England in August. It's my health now that I must see after.

How are you all at the Cave?—Ghita quite better? Grisha still there?—How is Gertler?—I often talked about him to Julian Huxley & Juliette, who really like him.

Tell me if there is any news.

Yrs

D. H. L.

---

1 This and the succeeding letters, many of them previously unpublished, show the extensive role played by Koteliansky in the distribution of *Lady Chatterley's Lover* in England.

VILLA MIRENDA
Scandicci
Florence
31 March 1928

Dear Kot

Orioli[1] sent you some more leaflets—hope you have them.
—And several booksellers, including Dulau, wrote asking for
invoices. We decided on 15% only. If they don't like it, I
can't help it. Booksellers want 25% discount, then they hang
on to the book, & sell it for £4 instead of £2. I don't care
vastly about them. It looks as if I'd sell the book alright [*sic*]
to individuals.—Orioli wrote Dulau & the others, the 15%.
I'll keep you No. 1 if I can, & Farbman 17. But you know
they should be shuffled, & taken at random, to be really fair.
We are sending printed receipt-slips, saying amount received.
I can't alter the leaflets now—they are nearly all sent out.
We intend to bind the book in hard covers, & print on the
cover a design of a phoenix rising from the nest in flames,
which I drew, & which the printer has already cast. I'll send
you a little slip with the design.—Do you remember my
same phoenix on the seal I gave to Murry that Christmas when
I came from Mexico? I wish I had it back from him. "Will
the bird perish, shall the bird rise." No rising for *him*.—But
it will look nice on the cover of the book. I shall mail by
registered book post—then there is no danger.

It's rather fun doing it—buying the special paper—going to
the funny little printer's shop.—But I haven't bought the
binding paper yet. Probably I'll get it from Milan.—Or do you
think people would as leave have the book just sewn, in
Continental fashion? Of course that would be cheaper.

Yrs

D. H. L.

---

1 Pino Orioli. See "The Lawrence Circle" in *C.B.*, III, 639–40. Orioli's letters to
Koteliansky are among the *Koteliansky Papers* in the British Museum.

---

299 [VILLA MIRENDA
Scandicci]
Florence
Tuesday [3 April 1928]

My dear Kot

What do you think of this letter of Shearman?[1] I felt rather mad—but send him his £10 at once. I can't remember the loan—& if he lent it, I'm sure he gave the impression of *giving* it.[2]

Curtis Brown & the publishers are very angry with me for publishing my novel—they say it will only do me harm—etc etc. They'll put any obstacle in the way they can.

Sad to think of Fox gone—I can't believe he is no more in the Cave.[3]

At last a day of sun.

D. H. L.

---

1 Shearman's letter to Lawrence is preserved among the *Koteliansky Papers* in the British Museum.

2 See Lawrence's letter to Shearman in *C.L.*, I, 544. The letter, dated 18 February 1918, begins: "Thank you very much for the £10."

3 A reference to the death of the Farbmans' dog.

VILLA MIRENDA
Scandicci
Florence
18 April 1928

Dear Kot

Thanks for your letter and the Behrens order.—We have
now got about 150 orders—eighty-odd paid—only two from
America, because they haven't had time—so these are all
English. A good many people haven't ordered who will do
so, I think—like E. M. Forster & his crowd—& W. J.
Turner & so on. People don't like ordering far in advance.—
Orioli says he will keep you No. 1 & 17, and let the rest go
out promiscuously—he's marked it down against your
order.—I'm sorry about Ottoline.—Tomorrow Lady
Colefax is coming to tea, I'll get her to help.[1]—And of course
I want to see American results.—I had a letter from Mrs.
Knopf yesterday liking the novel very much, & wanting to
publish it if they can get it possible for the public.—So if
they do it, no doubt they'll have English rights too. I think
Chattos are considering the MS. now—but I shan't let it go
to any other London publisher. If I can cover expenses before
the book appears, I don't mind. I put £130 in the bank
today—opening an English account here in Haskard &
Casardi's.

Dull weather here—rather gritty for the chest.

Awfully nice of you to take so much trouble.

Ever

D. H. L.

[PS.]
I enclose you a phoenix[2]—these I had printed just to use as
ex libris.

---

1 For a reference to Lady Colefax as "that remarkable hostess," see Cynthia
Asquith, *Remember and Be Glad* (London, 1952), p. 155.

2 The memento has been reproduced on the dedication page to this volume
of letters.

VILLA MIRENDA
Scandicci
Florence
16 May [1928]

My dear Kot

Time I wrote you again. We are still here—are keeping on this
house. The printer has at last got the *very nice* paper. Now
he's printing the first half of the novel—1000 copies on this
paper—then he'll have to break up the type & set up the
second half. Only enough type, & that rather ancient, for
half the book. What a go!—But now he really won't be long—
and the binder can start at once. I think we'll have 200 copies
ready to send out by 7th June.

We shall have to post everything registered book post: it's
much the safest: though I may try to slip 200 copies into
America in crates. The English have ordered already well
over 400 copies: very nearly all their half. And the Americans
are itching, but terrified I shan't get the book into the country,
but I shall, & then they'll have to pay $15 instead of $10.
He who hesitates pays more!

So we shan't get away probably till first week in June. But
the weather is very bad in Switzerland now, so I'm just as
well here.—We may stay in Paris a while in August—then
you could come over. Otherwise we'll see you in England.
I might take a house somewhere by the sea in England for
September, & let my sisters come there: & then you could
come too.

Dorothy Warren[1] asked me to send her my pictures to show
in her gallery. I've got seven big ones, four or five small
oils, & seven water-colours. I wonder very much if I should
send them. If you see Gertler, ask him what he thinks. I
think there's a certain something in the pictures that makes
them good—but you'd hate them.

It's very uneven weather here, rather cold, not right at all.
But I suppose it's everywhere alike.

D. H. L.

1 Mrs. Philip Trotter (1896–1954), who as Dorothy Warren "met Lawrence during World War I at Garsington, home of her uncle, Philip Morrell. In 1928 she married Philip Trotter, with whom she operated the Warren Gallery at 39a Maddox Street, London W.1. There, in the summer of 1929, she exhibited Lawrence's paintings, thirteen of which were removed by the police" (*C.L.* I, liv).

302 [VILLA MIRENDA
Scandicci
Florence]
7 June [1928]

Signed the last sheets for *Lady C.* today, so am free—expect you'll get your copy in about ten days. We leave on Sunday for the French Alps—muggy thunder here, no good.—Shall send address immediately we have one.

D. H. L.

303 GRENOBLE
[France]
Thursday [14 June 1928]

We are going up this evening to Hotel des Touristes

St. Nizier de Pariset
nr Grenoble
Isère, France

It's about 3000 ft up—edge of a plateau—queer country, lovely air—down here it's hot.

Will write.

D. H. L.

304 ST. NIZIER
[France]
Friday [15 June 1928]

Dear Kot

This place won't do—so don't write here. We are moving on to Switzerland.—

I will send address.

D. H. L.

---

305 GRAND HOTEL
Chexbres-sur-Vevey
Suisse
Tuesday [19 June 1928]

We got here Sunday, & are pretty comfortable, so I expect we shall stay a while. We are only 1800 [feet] above the sea—but the weather is rather cold, so it's quite enough for the moment. It's a lovely view across the Lake of Geneva. Frieda has gone off today to Baden for a week. Am anxious to hear from Florence.

D. H. L.

GRAND HOTEL
Chexbres-sur-Vevey
Switzerland
27 June 1928

Dear Kot,

I hear from Florence the first copies of *Lady C.* are ready, &
a good many will go off this week. Orioli will mail them as
they come from the binder—it's no good holding them—
the post office won't register a mass at once. So people will
get them in turn. But we shall send to America first. And now
let's trust in heaven.

Aldous & Maria are here for a few days—not so chirpy as
they were in Diablerets—but I expect that is big cities like
London & Paris. Frieda is back from Baden. I am pretty well—
much better than last year, thank heaven. This hotel is very
comfortable & pleasant—only about two thousand feet up.—
Probably in July we shall move up somewhere, over the
3000 line. But one does feel better in Switzerland.—This
afternoon Maria motored us to the Castle of Chillon—but
those show-places bore me.—I am thinking definitely of
sending my pictures to London, but am hesitating between the
Warren Gallery & Claridge's. Must decide directly.

The weather is mixed—was very hot—then thundered—now
is cool. But the hotel anyhow is pleasant.—I can't say
definitely about coming to London. If the altitude suits me
very much, the doctors say I should stay up till end of
Sept. But if it doesn't make a terrific difference to me, we shall
probably come to England end August. And we *may* go
to Egypt in the winter.

Hope you're all right—now I'll be all anxiety till *Lady C.* is
safely delivered.

D. H. L.

[PS.]
Do let Orioli know immediately you get *Lady C.*

KESSELMATTE
Gsteig b. Gstaad
(Bern)
12 July 1928

My dear Kot

Well here we are, having made a new move—this time into a
little peasant chalet on the mountain about a mile above
Gsteig village—& not many miles—six or seven—from
Diablerets, but on the other side of the Pillon Pass. It's very
peaceful, the stillness of the high mountains—& the people,
the peasants, seem very nice—more alive than the French
Swiss round Chexbres. We've got the place till end Sept.—
& I really ought to stay, & not come down—it's about 4000
ft—& really see if I can't cure my cough—which is still a
curse—though I'm pretty well in myself. But I can't climb
hills either.—I think I can be quite happy here for a while,
drifting around in the meadows & the pine-woods. I like to
be a good deal alone. And we're not by any means isolated—
our friends the Brewsters, from Capri—who were with us in
Ceylon—are staying in the hotel in Gsteig village, & they
come up.—So let's hope I really can get better, I'm so sick of
not being well.

I want to come to England end of September. Dorothy
Warren is going to show my pictures in early October—& I
want to see my sisters & everybody. I'm not sure what we
shall do in the winter. Have you seen Dobrée? is he in
London?

Have you got your copy of the novel?—Orioli is sending
them out. I am so anxious to know they arrive.—I don't
suppose you'll like the book—but never mind—every
man his own say, & some things must be said.

Will you stay in the Cave all summer—? and Sonia & Grisha
& Ghita?—Where will they be going?—How alone you will
be, even foxless! Imagine that that young rascal should now
be only a memory!

I hear Murry is writing again to Brett—*lamentoso*—& she is inviting him out, *en famille*, to New Mexico.—Do you have any news of him?

A thunderstorm, & massive rain suddenly! How are you?

D. H. L.

[PS.]
Orioli sends out the books twenty or so a day, as they come from the binder. If we sent a great mass at once, they are much more likely to be held up & inspected by the authorities. A few at a time should pass unnoticed, especially if nobody raises their voice.

KESSELMATTE
Gsteig b. Gstaad
Bern
30 July 1928

My dear Kot

Now the fun begins—the dealers—some—are beginning to
refuse to accept the books they ordered. Today I heard from
Orioli that Stevens and Brown, Booksellers, London—he
doesn't give me the address—say they must return the thirty-
six copies they ordered, and ask to be informed *at once* what
they shall do with them. They had already received 28 copies
at the time they cancelled their order—but also the remaining
eight were on their way from Florence.

Would you hate to fetch away those thirty-six copies for me?
I should be so glad. You could ring up the bookshop and
tell them you were speaking on behalf of Mr. Orioli of
Florence, & Mr. D. H. Lawrence—and that Mr. Lawrence
had written asking you to fetch away thirty-six copies of his
novel, the order for which they had cancelled.

I enclose £2 for taxi and expenses—but of course, don't do
it if you have any qualms.—I can have the books fetched away
from your house in a day or two if you wish. Not that there
is any risk so far.

I enclose a note to Stevens & Brown. You needn't tell them
your name.

Foyles also sent back six copies—& another man some.—
Damn them all, hypocrites.

D. H. L.

[PS.]
Did you receive your last copy, No 17? I do hope so.

[KESSELMATTE]
Gsteig [b. Gstaad
Bern]
Wednesday [1 August 1928]

My dear Kot

Your letter this evening. I asked Enid Hilton (Hopkin) to
fetch the Jackson books. She lives 44 Mecklenburgh Square
now, & I think she's room.—And I think they'd be safe
there.—But I haven't heard from her yet if she would do it.

I asked you to get the Stevens & Brown books—36. My sisters
don't know that I'm publishing that novel—I don't want them
to know—it would only upset them. Anyhow, if you will
get the 36 copies for me, I'll ask Richard Aldington to fetch
them in a taxi—down into the country—Malthouse Cottage,
Padworth nr Reading, Berks. You could let him know.

But I don't believe they will suppress the book—so till they do
there's no risk.

Perhaps you might send two copies to L. E. Pollinger,
Curtis Brown Ltd., 6 Henrietta St., Covent Garden. He asked
for two.—And Simpkin & Marshall wrote to Orioli for more
copies.—

This in haste.

D. H. L.

KESSELMATTE
Gsteig b. Gstaad
Bern
Saturday 4 August 1928

My dear Kot

I was very glad to have your express and to know the books
are safe. By the same post I heard from Enid Hilton that she
has the 74 books from Jackson in her flat.

Now I suppose Richard A. will write you about taking your
copies down to the country. But will you send two more
copies to L. E. Pollinger, of Curtis Brown's—making four
in all—and one copy to Bettina Von Hutten, 19 Whitehead's
Grove, Chelsea.—Is that the Baroness von Hutten?

I do wish you hadn't sent back my cheque. Will you, since
you are so proud, keep an account of what I've cost you, &
tell me.

I am writing now to Enid Hilton to ask her if she knows of
some safe place, where to store the books. For the life of me,
I can think of nowhere except Richard A. As I told you, my
sisters know nothing of this venture, and I don't want to tell
them.—But I shall ask Enid to keep about two dozen copies
in her flat, to distribute for me. I don't think there's any
risk—at least not yet.

I wouldn't trust Miss Beach¹ in Paris for a moment. We
must find some safe place to deposit the things, in England.
You might speak to Richard.

I myself shall raise the price before long. What would you
suggest about that?

Where are you going, in the country? I hope it'll be nice.

I'm very grateful to you for taking this trouble for me. I
expect we'll get it all smoothed out one day. I believe Orioli
sent to most of the booksellers without pre-payment—and some
seem to be deferring their paying—hoping, I suppose, to sneak
out if the thing is suppressed. What a world!

D. H. L.

[PS.]
Have you got your last copy—no. 17?

Be sure to let me know immediately if there is any move to suppress—& let Enid H. know, will you?

---

1 Sylvia Beach, who "published under the imprint Shakespeare and Co. at her bookshop first located at the rue Dupuytren, then at 12, rue de l'Odéon, Paris" (*C.B.*, III, 711).

311
Gsteig b. Gstaad
(Bern)
Wednesday 8 August 1928

My dear Kot

I'm glad you will keep the 36 copies by you. Richard A. said he had written for you to send them down there—but I presume you didn't.

Now Orioli says he has sent you some orders to distribute. Perhaps you have done it already. If not, send on the orders to Mrs. Lawrence Hilton, 44 Mecklenburgh Square W.C.1.— and ask her to do it. I don't trust the Jacksons either, & would much rather have that Jackson lot distributed. I have already asked Enid H. to send 40 copies in a box down to Richard. And I have asked Orioli to send all orders here to *me*, & I'll forward them to Enid H. He has another two dozen or so, he says. And if you hear of any action against the book, you'll let me know at once, won't you—& Enid H. too—& Richard.

I'm sending the cheque again: I beg you please to pay *all* expenses out of it. Don't please send it back again.

Did you send the two copies to Cornish Bros. of Birmingham? Orioli says he sent you their order for two copies, & then wrote to you they had *cancelled* it.—Dirty swine.—If you have *not* sent them the order, will you forward them their money back (I enclose cheque). But if you *have* sent their order, perhaps you can get the books back before you refund. I really think Orioli is too meek about accepting the cancelling of orders. I am trying to make Jacksons refund postage.

Well, you are probably gone away to the country by the time this reaches London. I hope you'll have a good time. It's marvellous weather here.

I'm most awfully sorry to give you such a lot of trouble. But now I hope it will be finished. And do pay all postage & everything from my cheque.

D. H. L.

[PS.]
Cornish Bros.—Booksellers. 39 New St. Birmingham.

KESSELMATTE
Gsteig b. Gstaad
(Bern)
10 August 1928

My dear Kot

Many thanks for yours. I have today send Enid H. a list of
twenty copies to send out. Hope she does it safely.—She
may have sent some copies down to Richard A.—if so, I
expect we shall soon exhaust what are left with her. But
I'll let you know.—Only if anything *definite* happens in the
confiscation line, you might make sure her lot is safe.
Otherwise don't you trouble any more. I'm awfully sorry
you've been bothered so much.—Now there is that final
bit of a nuisance with Cornish Bros.—Oh dear!

I'm sorry you're not going to the country—it might have
done you good. But perhaps you'll get your trip yet.

hastily

D. H. L.

[KESSELMATTE]
Gsteig b. Gstaad
[Bern]
Friday [17 August 1928]

My dear Kot,

Your card from Falmouth this evening. It's a pity if Cornish Bros. send all the way back to Florence. I ought to have suggested that they were sent to *me*, c/o L. E. Pollinger of Curtis Brown Ltd. Pollinger would have taken them in for me —& been quite safe. He is very friendly. However, I suppose it's too late now. I would have told Pollinger to hold the books for me.

Enid sent 32 copies to Richard, who has them safely. The others she has mostly distributed, according to orders—and collected cash in most cases. Mrs. Lahr took another twelve copies, & paid on the spot: seems very nice. I think, if Enid has distributed my final orders, she will have only one copy left. And I asked Richard to distribute ten: leaves him 22. Will you do the next batch of orders?—or shall Richard?— Pollinger has sold nine copies for me—nett [*sic*]—very nice. He may dispose of more.—Or do you think we can begin again sending out orders from Florence?—Foyles' kept their six copies after all: after cancelling order. They said they saw the little notice in the *Star*!!

There is no further news from America.

Here we had heavy thunder & rain, so now it is quite cold. But I don't mind.—My sister Emily, elder sister, is coming with her daughter of 20—they arrive on the 26th—Sunday week. I do hope it will be fine weather. By Sept. 15 I think we shall have had about enough of here—then probably go to Baden for ten days—then I want to come to England.

That Bettina von Hutten—Baroness or not—hasn't paid yet.

Enid was awfully good & smart delivering the things.— Orioli says it is bad business to demand payment on delivery from people we know are pretty safe—only with comparative strangers one should do it.

Did you have a nice holiday? My word, how I remember
Falmouth! Staying near there with the Murrys, in war-time:
and Murry trying to drown us all, one Sunday afternoon,
when we were rowing on that river & a sudden storm blew
up. That will always be war region to me.

D. H. L.

314 [KESSELMATTE]
Gsteig [b. Gstaad
Bern]
Thursday [23 August 1928]

My dear Kot

Many thanks for yours. I'm sorry the motor holiday was
expensive, but motor holidays always are. Was everywhere
very crowded? did Cornwall seem very spoiled? I've been
thinking so much about it lately—I loved Cornwall.

Would you mind sending these two copies to Simpkin
Marshal—they are paid. I asked Richard to send out about
18 or 20: and I'm sending him the provincial orders. Soon
we'll have no books in England. I've asked Orioli to tell me
how many he has left in Florence. *Do you think it's quite safe
to post to England from Florence?*

I do wish you didn't send the cheque back—why are you so
obstinate?

I had a fluttered & "interested" p.c. from Barbara.[1] How the
flutterings bore me!—My sister Emily & her daughter arrive
Sunday morning.—No word from O. about Cornish Bros.

D. H. L.

---

[1] Barbara Low

KESSELMATTE
Gsteig b. Gstaad
Switzerland
30 August 1928

My dear Kot

Thanks for yours. Am glad rumours have gone quiet. I wonder what "influential people," indeed?

Those Cornish Bros. stopped their cheque—it was returned to Florence unpaid. And they have *not* returned the two copies—not so far. Oh swine of people! So please burn my cheque to them.

Did you send the six copies to the A. L. Humphreys at the Devonshire Club, James St., S.W.1.—?—I thought we'd better draw on your little lot for him, as he paid the £12. in advance.

I enclose a letter from Miss Sylvia Raphael. I had her cheque & ordered her a copy, either from Enid or R. A., some weeks ago. I begged R. A. to send me his list of copies he'd sent out, people he'd sent to, but he didn't do it. And tomorrow he & Arabella are leaving for Italy—to be away all winter.

If he sent out all orders I forwarded to him, he would have not more than five copies left. These I asked him to send back to Enid. But I don't know what's happened.

Would you send this one copy to Miss Raphael.

The Vanguard Press in New York wanted to do a limited edition at $10—for subscribers only. As they can't *print* it in U.S.A., they want to do it by the photography process—& give me 10%. I suppose, considering all their expense & risk, it's worth it. At least one can supply orders. The U.S. authorities are holding up some copies. There was a paragraph in a California paper saying the book was obscene & the customs were not allowing it to go any further. But some copies have got in—we know of about 14. But Orioli sent 140 or so —probably most of them lost. Damn!

I want him to tell me how many copies we have left, but he doesn't do it. But he is back in Florence now. He has started sending a few copies to England again. I shall ask him to send you another twenty, two copies per day. Shall I put it that way? If you'd rather have it otherwise, write him direct. We won't ask you to send out any more, now he is posting from Florence.

My elder sister & my niece are here—but somehow I feel a bit remote & depressed. They are so far from my *active* life. And it pours with rain. And I've got a bit of cold, & write this in bed. And altogether, I wish the Lord would make a new man of me, for I'm not much to boast of now.

D. H. L.

[PS.]
Let Barbara write to Orioli for a copy!

KESSELMATTE
Gsteig b. Gstaad
Switzerland
5 September 1928

My dear Kot

Thanks for yours received today, with Cornish Bros cheque,
& list. I got a list from R. A.—he had only four copies left,
& he sent them to Enid: who had just got orders for four
from me—which clears up that bunch entirely.

Orioli wrote that Simpkin & Marshall wanted five more copies,
& wanted them delivered by hand if possible, & they wish to
pay on delivery. Do you mind doing it? If Enid had any
copies I'd ask her.

I hope Orioli is sending you the twenty copies. He still has
not told me how many copies remain in Florence.—Of the
American 140, I'm afraid about half were unpaid. But some
Americans are paying as they receive their copies. I'm afraid
we shall lose a number there, though.

If I don't let the Vanguard print, then someone else is *sure*
to pirate the book. You know Joyce was pirated, in sections,
in spite of Sylvia Beach's frantic efforts.—And if the Vanguard
print a 1000 at $10.—I don't see I break faith with the pur-
chasers of my edition. I didn't promise that no other edition
should ever be published.

My sister & daughter leave on Friday. It is sad to say I rather
suffered from them. But a gulf comes as one grows older.
And nowadays I can't bear to be stuck among several women,
alone. It just seems to annihilate one.

I expect we shall leave here for good on the 17th—go to
Baden-Baden for ten days or a fortnight—then I really ought
to come to England. Dorothy Warren is showing my pictures
from Oct 5th to 26th. She has had them framed, & says they
look lovely. Of course I'm pining to see them framed & hung.
Yet I don't know if I can drag myself to England.—I think she
will put about 15 gns. on the water-colours—& something a
bit more on the small oils—but on the big pictures I want her

to put a real high price, like £500, because I really don't want to sell them. I have so few, & we got so fond of them, as they hung in the Mirenda.

Are you all alone in the Cave?—I think it must be rather nice.

D. H. L.

317

My dear Kot.

Orioli was away from Florence for a time because of a family tragedy—but he is back now. I have asked him to send you 20 copies. He writes that there are about 210 copies left, that is 190 when yours are gone. And feeling very fierce because the book is selling for $50 in New York—there can't be very many copies there to sell—he has written to people ordering copies that the edition is sold out, Davis & Orioli have bought the remainder, & the price is four guineas. Since he's done it he's done it, I don't care very much: expecially as it is the *Americans* who are now rushing to order. We'll see how it goes off.

I wrote Dorothy Warren she could postpone the show if she likes, as I cannot think of sending the pictures to New York now. I'm afraid the silly ass has shown them to half London already. But if she wants to make a public show in Oct., let her. I've always had the same enemies. As for the painters, if my pictures aren't ten times better than Roger Fry's, then he's welcome to Fry [*sic*] them to his heart's content. My pictures are alive—and the little whipper-snappers will hate them for it.—Bah, if I'd spent my life considering my enemies, I should be a dumb dead fish long ago.

I sent you a stupid book which was sent me—*Why We Misbehave*—I thought, as it is only just published, & at $4 or $5, you might perhaps sell it in Charing X [Cross] Rd. one day when you're selling books you don't want. If not, throw it in the dust-bin.[1]

We leave here on Monday for Baden-Baden. I think we shall stay in Hotel Löwen, Lichtenthal bei *Baden-Baden*.

Autumn here now, chilly, cloudy—time to go. I doubt I shan't come to England—damn England. I didn't know Enid had her tragedy up her sleeve—or had a tragedy at all.

Her husband isn't thrilling, but quite nice. Perhaps she
was only being impressive.

Gute Nacht!

D. H. L.

---

1 *Why We Misbehave* by Dr. Samuel Daniel Schmalhausen was published in New
York by Garden City Publishers (1928).

---

318 [HOTEL LÖWEN
Lichtenthal b.
Baden-Baden]
29 September [1928]

I am leaving on Monday for South of France—not quite sure
where. Frieda is going direct to Florence to get rid of the
Mirenda. I shan't go back there—it really doesn't suit my
health. I shan't go to Paris just now, but later we may, &
I'll write you. The picture show is postponed a while—I
think Frieda will come over.—Has Orioli sent you the books?
Did you see the article in *T. P.'s.*[1] Will send address.

D. H. L.

---

[1] Probably a reference to Lawrence's "Laura Philippine," which was published
in *T. P.'s and Cassell's Weekly* (7 July 1928). For his other contributions to this
periodical see Items C108 and C150 in *B.*, pp. 265, 273. "Laura Philippine" has
recently been reprinted in *Phoenix II* (New York, 1968), pp. 523–26.

319 LE LAVANDOU
Var. [France
5 October 1928]

Nice down here by the sea, sunny & fresh & so easy-seeming.
Frieda is in Florence—I am alone for the moment. I may go
over to the island of Port-Cros, so will send address in a
day or two.

D. H. L.

---

320 LA VIGIE
Ile de Port-Cros
Var. [France]
Sunday [14 October 1928]

We are going over to the island tomorrow, & this is to be the
address. Send me a line.

D. H. L.

LA VIGIE
Ile de Port-Cros
Var. France
31 October 1928

My dear Kot

Have I written to you since we are here, or haven't I? I've
lost track. But Frieda arrived from Florence with that Italian
flu, & of course I got it, & have felt bad these two weeks.
But am a lot better.

I had your letter here—& yesterday came cuttings from *John
Bull, Sunday Chronicle* etc.[1]—& what a tin-pot shindy!
What fools altogether!—But what about those customs
confiscations? was it your copy? I hope no trouble to you,
anyhow. How bored one gets by endless mob-stupidity.—
But let me know. I seem to know nothing here—mail comes
three times a week, when the sea is not rough. Today it's a
storm, so probably tomorrow no boat.

I should like it here if I had shaken off this cold. It is very
quiet. Richard Aldington & Arabella & Mrs. Patmore, & an
Italian man to do the fetching & carrying—that's all. For
the rest it is a fortified hilltop on an island covered with
pine-trees. There is one hotel, one little port with eight or
nine houses—nothing else but hills & trees, & sea & other
islands & mainland ten miles or so off. The hotel is nearly
an hour's walk. I have not been down since we are here. All
being well, we shall stay till towards Christmas, then I don't
know where.

I ordered you a copy of my poems[2]—suppose you'll get them.

How are you? Are the Farbman's [*sic*] back, and is there
any news? *Where* does Murry want to go? Brett threatens
to come to Europe—hope she'll go to him. We get on very
well here—manage to get good food & all that.—I still haven't

heard if Dorothy Warren is actually in London: Frieda might come in Nov. if she shows the pictures. I feel very indifferent to almost everything.

tante cose!

D. H. L.

---

1 These articles on *Lady Chatterley's Lover* are reprinted in *C.B.*, III, 262-65.

2 *The Collected Poems of D. H. Lawrence*, 2 vols. (London, 1928). These were published in September 1928 by Secker.

---

322 HOTEL BEAU RIVAGE
Bandol
Var. [France]
Saturday [17 November 1928]

Got here today—think we shall stay this month out. Glad to be off that poky island—but we had such a bad crossing, still feel shaky inside. Will write—I had your letters—no news here.

D. H. L.

HOTEL BEAU RIVAGE
Bandol
Var. France
3 December 1928

My dear Kot

How are you now, and how are things? We have been sitting here quietly, with good sunny weather, this last fortnight, and really I think I'm getting stronger. Only my cough is a curse, but my real health seems genuinely better. Which to me is the chief thing.

Lady C. continues her sad course. I hear there are *two* pirated editions out in America—Lahr [1]—the Red Lion St. bookseller —wrote me he bought a copy for 30/- —and Stieglitz [2] wrote they are selling it in New York, the pirated edition, as the Original, at $10: pretending it is the original. So you see my plan to agree with the Vanguard people to take 10% would have been best, since now I get *nothing*, & they do as they like.—

Then I hear nothing lately from Orioli—he was not well when he last wrote—and any copies I asked him to send out, lately, he has *not* sent. Something is wrong. I expect I shall have to go to Florence.

Did I tell you that when I printed *Lady C.*—as they had only enough type to do *half* the book at a time, I had them print two hundred copies on ordinary paper. These 200 copies are bound up in paper binding—brochure—and I wish I could put them on the market at £1.—to undersell the pirated copies. I wrote to Charles Lahr about it, as he seemed friendly—you remember you once went there "Miss Archer" [3] —but he hasn't answered.

How has Aldous' book gone in England? [4] I heard it sold 80,000 in America. It's the modern sort of melodrama, what *East Lynne* was in its day. [5]

I am hung up here waiting to see if I've got to go to Florence —I don't want to go. If I needn't, I think we shall go to Spain. Unless also I am forced to come to London to take my pictures away from Dorothy Warren—I can't have her keeping them there in this fashion. I may have to come just for Christmas—though I dread London, with its darkness and squalor.

How are you all? Sonia & Grisha & Ghita? Things don't get much brighter in the world, do they? That's why one sticks to the Mediterranean, with its sun. But I hope you are well. The thought of St. John's Wood is gloomy to me.

D. H. L.

---

1 Charles Lahr was later involved in the publication of an unexpurgated edition of Lawrence's *Pansies*. For details see *I.H.*, p. 399.

2 Alfred Stieglitz, the "American photographer and art exhibitor." See *C.L.*, I, liv and *C.B.*, III, 702. Two letters from Lawrence to Stieglitz are printed in *C.L.*, II, 1076–77, 1089–90.

3 I have been unable to identify "Miss Archer."

4 Aldous Huxley's *Point Counter Point* (London 1928).

5 *East Lynne* (London, 1861) was an immensely popular novel by Mrs. Henry Wood. Its heroine, Lady Isabel Vane, after running off with another man, returns to her remarried husband disguised as a nurse to care for her own children. She keeps up this pretense for a considerable time but is at last reconciled with her husband.

HOTEL BEAU RIVAGE
Bandol
Var. [France]
Sunday [9 December 1928]

My dear Kot.

I heard today from Charles Lahr, 68 Red Lion St. W.C.1.
He says he can handle *all* the 200 edition: give me 21/–,
and sell to the trade for 24/–, and private people for 30/–.

Also he says he can dispose of several of the £4-copies: give
me £4 and sell for £5—I believe he is absolutely honest, &
I like the sound of him. Rhys Davies, a young Welsh writer,
was here a few days—nice fellow.[1] He knows Lahr very well
& has a great respect for him.

I told Lahr I would ask you to call and see him. Will you
go?—and supply him with a few of your copies if he wants
them.—But go and talk to him.—I told him if you let him
have copies he could put the money in the bank.

Then Orioli could fill up your 25 again. And I am asking
Enid if she'll take 25. Somehow I feel now as if I'd rather have
the books in London. Orioli is perhaps not so interested any
more.

I told Lahr I had only a few copies of the first edition—that
Orioli was responsible for the last hundred. So stick to that.

No, I've heard of no copy confiscated.

Orioli says the men of the Fanfrolico Press told him they
would like to do a portfolio of reproductions of my pictures.
What do you think? I would have to get them photographed.

Today it's rainy here too—but not unpleasant. We may stay
here over Christmas. Not a bad place. Remember me to
Sonia & Grisha.

D. H. L.

---

1 For an account of this visit by Davies, see *C.B.*, III, 270–81.

HOTEL BEAU RIVAGE
Bandol
Var., France
14 December 1928

My dear Kot

Yours today—hope you got on all right with Lahr.

Could you post me the enclosed letter to Jack Lindsay?[1]
I leave it open for you to read.

Would you either go and see L. E. Pollinger of Curtis Browns,
and take him three copies of *Lady C.*—or just leave the copies
for him? He pays the £4 into my bank & is perfectly safe.
I told him you'd call, but if you'd prefer merely to leave the
books, do that. And I'll ask Orioli to send you ten more copies.

And you *must* let me pay you, some way.

D. H. L.

---

[1] "Australian-born writer, long resident in England. With P. R. Stephensen,
operated Fanfrolico Press with offices at 71, High Holborn, London (1926–1930).
Declined to publish Lawrence's *Paintings*, encouraged Stephensen to found
Mandrake Press" (*C.B.*, III, 638).

HOTEL BEAU RIVAGE
Bandol
Var. [France]
21 December 1928

My dear Kot

Stephensen[1] was here of the Fanfrolico. I *liked* him: not limp
at all—been a bit taken in by the "culture" of the other lot, I
fancy. They are starting a new Press in [*sic*] New Year—The
Mandrake Press—& are going to publish ordinary books,
from 3/6 to 10/6 also—& say they will be glad to do
Fallen Leaves.[2] He said he'd write you: but if he doesn't,
say nothing, and remind *me* to nudge him, when the time
comes. He says he'll do my pictures—he's the *man* of the
show, & has whatever money they have—& Edward
Goldston of Museum St.[3] is to back them. He talks of doing
my pictures 500 copies at ten guineas. Seems to me very
dear. But we'll see what actually happens: talks of giving me
an advance of £250. *Avanti Italiani! Don't mention this*—I
want to write a foreword. Could you ask any of the booksellers to send me *at once*, with the bill, a copy of Roger Fry's
Cézanne book. It would make a good starting point for me to
write a good peppery foreword *against* all that significant
form piffle. And if you can easily lay hands on a cheap copy
[of] Tolstoi's *What is Art?* send me that too, *with the bill.
I must pay for them.*

Would you care to have a copy of *Lady C's* second edition.
I'll give you one for Christmas.

D. H. L.

---

1 P. R. Stephensen, an "Australian writer and editor. With Jack Lindsay,
operated Fanfrolico Press in London (1926–1929); thereafter with Edward
Goldston, bookseller, The Mandrake Press, which published Lawrence's *Paintings* (June, 1929) and *A Propos of Lady Chatterley's Lover* (June, 1930). The
privately printed, unexpurgated *Pansies* (August, 1929) carries the Stephensen
imprint. Visited Lawrence at Bandol, December, 1928—January, 1929. Returned
to Australia in 1930's" (*C.B.*, III, 641).

2 This is V. V. Rozanov's *Fallen Leaves* [Bundle One], translated from the Russian by S. S. Koteliansky with a foreword by James Stephens. It was published in London by the Mandrake Press in 1929. See Lawrence's review of this book in *Phoenix* (New York, 1936) pp. 388–92. The review was published originally in *Everyman* (23 January 1930). There is no evidence that Lawrence helped Koteliansky with the translation of *Fallen Leaves*.

3 "Edward Goldston, the Jew bookseller of Museum St" (*C.L.*, II, 1142).

HOTEL BEAU RIVAGE
Bandol
Var. [France]
Friday 11 January 1929

My dear Kot

Pollinger says he wants more copies of the first edition—will
you let him have whatever he wants—and if you like, Orioli
will always send you further copies to make up your twenty-
five. He sent some to Mrs. Patmore—Brigit—but I don't
know if she's very stable—may go away anywhere—so I
think I'll ask her to let Lahr have them to hold. They are
only about ten. Then I'll get my sister to have twenty. I had
to send them the book at last. Ada—in Ripley—has read it,
and says she feels I've always hidden part of myself from her.
If people refuse to see, what can one do?

Lahr has paid into my bank ninety guineas for 90 copies of the
second edit. I think Orioli sent him in all 112—but O. is a
bit vague. There are only 18 copies or so left—& I want to
keep a few.

Stephensen was here again—of the Fanfrolico and he seems
to be going ahead with my pictures. He is combining with
Edward Goldston. There will be no Lindsay—either father or
son—in the Mandrake Press.—I have written the "Introduction"[1]—about 10,000 words—slain Clive Bell. I got Fry's
Cézanne and Bell's *Art* from Bumpus, but no invoice. I wish
they'd send it at once, before we leave. What a fool Clive
Bell is!

Did you see Pollinger, and what did you think of him?

Barbara Weekley leaves tomorrow for London. She's got
herself into a nasty state with those messy second-rate
Studio crowd—really spoilt herself. Wish she'd get out of it.

I expect we shall stay here another two weeks, as Aldous
& Maria are probably coming for a bit, on their way to Italy.
But there's no news.—I forgot to mention Rosanov [*sic*] to

Stephensen—but he's only just got back to London—so let him get started with his Mandrake—he'd do it in that press.

D. H. L.

---

1 "Introduction to These Paintings," which is reprinted in *Phoenix* (New York, 1936), pp. 551–84.

HOTEL BEAU RIVAGE
Bandol
Var. [France]
18 January 1929

Dear Kot,

Lahr wrote tonight his plan of having *Lady C.* printed in
Berlin or Vienna, & having orders go to Orioli & be forwarded from Florence to Berlin. In some ways it is good, but
as you suggest, I want to get the thing *finished* at Florence.
Orioli is going to publish a story by Norman Douglas, and
a translated cook-book by Faith Mackenzie, and he'd just
get into a muddle. So we must leave him out of count. If
we were going to print in Berlin, it would, in my opinion,
be better to have someone there to receive orders. I have a
cousin there married to a German, Max Hunger, who spent
most of his younger life in England—he would probably
do it—though I am not keen to ask him. And would the
English want to send orders to Berlin? I suppose so. Lahr
said his friend Ehrenstein would do the despatching of orders.
Did you see him?—What do you think of the German plan,
anyhow? I should like to get out another edition, *as quickly
as possible.* Do you think 15/- about right for price?

I wondered once if you'd like to go to Paris & do the thing—
and we could arrange it all between us. But probably you
wouldn't want to. And perhaps there'd be passport difficulties.

Did you get the copy of the second edition which Orioli
sent you, as my Christmas card? You don't mention it—so
I hope it's not gone lost. Six copies were also sent to Pollinger,
& *he* hasn't acknowledged them. And six copies of the *first
edition* were sent to Mrs. Brigit Patmore, to hold for me,
and though I have written to her, I get no word from her.
Would you mind ringing her up, if she is on the telephone—
and then if she's got the six copies, perhaps you would call
and take them over to Lahr, for him to keep, as it is just
near. The address is 4. Milman St., Bedford Row. Did you
meet Brigit Patmore in Mecklenburgh Square days?[1] She was
rich then, but is quite poor now, has left her husband & is
living with her two sons.

I'm a little afraid now of mail difficulties, till I hear that your copy, & Brigit Patmore's & Pollinger's are safely arrived. I hear that the police stopped a copy of Douglas' *Limericks* in the post, and the Chief of Police went to interview the man it was addressed to, somewhere in Sussex. But then I think the limericks are just indecent. Why didn't Douglas keep them out of the post?—so bad for everybody else.

Stephensen is rushing round getting his new thing started. He won't print any ordinary Mandrake books till autumn, but go and see him if you wish—or, when I write to him—he's supposed to be sending me a colour-proof of one of my pictures—I will remind him to see you about Rosanov [*sic*]. I thought it best to let him get going first.

I'm not sending any copies to my sister till I hear the post is really safe. But do, if you can, take those six copies from Brigit —I hope she's got them safely.

Orioli sent 10 copies 2nd edition & 2 copies first edition to Sylvia Beach, Paris, just after Christmas. The first arrived & are sold—but the second have not arrived—they are lost somewhere. I have asked Orioli to start enquiries. I do hope the post won't go wrong.

Bitter cold wind here, hard frosts at night, but sunny days. I hear London is dismal. You might really enjoy going to Paris and taking two rooms and publishing the Paris edition of *Lady C.*

D. H. L.

[PS.]
Frieda sent to Barbara Weekley your comments on her!!— which I heartily agree with.

[PPS.]
I wonder if perhaps the French are getting a bit scared of English "improper" books printed in their country. Perhaps they are. The MSS I send from here seem to be held up too. I sent copies of my poems *Pansies* to Pollinger twelve days ago, and they are not there yet. Perhaps the German idea is best—France getting uneasy.

---

1 Lawrence lived at 44 Mecklenburgh Square during October–December 1917. See *P.R.*, p. 47.

HOTEL BEAU RIVAGE
Bandol
Var. [France]
21 January 1929

Dear Kot

Have you heard that two Scotland Yard fellows called on
Pollinger & told him six copies of *Lady C.* had been sent him
& making enquiries—& saying all copies of the book sent
would be confiscated. So that's that! I am wondering about
Mrs. P's—expect it's the same there.—Also the two *MS.*
copies of my poems *Pansies*, sent to Pollinger, are being held
up. What rights have they over MSS, I should like to know?

I am writing Stephensen & shall mention Rosanov [*sic*].

D. H. L.

HOTEL BEAU RIVAGE
Bandol
Var. [France]
1 February 1929

Dear Kot

There is no real news here—except that the man of the
Pegasus Press wrote this morning saying he hadn't got the
information yet from his distributing agents, but that he
agreed to give me 40 frs. per copy if they do an edition of a
thousand to sell to trade at 100 frs:—but if they do 2000,
then on the second thousand I am to have only 30 frs. I
shall write it will be better to do 1000 only. *But how am I
to keep a check on him?*—Nothing of course is settled yet,
but he says the pirated edition is selling in Paris normally at
300 frs—price to the trade 200 frs—but that lately the pirates
have delivered copies to the trade at 150 frs & even at 100
frs.—& he talks as if we would have to come lower. But of
course I am not sure that his figures are correct.

Aldous & Maria left this morning—both rather seedy, I thought—Aldous very sympathetic. He wrote to Jack Hutchinson about the MSS of the *Pansies*—& Jack will talk it over with Moseley [*sic*],[1] the Socialist with whom he is great friends, & who can ask questions in the House if necessary.[2] I will let you know the results.

When I have got things settled up, I want to go to Majorca— I feel like moving on. But there are various things to do.

Did you see Murry's effusion over me in his *Adelphi*? *Semper idem!*

You might perhaps have a talk with C. L.[3] about the Pegasus. Curtis Browns have a sort of connection agency in Paris, but I don't know if one could use them to make an agreement—or if they are much good.

Aldous & Maria brought us both bad colds—but the weather's nice.

D. H. L.

---

1 Sir Oswald Ernald Mosley who sat as a Labour M.P. (1924–30), but who, in the early part of 1931, seceded from the Labour Party and formed a new party known as the British Union of Fascists.

2 For a transcript of the 28 February 1929 "Parliamentary Debate on Seizure of *Pansies* MSS" see *C.B.*, III, 308–12.

3 Charles Lahr.

HOTEL BEAU RIVAGE
Bandol
Var. [France]
7 [February] 1929

My Dear Kot

I suppose you haven't seen Pollinger—I wish you saw him &
had a talk with him.—The men from the Yard admitted that
they had the MSS of *Pansies* and they consider them indecent
& obscene—which is a lie. Apparently by law, *if* the things
are so considered, they are in the right. But I am having CB's [1]
solicitors apply for the release of these MS. [*sic*]—I haven't
heard anything from Jack H. [2]—and there is nothing further.
Mail seems to go through normally, even to CB's office—on
which the Yard seems to have concentrated all its efforts.
CL thinks they suspect CB's of having handled the whole
edit.—but I doubt it. I wonder if old CB has his finger in
other pies.—

The Pegasus have not written anything further, so things are
where they were. I haven't Nancy Cunard's address—have
you? If you sent it me I'd write her myself. Aldous &
Maria evidently are quite out of touch with her.

They—Aldous & Maria, left a week ago for Florence, where
they want to sell the car. On Saturday they broke down at
Albenga near Savona and I've not heard a word since. They
both seemed rather seedy & run down, I thought. Aldous is
really nicer—getting older & a bit more aware of other
people's existence.

Spain seems really rather upset—anyhow a great deal of
police-watching going on—so I think we'll not go there just
yet. I want to move from here soon—though it's on the whole
sunny & pleasant—but perhaps go to Italy & find some little
house—& then go to Spain later—or somewhere else.—I
shall soon have finished typing out the *Pansies* again &
correcting them.

Yes, it would be a good thing if someone were in Paris whom
one could trust, to do an edition & keep it going.

Ottoline writes very friendly—says she has such a lot of pain nowadays.

We've both had a bit of flu—not bad—but it gets at my chest of course.

I had a typescript copy of the "Introd. to the Paintings" from Pollinger, & returned it corrected. They are to give me 250 down, for the pictures, and a royalty of 5%—quite decent.

How are you & what are you doing?

D. H. L.

---

1 Curtis Brown, Lawrence's literary agents.

2 St. John [Jack] Hutchinson, K.C., who had known Lawrence during the war years and who in 1929 acted as Dorothy Warren Trotter's defence counsel in the trial over her exhibition of Lawrence's paintings.

[HOTEL BEAU RIVAGE]
Bandol
[Var. France]
1 March 1929

My dear Kot

We had intended to leave tomorrow, but are staying on a few
more days—probably till Wednesday—then I think we shall
really go to Spain—probably stay in Palma—Majorca—for a
while. Frieda wants to find a house—we might do so there.
Who knows! I would rather like to go to America for the
summer, to sell the ranch & settle up there—but don't
know really if I'm well enough.

The fuss about the *Pansies* and the rest seems to go on. I
get bored even by the thought of it. It is all so artificial &
stale, and they are all so feeble. But let us hope they can
fix Jix¹ up a bit—it's too childishly silly.

My sister was here about two weeks—seems changed—a good
deal sadder, but I doubt not much wiser. Perhaps sadness &
wiseness no longer go together.

But of course those mining districts *are* depressing now,
trade all gone to pieces, and no real hope.

Secker wants me to go back to Italy to finish my *Etruscan
Sketches*, but I don't want to. He very much wants me to
give him a book for the autumn—but I've got none, & all this
jixing business has put me out of temper for writing. I
wonder if you could take him round a little parcel² that he
keeps asking for. He is a funny chap—quite perky now he has
made money with the German translations.

I am correcting the "Foreword" to my paintings—proofs—I
think Stephensen is having a bit of a struggle.—It's gone a
bit colder again here—time now that spring began to come—
all plants & flowers—most trees frozen dead down here—a
great loss, & very sad.

D. H. L.

1 Sir William Joynson-Hicks, the Home Secretary at this time. For a brief discussion of the *Pansies* censorship problem, see Harry T. Moore's "Introduction" to *D. H. Lawrence: Sex, Literature and Censorship* (New York, 1953), pp. 21–22.

2 A covert reference to *Lady Chatterley's Lover*.

[HOTEL BEAU RIVAGE]
Bandol
[Var. France]
Friday 8 March [1929]

My dear Kot

We are still here—leave on Monday—Frieda for Baden, I
for Paris, to attend to a new edit. of my novel—which I
shall probably produce myself, but which will be distributed
& put on the market by the Librairie du Palais Royal—
Groves & Michaux.[1] I have a letter from Mr. Groves—
sounds all right—but I'd better see to it personally. Shall try
to do a pocket edition, to sell to trade at 50 frs. Galignari's
wrote me, they are now selling a *German* reprint—pirated!
Must stop that.

I only wanted you to send a copy of my book[2] round to
Secker, & deliver it into his hands. He seems to want one
very particularly.

Shall send an address from Paris—or c/o Aldous—3 rue du
Bac. Suresnes (Seine) will do.

Yrs.

D. H. L.

---

1 For a description of this edition of *Lady Chatterley's Lover*, see Item 42c,
B., p. 92. It was published in May 1929.

2 Koteliansky seems to have missed the oblique reference to *Lady Chatterley's
Lover*. See note 2 to Letter No. 332.

---

334 HOTEL PRINCIPE ALFONSO
Palma de Mallorca
Spain
17 May 1929

My dear Kot

So long I haven't written to you—but then you didn't write
to me. And we have been on this island a month—very
agreeable, so calm & so sunny. But humanly it's a bit dead—I
believe all Spain is—so I don't want to live here. We want to
leave at end of this month, & can't make up our minds
whether to do a trip in Spain—Alicante, Bourgos, Granada,
Sevilla, Toledo, Madrid—or whether to take the boat straight
to Marseille. Frieda is moaning again for a house—& now it's
a year since I left Italy. So I think we shall go back to Italy &
look for a house there. All in all, it seems the best place.

What do you think Lahr wants to do about the poems?
I can't quite make out. Secker is omitting about a dozen, so
he said—but I have no proofs from him yet, so can't verify.
I don't mind much what Lahr does, whether the complete
MS. or only those left out by Secker. And I feel hesitant about
a broadside for electioneering purposes—it's not quite my
line.—But do get the original MS. of *Pansies*[1] from Jack
Hutchinson if you can, & keep it for me.

I have seen proofs of nearly all the pictures from
Stephensen—some very nice, some smudgy. But I believe
they'll make a fine book—they have already got orders for 200
or so copies: & *all* the vellum copies at £50 ordered! Now I
want to know if Dorothy Warren will really hold her show.

What's your news? None as usual? Are you staying in the
Cave all summer? Or will you get away a bit? Pity you can't
come abroad, it's really better.

many things!

D. H. L.

---

1 This MS of *Pansies* is now at the University of Texas. The corrected typescript is in the possession of George Lazarus. See Item E302 in *B.*, p. 343.

335
Palma de Mallorca
Spain
25 May 1929

My dear Kot

Don't take any notice of my not having written—it was that
I had grippe when I stayed with the Huxleys, & felt pretty
rotten when I was with them, so lost track of most things
for the time. I think one shouldn't stay with people—though
they were very kind;—but it is best to keep one's very own
atmosphere about one, and not be plunged in other people's.

I think Jack Hutchinson must yield up that typescript[1]
to you complete. He has no further right to it—he achieved
very little—and of course it will have a certain value now,
after all the fuss. Not that I care about *that*. Neither do I
want the MS trailing round in Hutchinson's possession.

I am a bit puzzled what to do about the poems.[2] Secker sent
me the proofs the other day, and wants to come out with his
edition at 10/6 on June 30th or thereabout. He also wants
to do 250 copies at two guineas. I had agreed to 150 copies,
so he stuck in another 100 copies *at the* same price. Of course
I jibbed—& shall not sign 250 unless the price is forthcoming.
But the trouble is, I only stipulated to print myself—that is,
the Lion—250 copies, and I don't like to go back on my word.
—Of course Knopf is publishing the book identical with
Secker's in U.S.A.—so that the copyright will be secured in
both countries. I shall be my own pirate, this time. What do
you think?

I think Stephensen will do pretty well with the book of
paintings, if there is no interference. The reproductions are
rather poor, in some cases—but it is very difficult getting them
true.

We think to sail to Marseille on June 4th. Frieda is very
anxious now to find a house, and on the whole, I think
Italy is the best place. So we shall go there and look round,
before the weather gets too hot. It's not at all hot here yet,

but very nice—and I am pretty well, save that my cough is a curse and a nuisance.

I can hardly imagine the Cave nowadays—it seems so remote. Murry wrote me a loving letter, but I told him it was no good. I think he's about at the end of himself. I wonder if the election[3] will make any difference? it may.

D. H. L.

[PS.]
I hear the Bibescos are on the island—hope they don't find me out.

---

1 *Pansies*; see note 1 to Letter No. 334.

2 *Pansies*, published by Secker, July 1929. See Item A47 in *B.*, pp. 113–19, for details of the publication.

3 See note 2 to Letter No. 336.

HOTEL PRINCIPE ALFONSO
Palma de Mallorca
Spain
5 June 1929

Dear Kot,

I'm still waiting final news of Secker's *Pansies*—also of
Stephensen's book of pictures, also of the Warrens Show.
Do tell me if you can find out anything about the picture-book
& the show. Stephensen is not *too* dependable, either.

I think I shall agree to the Lion's 500 of the poems—& we
needn't number them. But the price is best two guineas, not
three—and I do want him to take a proper percentage. I
say if I take £1 a copy that is already huge. I hope he'll
choose nice paper. Do overlook him a bit—& what do you
really think are his weak points, besides enthusiasm? I do wish
you also would take a little percentage, for all the trouble.
Say you will.

Knopf wouldn't do my *Collected Poems*—he wouldn't buy
back the rights from Huebsch & Seltzer. So I'm going to
leave him as soon as I have fulfilled my contract with him.
Cape made a pretty mean contract for the *Poems*—but I did
want them rescued from the Huebsch-Seltzer-Kennerley
scrap-heap in U.S.A.

Wonder if you have seen Hutchie.[1] Wonder if he got in!
But he didn't. If there is any interesting election-govt. news,[2]
do tell me. I am interested in it.

Just heard from Curtis B.—Secker is doing 250 *Pansies*—and
agrees to my doing 500 if they *follow* his edition. So tell the
Lion 500 O.K.—but not till after Secker is out—& nothing
to America till after Knopf is out too with his edit. Secker
fixes June 30th for his date.—Tell the Lion I'll try about a
photograph or a drawing—perhaps a drawing by an artist
here.—Must hurry off to Palma.

D. H. L.

[PS.]
Tell Lion we stay till 18th.

1 St. John Hutchinson. See note 2 to Letter No. 331.

2 The British Parliamentary election of June 1929 in which the Conservatives, under Lloyd George, won 260 seats, the Liberals 59 seats, and the Labour Party 288 seats. On 5 June 1929, Ramsay MacDonald became Prime Minister of the Labour minority government. Margaret Bondfield (see Letter No. 139), the first woman to enter the cabinet, was named Minister of Labour. See A. J. P. Taylor, *English History, 1914–1945* (Oxford, 1966), pp. 270–75.

337

HOTEL PRINCIPE ALFONSO
Palma de Mallorca
Spain
12 June 1929

My dear Kot

We want *really* to sail next Tuesday, 18th, to Marseille. Frieda wants to come to England to see about my pictures. Somebody must see about them—Dorothy Warren can't be trusted. I shan't come because of the long journey. Probably I shall go to North Italy & wait there. Tell Lahr not to write here any more.—He will have had my letters saying print the 500—& I'll send a drawing or photograph this week.

I'll write you as soon as I get somewhere.

D. H. L.

[PS.]
I asked Stephensen to give you a copy of the picture book.[1]

1 *The Paintings of D. H. Lawrence*, privately printed for subscribers only (London, 1929). For other editions see *B.*, pp. 109–13.

KAFFEE ANGERMAIER
Rottach-am-Tegernsee
Oberbayern [Bavaria]
10 September 1929

My dear Kot

I have not written for so long because I knew, with all the
police & pictures fuss,[1] you preferred not to receive letters.
However, that idiocy has died down again, and everybody
knows once more what idiocy it was. And as a matter of fact,
in spite of Hutchinson & the rest, I don't believe my mail is
interfered with at all. Hutchinson's letter to me was returned
to him simply because he failed to put the name of the city—
Baden-Baden—on the address. So it could not be delivered.

I suppose you have seen the Lion and his edition of the
poems.[2] As a piece of book-making, I confess I was disappointed with it—as I told him. But I suppose he must live
and learn. Only he has no experience in matters of *taste*.
He is a good man, but a wee bit of a muddler, and careless in
details. Still he is a man in ten thousand, and I am very
grateful to him for his pluck and energy.—I wish though,
that he would wind up soon with the poems. He talks of
holding over the vellum copies till towards Christmas. And
I wish he would produce the few out-of-series copies to give
away. Have you had a copy, by the way? I asked him to
give you one. He never tells me in any detail what he does.

We are here in the mountains—and I really don't like
mountains. But we want to go down to Italy next week,
perhaps for a little while to Venice, then really to look for a
house to settle down. I feel I am really fed up with moving
about, and should be glad to have a place of my own. My
health is about the same—a curse & a nuisance. The doctor
says I am really better. New & different doctors descended
on me from München, & say I only need diet—and no salt.
It's a great stunt, the no-salt and *Rohkost*, raw food diet. I
suppose there is something in it.

Frieda's foot is better. The bone-setter, a farmer, came from a
near village & pushed the bone into place in half a minute.

Now she goes all right. And I paid that specialist in Park Lane 12 guineas & the *Medizinabrat* in Baden another lot. —Swine, these doctors.

I was thinking, one day we must rescue the Shestov translation from Martin Secker. If the Mandrake have any success with Rozanov,³ we ought to follow it up with a new edition of *All Things Are Possible*. I suppose Secker has let the thing lapse out of print long ago, and no intention of reprinting. One day you must write a letter & ask him.

Let me know how you are. If you don't care to write direct to me, you can enclose me a letter addressed Dr. Max Mohr, Wolfsgrube, Rottach-am-Tegernsee.

Yrs

D. H. L.

---

1 The exhibition of Lawrence's paintings was scheduled from 14 June to 5 July 1929. A detailed account of the exhibition and its aftermath, i.e. "fuss," is given by Philip Trotter and others in *C.B.*, III, 326–400.

2 *Pansies.* See Items A47, c, d, e, in *B.*, pp. 114–16.

3 *Fallen Leaves.*

VILLA BEAU SOLEIL
Bandol
Var. [France]
10 October 1929

My dear Kot

Yes, I had your two letters at Rottach—didn't I answer?
But there was nothing to say—and I felt so *awfully* ill in
Germany—in spite of doctors & attention—they gave me
arsenic, the beasts—of course pure poison—that I wonder I
ever managed to crawl away. Here I feel much better, & we
have got a nice little house on the sea, & I sit on the terrace
in the sun, & there is a good woman to cook—so I feel much
serener & better. I never want to come north again, while I
live.

Curtis Browns seem very huffed with me for making money on
the private edition, apart from them. But they had such a
scare over *Lady C.* how can they possibly handle the stuff I
do in private. Did I tell you Heinemanns wanted to do
Man Who Loved Islands—signed contract, & were paying me
£300 down—for a private ed. of 500—when Compton
Mackenzie descended on them with a shriek, threatening a
suit for libel, & they withdrew.

Do you still have that book *Early Greek Philosophers* which
I bought when I was last in London? if so, would you send it
me, I want to do some work on the Apocalypse, & consult it.
If you haven't got it, no matter.

So there is now Smerdyakov on God![1] I feel it's about time
the Great Dragon swallowed that small fry of treachery. But
England will stand hypocrisy for ever.

D. H. L.

---

1 A reference to J. M. Murry's book *God* (London, 1929). See note 4 to Letter
No. 252.

VILLA BEAU SOLEIL
Bandol
Var. [France]
25 October 1929

My dear Kot

Thanks for your letters. About coming to England to be near Mundesley,[1] I could never do it. But if my health gets very tiresome, I could go to live near some sanatorium down here, if I knew of a good one, & be under supervision. I would do that. But you see it's quite different supervising lungs, which are straightforward, from supervising what is my real trouble, chronic inflammation of the bronchials & all the breathing passages.[2] The doctors say they think the lung is healed again—the local doctor here said the same—but the bronchitis & asthma are bad—& they don't know what to suggest.

I feel as you do about the Lion. In fact I had already asked him to make a proper bill & square up & finish altogether with the poems. But for some time I haven't heard from him at all. I know he's perfectly honest—but not calm enough. I don't think I shall have him print anything else. I wonder why he's not written lately.

Stephensen sent me the 3/6 books—so I suppose Rosanov [sic] will come along in time. I still think, if Rosanov goes, we might rescue Shestov from Secker. I could do it.

We are settled in our little house—very pleasant—we have for once all the conveniences, bath-room, & central-heating plant. They say it works well. The Brewsters—friends from Capri—are here, & probably will take a house for the winter—& the Huxleys, who are now in Spain, say they will come in November. I haven't heard again from Frederick Carter.[3]

I should be quite happy if only my health were better—my miserable bronchials.

My regards—& I hope you are all right.

D. H. L.

---

1 The sanatorium in Norfolk.

2 Lawrence stubbornly refused to admit that he was suffering from tuberculosis.

3 See Carter's memoir of Lawrence in *C.B.*, III, 410–18.

341 [VILLA] BEAU SOLEIL
[Bandol
Var. France]
Wednesday [27 November 1929]

Dear Kot

Didn't I answer your letter?—I got Rosanov [*sic*],¹ & some of
it I think really good—the latter half. I did a small article on it,
& sent [*sic*] to Curtis Brown, but probably they'll not be able
to place it. I said in it that Rosanov died a few years later
than *Fallen Leaves*—1912—That's right, isn't it?²

I don't know what to say about your doctor.³ It's a great bore
for him to get out at Toulon & come back here—about 8
miles—& then next day or so go on to Cannes or wherever
he is going—some hours from Toulon. And I simply don't
want to make a three or four hours' journey to talk with a
doctor who will want to talk about lungs when the trouble is
bronchials. If I knew a doctor who understood bronchials!—
but they are much more difficult than lungs!

Carter is here, & we've had various talks about everything
going. He makes me feel that all is very dreary & dead in
that literary London, & the young have no life in them at all.

I'm glad you could let Curtis Browns have the *Adelphi*
copies. Murry was trying to frustrate me there. You will
know by now they want to publish those essays in a vol. of
collected newspaper & magazine articles.⁴—I don't want any
more limited editions of me to appear just now.—There is
*Manente*⁵ and the *Escaped Cock*⁶—people will be tired. I
wish I could have sent you a *Cock*, but I myself only got one
or two. I shall try to secure others. It will have to appear in
England later—but I am not arranging anything so far with
C. L.⁷ The Mandrake is, I believe, as good as dead.—Carter is
taking a copy of the *Cock* to the Lion—promised from the
first, so I must keep my promise.

I'm glad Murry has decided there is no God. It makes one
know that there *is*.

I shall have to think of somebody for an edition of the *Cock* next year.

Do you ever hear of Margaret Radford?

ever

D. H. L.

---

1 *Fallen Leaves.*

2 Rozanov did not die until 1919. Lawrence's review was published in the periodical *Everyman* (23 January 1930). It is reprinted in *Phoenix* (New York, 1936), pp. 388–92.

3 Dr. Andrew Morland.

4 These essays were collected and published after Lawrence's death as *Assorted Articles* (London, 1930). See *B.*, pp. 128–30.

5 *The Story of Doctor Manente*, translated by Lawrence and published in March 1929. See *B.*, p. 107–8.

6 *The Escaped Cock*, later called *The Man Who Died*. For publication history see *B.*, pp. 123–26.

7 Charles Lahr.

[VILLA] BEAU SOLEIL
Bandol
Var. [France]
23 December [1929]

Dear Kot

Well here is Christmas! We had a great storm yesterday, so today is grey & sulky. I am in bed, as usual, my bronchials really behaving very badly this winter. Am so tired of them.

I shall be pleased to see Dr. Morland if he stops off here but don't at all like the thought of troubling him & interrupting his journey. It is very kind of him to say he will see me.

I wrote Pollinger about *Pansies* pirates & he has tried to see Goldston, without success. Goldston is getting a difficult bird too.

There is nothing new in the world. I wish my health was better: hope yours is all right. There are various friends here in the hotel, so we shall have a certain amount of Christmas fuss. I hate it, but Frieda seems to think it is essential.

Excuse this poor letter—

D. H. L.

343 [HOTEL] BEAU RIVAGE
Bandol
Var. [France]
9 January 1930

Dear Kot

I was just writing about the impossibility of fitting the Christian religion to the State.—Send me the *Grand Inquisitor*, and I'll see if I can do an "Introduction."[1] Tell me how *long* you'd like it. I did about 6,000 words for Carter's Apocalypse book.[2] For the "Introd." to Dahlberg's *Bottom Dogs* I got £20—but that is a bit low.[3] It depends on the publisher, & the price of the edition etc. Tell me what the plan is. We can arrange all right.

Dr. Morland is due to arrive here on the 15th—and so is Pollinger, travelling straight from London. Pollinger is staying about a week—he's not well either. I don't know whether he'd like to travel with the Morlands—.

Weather rather bad—health so-so. I do hope you're feeling better than in your other letter, & no serious troubles. I do hope too that Sonia is better. Everybody seems to be ill.

Send me your translation.

D. H. L.

---

1 Koteliansky's translation of Dostoevsky's *The Grand Inquisitor*, a section from the novel *The Brothers Karamazov*, was published by Elkin Mathews and Marrot in July 1930. See the description of this edition, which includes Lawrence's "Introduction," in *B.*, pp. 215–16.

2 Lawrence wrote an Introduction to Frederick Carter's *Dragon of the Apocalypse* (London, 1932), which was published separately in the *London Mercury*, XXII (July 1930), pp. 217–26. For further details, see *B.*, p. 283.

3 Edward Dahlberg, *Bottom Dogs*, with an Introduction by D. H. Lawrence (London, 1929).

344

Dear Kot

Just a word to say I have the *Inquisitor* & will try to do a
nice little introduction[1]—though I shall never be able to
squash myself down to a thousand words.

Pollinger arrived today, but we haven't talked business at all
yet. He says he must leave Monday. Dr. Morland arrives with
his wife on Friday. Shall let you know what he says.

ever

D. H. L.

[PS.]
By the way, how do we stand with regard to copies of my
novel? Did the Lion have them all? and did he sell them all?

---

1 There is no hint that Lawrence was asked to work over Koteliansky's translation of *The Grand Inquisitor*. Hence the speculation by Bertram Rota that Lawrence
edited the translation of *The Grand Inquisitor* is unfounded. For Rota's remark
see *B.*, pp. 41–42.

---

345 [VILLA] BEAU SOLEIL
Bandol
Var. [France]
Saturday [26 January 1930]

Dear Kot

Dr. Morland said I must lie still & see no one & do no work
—the lung trouble active, but the bronchitis the worst, and I
must get it down—they aggravate one another. So I am lying
quite still, & already feel rather better.

Pollinger took the "Introd." back with him—about 4000
words I suppose. He thinks Mrs. Henderson[1] is all right.

I won't write any more—but hope you'll like the "Introd."

D. H. L.

---

1 Unidentified.

Vence
A.M.
9 February 1930

Dear Kot

Well I came here last Thursday—and it's no different from being in an hotel, not a bit—except that a nurse takes my temperature. I have the ordinary hotel food—and do just as I like—and am far less "looked after" than I was in the Beau Soleil. So much for a sanatorium. The doctors don't seem to think my case desperate—they don't seem to think anything of it at all—I have no fever—& weigh under 45 kgr.—90 lbs. But I think I'll be all right.

Yes, we both liked Dr. Morland.

If you see Mrs. Henderson, thank her for her letter, & tell her I'll answer it—tell her how I'm fixed. Send me her address.

Yes, you can leave out Murry's name—put Katharine's instead, if you like.[1]

It rains today.[2]

D. H. L.

---

1 The reference is to the "Introduction to the *Grand Inquisitor*," in which Lawrence had noted: "It is a strange experience, to examine one's reaction to a book over a period of years. I remember when I first read *The Brothers Karamazov*, in 1913, how fascinated yet unconvinced it left me. And I remember Middleton Murry saying to me: 'Of course the whole clue to Dostoievsky is in that Grand Inquisitor story.' And I remember saying: 'Why? It seems to me just rubbish.' Since then I have read *The Brothers Karamazov* twice, and each time found it more depressing because, alas, more drearily true to life" (*Phoenix* [New York, 1936], p. 283).
2 On 1 March 1930, Lawrence was moved from the Ad Astra sanatorium to the Villa Robermond, where he died on 2 March 1930. The British United Press carried the following announcement on 3 March 1930: "*Nice*. Mr. D. H. Lawrence, the novelist and poet, died at Vence, near Nice, at nine o'clock last night after a short illness. He had been suffering from tuberculosis. News of his death was kept secret until this afternoon by his literary friends, who were at his death-bed" (*C.B.*, III, 446). For obituary notices and several accounts of Lawrence's final days see *C.B.*, III, 447–90.

Postscript[1]

W HEN HARRY T. MOORE was preparing *The Intelligent Heart: The Story of D. H. Lawrence,* he obtained from Dr. Andrew Morland an account of the doctor's visit with Lawrence in Bandol during the latter part of January 1930. Dr. Morland's recollection of this visit was written in 1952 and published in part by Moore in 1954;[2] a longer version of the visit was included by Edward Nehls in the third volume of *D. H. Lawrence: A Composite Biography* (1959).[3]

Among the *Koteliansky Papers*[4] in the British Museum, I recently located four previously unpublished letters written by Dr. Morland; three of these are addressed to S. S. Koteliansky and one to Mark Gertler.[5] The letters, written between 11 February 1930 and 9 March 1930, are published here through the courtesy of the Trustees of the British Museum and with the kind permission of Mrs. Dorothy Morland, the widow of Dr. Andrew Morland.

A former head of the Department of Chest Diseases at University College Hospital, London, Dr. Andrew John Morland (1896–1957) was a superbly qualified medical expert. Something

1 This Postscript was originally published as "The Last Days of D. H. Lawrence: Hitherto Unpublished Letters of Dr. Andrew Morland," *The D. H. Lawrence Review,* I, No. 1 (Spring 1968), pp. 44–50. I wish to express my appreciation to James C. Cowan, the editor of that review, for allowing me to reprint the material here.

2 *I.H.,* pp. 427–28. My authority for the date when the memoir was written (1952) is Edward Nehls. See note 400 in *C.B.,* III, 729.

3 *C.B.,* III, 423–25.

4 The original Morland letters are to be found in Add. MSS 48974 (Vol. IX), ff. 146–150v.

5 The best account of Mark Gertler's life and his friendship with Lawrence and Koteliansky may be gathered from *Mark Gertler: Selected Letters,* edited by Noel Carrington (London, 1965).

of the impressive nature of his medical credentials may be gathered from the following summary of his career:

The son of John Coleby Morland, he was educated at Sidcot Grammar School, University College, London, and at University College Hospital. He also studied at Lausanne University. He became M.B. and B.S. in 1923 (in the latter he took honors and a distinction), M.R.C.S. Eng., and L.R.C.P. Lond., in the same year, M.R.C.P. and M.D. in 1930, and F.R.C.P. in 1941. For a spell in 1924 he was house physician at the Brompton Chest Hospital and then went to Montana for four years. In 1928 he went to Mundesley as a resident physician at the sanatorium and had the benefit of seven years' association with that remarkable man Dr. S. Vere Pearson, who was something of a pioneer in the treatment of tuberculosis. During this period of his career he wrote *Pulmonary Tuberculosis in General Practice*. In 1935 he went to the French Hospital, London, and two years later took up an appointment at University College Hospital. He was made a Chevalier of the Legion of Honour in 1950. He married in 1928 Dorothy Saunders, by whom he had a son and a daughter.[6]

D. H. Lawrence first mentions Dr. Morland in a letter to Mark Gertler dated 23 December 1929: "I shall be pleased to see Dr. Morland, if he really wants to take the trouble to stop off here. But I don't like the thought of troubling him" (*C.L.*, II, 1225). And writing to Koteliansky on the same day, Lawrence says: "I shall be pleased to see Dr. Morland if he stops off here but don't at all like the thought of troubling him & interrupting his journey. It is very kind of him to say he will see me" (Letter No. 342). On 9 January 1930, Lawrence writes to Koteliansky: "Dr. Morland is due to arrive here on the 15th" (Letter No. 343).

Dr. Morland did not see Lawrence until Monday, 20 January 1930. In a letter to Mabel Luhan dated 21 January 1930, Lawrence says: "The doctor from England came on Monday—says the bronchitis is acute, and aggravated by the lung. I must lie still for two months.—Talks of my going into a sanatorium near Nice, but I don't know if it's suitable. And I don't know if I shall go" (*C.L.*, II, 1235). Lawrence was reluctant to enter the sanatorium at Vence, although he readily accepted Dr. Morland's recommendations of "absolute rest—no work—no seeing people" (*C.L.*, II, 1238). He wrote to the doctor on 30 January 1930 saying: "If I make good progress as I am, I shan't go to Vence: if I don't I shall" (*C.L.*, II, 1238). By the 2nd of February he was apparently not satisfied with his progress, for writing to

6 See *The Times* (15 July 1957), p. 14.

Mrs. Margaret Needham, he says: "I'm not really any worse, but Dr. Morland assured me I should get better so much more quickly in a sanatorium, and be able to *walk* again—and that is what I want. I want my legs back again" (*C.L.*, II, 1239). The next day, 3 February 1930, Lawrence writes to his sister Ada: "I have decided to go to the Sanatorium that Dr. Morland recommended—Ad Astra, Vence, A.M." (*C.L.*, II, 1239).

The letters published here record Dr. Morland's diagnosis of Lawrence's condition in those crucial days just a month and a half before his death. The letters also point to Koteliansky's and Gertler's concern for Lawrence's welfare and reveal how instrumental these two were in arranging the visit. Lawrence, who never took kindly to any sort of medical advice, seems to have appreciated Dr. Morland's attempt to help him; in a letter to Koteliansky dated 9 February 1930, Lawrence said that he and Frieda "both liked Dr. Morland" (Letter No. 346). Mrs. Dorothy Morland still recalls: "meeting Lawrence was a memorable experience as I was just married, very young and had T.B. myself—there was an instant rapport between us." [7] Had Lawrence's general condition not been so rundown, it is possible that he might have recovered. But, as Dr. Morland explains: "for a long time his [Lawrence's] will had lashed his failing body to further efforts until finally the collapse came."

7 From a letter to the editor dated 22 June 1967.

To S. S. Koteliansky

THE SANATORIUM
Mundesley, Norfolk
11 February 1930[8]

Dear Koteliansky,

I am indeed relieved to hear Lawrence has gone to Vence.[9]
It is not that his treatment will be so very much different up
there but one feels so much happier to think that he will
have proper nursing & attention. I am particularly glad he
has gone so soon; when I wrote last week I again advised
him to go so I hope it is this rather than any relapse on his
part that has made him decide. He had almost consented to go
previously.

I will certainly give him any help I can in the way of advice—
I am afraid a really long period of strict rest is the only
possible treatment now & it will not be easy to get him to
submit to it.

I have written to the doctor who will be looking after him &
hope to get a report from him before long. I will then write
to you again.

Yours sincerely,

Andrew Morland

---

8 When this letter was originally published in *The D. H. Lawrence Review*,
I, No. 1 (Spring 1968), p. 46, the date was erroneously given as 2 February 1930.

9 Lawrence apparently entered the sanatorium on 6 February 1930.

To Mark Gertler

THE SANATORIUM
Mundesley, Norfolk
25 February 1930

My dear Mark,

I have at last heard from Dr. Medinier of Vence about Lawrence. I am afraid his report is none too good. Both lungs appear to be affected with moderate severity but it is his general condition which is causing the greatest amount of anxiety; his appetite is poor & he does not seem to be responding to treatment. It is obvious that his case is not suitable for any special treatment & that reliance will have to be placed on prolonged rest & good food. I feel that for the present he is best in the sanatorium but doubt if he will stay there very long. I do not think much of French sanatoria & think that it would not be wise to urge him to stay on there very much longer. The difficulty will be to know what to do when he leaves. If he would consent to come to Mundesley I think that would be best provided he is not too ill to travel. It is unfortunate that I shall be away until July but he is not likely to be out of his room much for several months to come & his main requirements of good food & nursing should be satisfied as well here as anywhere.

If Mundesley cannot be arranged I suppose he would take a villa somewhere near Vence. Should he do this I think it important that he should have a good nurse & a good cook. I could probably find the former. Dorothy[10] will be seeing him in about a weeks time & I shall then know better how the land lies.

Will you pass this on to Koteliansky[11]—I have written more than etiquette allows but I know you will both exercise discretion.

Yours

Andrew Morland

---

10 Dr. Andrew Morland's wife.

11 This explains how this letter happens to be preserved among the *Koteliansky Papers*.

To S. S. Koteliansky

COOK'S HILL
Mundesley on Sea
Nr Norwich
Mundesley 4
4 March 1930

Dear Koteliansky,

How terrible it is that Lawrence is dead. I hardly thought he could recover after I had heard from the doctor at Vence but had no idea he would go so soon. I feel certain that for a long time his will had lashed his failing body to further efforts until finally the collapse came.

I wish now that I had never urged him to go to Vence as I am afraid my efforts only made his last weeks more unhappy.

What absurd lack of perspective our papers show in only giving 1/4 of a column on a back page to Lawrence while the trivial malaria of the Prince of Wales gets all the lime light.

Yours ever sincerely,

Andrew Morland

To S. S. Koteliansky

COOK'S HILL
Mundesley on Sea
Nr Norwich
Mundesley 4
9 [March] 1930[12]

Dear Koteliansky,

When I saw Lawrence at Bandol he was certainly ill—very ill & I realised that unless he began to look after himself at once he could not expect to live many months. It was not possible for me to form any very definite impression of his chances of arresting the progress of the disease as in such cases it is usually impossible to say how a man is going to respond to treatment. One comes across cases in which the general condition is as bad as Lawrence's was in which a period of strict rest is followed by remarkable improvement & eventually recovery. Others less ill, fail to respond. When I heard from the doctor at Vence that L. was not responding to treatment I feared that there was little chance of recovery but I certainly had no expectation of the end coming so soon. I am afraid he was very unhappy during his last week or two at the sanatorium, chiefly on account of his lack of progress & the effort of leaving may have produced a further setback. I doubt if any other disease was present.

Yours sincerely,

Andrew Morland

---

12 Dr. Morland dates this letter 9 February 1930. My conjecture is that the letter should have been dated 9 March 1930. The letter obviously follows that dated 4 March, for it appears to be Dr. Morland's reply to a letter from Koteliansky asking about the possibility of another disease being present which may have precipitated Lawrence's death. The reference to Lawrence's "last week or two at the sanatorium" clearly points to an error in Dr. Morland's dating of this letter.

Appendix I

A BIBLIOGRAPHY OF

S. S. KOTELIANSKY'S TRANSLATIONS OF

RUSSIAN WORKS INTO ENGLISH

BUNIN, IVAN. "The Gentleman from San Francisco." Translated by
S. S. Koteliansky and D. H. Lawrence. *The Dial* (January 1922),
pp. 47–68.
————. *The Gentleman from San Francisco and Other Stories*. Trans-
lated from the Russian by S. S. Koteliansky and Leonard Woolf.
["The Gentleman from San Francisco" is translated by D. H.
Lawrence and S. S. Koteliansky. Owing to a mistake Mr. Lawrence's
name was omitted from the title page. The three other stories are
translated by Mr. Koteliansky and Mr. Woolf.] Richmond: The
Hogarth Press, 1922.
————. *The Gentleman from San Francisco and Other Stories*. Trans-
lated from the Russian by D. H. Lawrence, S. S. Koteliansky, and
Leonard Woolf. New York: Thomas Seltzer, 1923.
CHEKHOV, A. P. *The Bet and Other Stories*. Translated by S. S. Koteliansky and J. M. Murry. London and Dublin: Maunsel and Co.,
1915.
————. *The House with the Mezzanine and Other Stories*. Translated
by S. S. Koteliansky and Gilbert Cannan. New York: Charles
Scribner's Sons, 1917.
————. *My Life and Other Stories*. Translated by S. S. Koteliansky
and Gilbert Cannan. London: C. W. Daniel, 1920.
————. *The Note-Books of Anton Tchekhov Together with Reminis-
cences of Tchekhov by Maxim Gorky*. Translated by S. S. Koteliansky
and Leonard Woolf. Richmond: Hogarth Press, 1921.
————. *The Life and Letters of Anton Tchekhov*. [With portraits and
biographical memoirs by E. G. Zamyatin and M. P. Chekhov.]
Translated and edited by S. S. Koteliansky and Philip Tomlinson.
London: Cassell and Co., 1925.

CHEKOV, A. P. *The Wood Demon: A Comedy in Four Acts.* Translated by S. S. Koteliansky. London: Chatto and Windus, 1926.

——. *Anton Tchekhov: Literary and Theatrical Reminiscences.* [Unpublished works of Chekhov, together with miscellaneous essays and reminiscences by various authors.] Translated and edited by S. S. Koteliansky. [With a portrait.] London: G. Routledge and Sons, 1927.

——. *Plays and Stories.* Translated by S. S. Koteliansky. London: J. M. Dent and Sons (Everyman's Library), 1937.

——. *Three Plays.* [*The Cherry Orchard, The Seagull, The Wood Demon.*] Translated by S. S. Koteliansky. Harmondsworth: Penguin Books Ltd., 1940.

——. *The Lady with the Toy Dog,* and *Gooseberries.* Translated by S. S. Koteliansky. London: Todd Publishing Co. (Polybooks), 1943.

DOSTOEVSKAYA, A. G. *Dostoevsky Portrayed by His Wife: The Diary and Reminiscences of Mme Dostoevsky.* Translated from the Russian and edited by S. S. Koteliansky. [With plates.] London: G. Routledge and Sons, 1926.

DOSTOEVSKY, F. M. *Pages from the Journal of an Author.* Translated by S. S. Koteliansky and J. Middleton Murry. London: Maunsel and Co., 1916.

——. *Stavrogin's Confession.* [Three hitherto unpublished chapters of the novel *The Possessed* and the plan of *The Life of a Great Sinner.*] Translated by S. S. Koteliansky and Virginia Woolf. Richmond: Hogarth Press, 1922.

——. *Dostoevsky: Letters and Reminiscences.* Translated from the Russian by S. S. Koteliansky and J. Middleton Murry. [With a portrait.] London: Chatto and Windus, 1923.

——. "New Dostoevsky Letters." Translated and edited by S. S. Koteliansky. *Virginia Quarterly Review,* II (July–October 1926), pp. 375–84, 546–56.

——. *New Dostoevsky Letters.* Translated by S. S. Koteliansky. London: The Mandrake Press, 1929.

——. *The Grand Inquisitor.* [Book V, Part III, Chapter V of *The Brothers Karamazov.*] Translated by S. S. Koteliansky with an Introduction by D. H. Lawrence. London: Elkin Mathews and Marrot, 1930.

——. *Stavrogin's Confession.* Translated by Virginia Woolf and S. S. Koteliansky. [With a psychoanalytic study by Sigmund Freud.] New York: Lear Publishers, 1947.

GOLDENVEIZER, A. B. *Talks with Tolstoi.* [Selected from 'vblizi Tolstova.'] Translated by S. S. Koteliansky and Virginia Woolf. Richmond: Hogarth Press, 1923.

GORKY, M. [A. M. Pieshkov.] *Reminiscences of Leo Nicolayevitch Tolstoi.* Authorized translation by S. S. Koteliansky and Leonard Woolf. Richmond: Hogarth Press, 1920.

―――. *Reminiscences of Anton Chekhov.* [By Maxim Gorky, Alexander Kuprin, and I. A. Bunin.] Translated by S. S. Koteliansky and Leonard Woolf. New York: B. W. Huebsch, Inc., 1921.

―――. *Reminiscences of Leonid Andreyev.* Authorized translation by K. Mansfield and S. S. Koteliansky. London: William Heinemann, 1931. [This work was serialized in *The Dial* as follows: June 1924, pp. 481–92; July 1924, pp. 31–43; August 1924, pp. 105–20.]

―――. *Reminiscences of Tolstoy, Chekhov, and Andreyev.* Authorized translation by K. Mansfield, S. S. Koteliansky, and Leonard Woolf. London: Hogarth Press, 1934. [Compass Books edition issued in 1959 by the Viking Press, Inc.]

HIPPIUS, ZINAIDA, N. (*See* Merezhkovskaya)

KOTELIANSKY, S. S. *Russian Short Stories.* [Selected by S. S. Koteliansky.] Harmondsworth: Penguin Books Ltd., 1941.

KUPRIN, I. A. *The River of Life and Other Stories.* Translated by S. S. Koteliansky and J. M. Murry. Boston: Luce, 1916.

MEREZHKOVSKAYA, ZINAIDA, N. (née Hippius). *The Green Ring.* [A play.] Translated by S. S. Koteliansky. London: C. W. Daniel, 1920.

ROZANOV, V. V. *Solitaria.* [With an abridged account of the author's life by E. Gollerbach. Other biographical material and matter from "The Apocalypse of Our Times."] Translated by S. S. Koteliansky. London: Wishart and Co., 1927.

―――. *Fallen Leaves.* [Bundle One.] Translated from the Russian by S. S. Koteliansky with a Foreword by James Stephens. London: The Mandrake Press, 1929.

SHESTOV, LEO. [Lev Isaakovich Swartzman.] *All Things Are Possible.* Translated by S. S. Koteliansky with a Foreword by D. H. Lawrence. London: Martin Secker, 1920.

SHESTOV, LEON. [Lev Isaakovich Swartzman.] *Anton Tchekhov and Other Essays.* Translated by S. S. Koteliansky with a Foreword by J. M. Murry. London: Maunsel and Co., 1916. [Published in the United States as *Penultimate Words and Other Essays.* Boston: J. W. Luce, and Co., 1917.]

TOLSTAYA, SOFIYA A. *The Autobiography of Countess Sophie Tolstoi.* [With a Preface and Notes by Vasilli Spiridonov.] Translated by S. S. Koteliansky and Leonard Woolf. Richmond: Hogarth Press, 1922.

TOLSTOY, L. N. *Tolstoi's Love Letters* [To Valerya Arseneva. With a study of the autobiographical elements in Tolstoi's work by

Paul Biruykov.] Translated by S. S. Koteliansky and Virginia Woolf. Richmond: Hogarth Press, 1923.

TOLSTOY, L. N. *Notes of a Madman and Other Stories.* Translated by S. S. Koteliansky. London: Todd Publishing Co. (Polybooks), 1943.

Appendix II

D. H. LAWRENCE'S AND
S. S. KOTELIANSKY'S CONTRIBUTIONS
TO *THE ADELPHI*

"The Wood Demon," by Anton Tchehov, translated by S. S. Koteliansky, I (June 1923), 42–48.

D. H. Lawrence, "Trees and Babies and Papas and Mamas," I (June 1923), 20–33.

"More Recollections of Tolstoy," by Maxim Gorky, translated by S. S. Koteliansky, I (July 1923), 111–14.

D. H. Lawrence, "Education and Sex," I (July 1923), 123–36.

"Recollections of Tchehov," by Maxim Gorki, translated by S. S. Koteliansky, I (August 1923), 217–23.

"The Saint Joseph's Ass," by Giovanni da Verga, translated by D. H. Lawrence, I (September 1923), 284–97.

D. H. Lawrence, "On Love and Marriage," I (September 1923), 307–15.

"From My Diary," by Maxim Gorki, authorized translation by S. S. Koteliansky, I (October 1923), 383–88.

D. H. Lawrence, "Three Poems," I (October 1923), 368–77.

"Across the Sea," by Giovanni Verga, translated by D. H. Lawrence, I (November 1923), 466–75.

D. H. Lawrence, "Indians and an Englishman," I (November 1923), 484–94.

"Letters of Tchehov to Gorki," translated by S. S. Koteliansky, I (November 1923), 504–10.

D. H. Lawrence, "The Proper Study," I (December 1923), 584–90.

D. H. Lawrence, "On Being Religious," I (February 1924), 791–99.

"Reminiscences of Leonid Andreyev," by Maxim Gorki, authorized translation by Katherine Mansfield and S. S. Koteliansky, I (February 1924), 806–20.

D. H. Lawrence, "On Human Destiny," I (March 1924), 882–91.

"Reminiscences of Leonid Andreyev," by Maxim Gorki, authorized translation by Katherine Mansfield and S. S. Koteliansky, I (March 1924), 892–905.

"Reminiscences of Leonid Andreyev," by Maxim Gorki, authorized translation by Katherine Mansfield and S. S. Koteliansky, I (April 1924), 983–89.

L. H. Davidson, "A Review of *The Book of Revelation* by Dr. J. Oman," I (April 1924), 1011–13 [Attributed to D. H. Lawrence by J. M. Murry; see *B.*, item C118, p. 267.].

"Liberty," by Giovanni Verga, translated by D. H. Lawrence, I (May 1924), 1051–59.

"A Letter of Anton Tchehov," translated by S. S. Koteliansky and Katherine Mansfield, II (June 1924), 38–45.

D. H. Lawrence, "The Dance of the Sprouting Corn," II (August 1924), 208–15.

"Tchehov and His Wife," Letters translated by S. S. Koteliansky, II (August 1924), 224–35.

D. H. Lawrence, "On Being a Man," II (September 1924), 298–306.

"In Defence of Countess Tolstoy," by Maxim Gorky, authorized translation by S. S. Koteliansky, II (October 1924), 395–412.

D. H. Lawrence, "Indians and Entertainment," II (November 1924), 494–507.

D. H. Lawrence, "The Hopi Snake Dance (1)," II (January 1925), 685–92.

D. H. Lawrence, "The Hopi Snake Dance (2)," II (February 1925), 764–78.

D. H. Lawrence, "Corasmin and the Parrots," III (December 1925), 480–89.

D. H. Lawrence, "Review of Baron Corvo's *Hadrian the Seventh*," III (December 1925), 502–6.

D. H. Lawrence, "Review of Marmaduke Pickthall's *Saïd the Fisherman*," IV (January 1927), 436–40.

D. H. Lawrence, "The Mozo," IV (February 1927), 474–87.

D. H. Lawrence, "Walk to Huayapa," IV (March 1927), 538–54.

Appendix III

Listed below are the letters which have already been published as follows:

"D. H. Lawrence: Letters to S. S. Koteliansky," *Encounter*, I, No. 3 (December 1953), pp. 29–35.

The Selected Letters of D. H. Lawrence, edited with an Introduction by Diana Trilling (New York: Farrar, Straus and Cudahy, 1958).

The Collected Letters of D. H. Lawrence, edited with an Introduction by Harry T. Moore, 2 vols. (New York: Viking Press, 1962).

"D. H. Lawrence: Letters to Koteliansky," edited by George J. Zytaruk, *The Malahat Review*, I, No. 1 (January 1967), pp. 17–40.

The letter numbers are those assigned to the letters in the present volume; the page numbers refer the reader to the previous places of publication. *C.L.* is the abbreviation for *The Collected Letters of D. H. Lawrence* cited above.

No.		No.	
1	*C.L.*, 288	26	*Malahat*, 21
4	*C.L.*, 289	27	*C.L.*, 306
6	*Malahat*, 19	30	*Malahat*, 21–22
7	*C.L.*, 292	34	*C.L.*, 313
11	*Malahat*, 19	35	*C.L.*, 321
14	*Malahat*, 20	38	*C.L.*, 328
19	*C.L.*, 295	40	*Malahat*, 22
21	*C.L.*, 297	43	*Encounter*, 29;

Index

422

Mackenzie, Compton, 200–3, 328, 390
Mackenzie, Faith, 374
McLeod, A. W., 23n.2
McQueen, 39
Madrid, 383
Magnus, Maurice, 266n
Maimonides and Aristotle, xxviii
Maisie (Horne), 50, 172, 274
Malahat Review, The, xxiii
Malthouse Cottage, 349
Manchester, 46
Mandrake Press, 369n, 370, 372–373, 389, 392
Mansfield, Katherine, xvi, xvii; recalls Law Bureau, xviii; xxvii, xxix; Gorky's *Reminiscences*, xxix–xxx; xxxv, 2n; return from Paris, 31; 34, 36; letters are jarring, 42; and her brother, 51; 71, 75, 78; 'needs ... to learn to live alone', 86; 87–92; rescues *Amores*, 92n; 93, 122, 152n.3, 156, 162–64, 167, 175n.2, 179, 181, 193, 200, 201n.2, 204, 216, 229, 242, 249; death, 251, 259, 398
"Man the Hunter," 280n.1
Man Who Died, The, 309n, 393n.6
Man Who Loved Islands, The, 325, 390
Mark Gertler: Selected Letters, xxivn, 6n.2, 114n, 155n.4
Markham, Edwin, 260n.2
Marryat, Captain, 75, 98
Marseille, 383–84
Marsh, Edward, 5n.1, 133n.1, 248
Mastro-don Gesualdo (Verga), 256
Matlock, 157, 175
Mayo, Katherine, 325n.3
Mecklenburg Square, 219
Medinier, Dr., 403
Melville, Herman, 75, 81, 98, 192n
Memoirs of the Foreign Legion (Magnus), 266; L.'s introduction, 266n; 268, 271
Mencken, H. L., 260n.2

Mendel: A Story of Youth (Cannan), 96, 98, 204n.2
Meredith, Professor H. V., 55
Merezhkovskaya, Zinaida, 197n.2
Merrild, Knud, xii, 259
Mexico City, 252
Meynell, Viola, lends L. her cottage, 23; 39, 44
Meynell, Wilfred and Alice, 25, 26
Middleton-by-Wirksworth, 141–147, 150, 153–59, 166–76
Mill, John Stuart, 179n.2
Moby Dick, 81, 111
Mohr, Dr. Max, 389
Moleschott, Jacob (1822–93), 186
Monck, Nugent (1878–1958), 309
Mond, Henry, 206
Monk, Violet (Mrs. Stevens), 225
Monroe, Harriett, 53
Monte Carlo, 281
Montreal, xv
Moore, Harry T., xii, xiin, xiii, xix, xixn, xxv, 23n.2, 29n.2, 40n.2, 99n, 124n.4, 135n, 141n.2, 151n.2, 167n.1, 177n.1, 181n.3, 183n, 194n.1, 196n, 227n, 248n, 381n.1, 399
Morgenrot, 38, 45n.4
Morland, Dr. Andrew, 392, 393n.3, 394–98; biographical details, 399–400; diagnosis of L.'s condition, 401–5, 405n.12
Morland, Mrs. Dorothy, 399, 403
Mornings in Mexico, 315
Morrell, Lady Ottoline, xvi, 23n, 24, 26–28; Kot's introduction to her, 29n.3; 39, 45n.4, 66, 74, 79n.4, 95, 109, 128n, 131, 136, 137, 142, 156, 248, 251, 317; 'again friendly', 379
Morrell, Philip, 343n
Morrison, Miss, 296
Moscow, 283
Mosley, Sir Oswald Ernald, 377
Mountain Cottage, 141–47, 150, 153–59, 166–76
Mountsier, A. Bobert, 52, 220–221, 227–28, 252